C0-AUF-137

# Promoting Global Competence and Social Justice in Teacher Education

# Promoting Global Competence and Social Justice in Teacher Education

*Successes and Challenges within Local and International Contexts*

Edited by David Schwarzer
and Beatrice L. Bridglall

LEXINGTON BOOKS
Lanham • Boulder • New York • London

LB
1715
.P775
2015

# 898161619

Published by Lexington Books
An imprint of The Rowman & Littlefield Publishing Group, Inc.
4501 Forbes Boulevard, Suite 200, Lanham, Maryland 20706
www.rowman.com

Unit A, Whitacre Mews, 26-34 Stannary Street, London SE11 4AB

Copyright © 2015 by Lexington Books

*All rights reserved.* No part of this book may be reproduced in any form or by any electronic or mechanical means, including information storage and retrieval systems, without written permission from the publisher, except by a reviewer who may quote passages in a review.

British Library Cataloguing in Publication Information Available

**Library of Congress Cataloging-in-Publication Data**

Library of Congress Cataloging-in-Publication Data Available

ISBN 978-1-4985-0435-5 (cloth : alk. paper)
ISBN 978-1-4985-0436-2 (electronic)

♾ ™ The paper used in this publication meets the minimum requirements of American National Standard for Information Sciences Permanence of Paper for Printed Library Materials, ANSI/NISO Z39.48-1992.

Printed in the United States of America

# Contents

# Acknowledgments

Editing a book is a serious and prolonged process where several colleagues, friends, and family members have helped in various ways. It is impossible to note all of them, but we would like to thank a few of them.

David Schwarzer would like to thank Provost Willard Gingerich for sending him as a representative of Montclair State University to the symposium for the internationalization of teacher education at the National Association of Foreign Students Advisors (NAFSA). That event was the biggest impetus for this book.

He would like to thank Christian Acosta, his graduate assistant, for helping with all the aspects of the editorial work for the book. His organizational skills, his technological knowledge, and his endless versions of the literature reviewed in the book made this book strong. Also his new new graduate assistant, Michael Molino for his help on this project. Muchas gracias por todo.

Finally, David would like to thank his wife, Taly, and his three children (Noa, Ariel, and Tamar) for listening to endless conversations about this project during dinnertime. Toda raba!

Beatrice L. Bridglall would like to thank all of the contributors for taking time to share their perspectives regarding reorienting teacher education to include the development of global competencies.

We would also like to thank our editor, Alissa Parra, and other colleagues at Rowman & Littlefield Publishers for working with us to bring this work to fruition. Thank you all for your collaborative spirit.

# Introduction

*Internationalizing Teacher Education: Successes and Challenges within Local and International Contexts*

## David Schwarzer and Beatrice L. Bridglall

This book is an edited volume showcasing attempts of successful (and less successful) internationalization experiences in teacher education programs. It focuses on internationalization efforts that are centered on a social justice component. This book provides a framework for teacher educators and program directors to reconsider their practice in the context of offering teacher candidates with exposure to international experiences.

This introduction details key theoretical differences between internationalization, globalization, glocal perspectives, and cosmopolitan education, which is followed by a succinct theoretical review of social justice perspectives in teacher education in the United States and in the world. We conclude with an overview of the content of the book, which is organized in three sections study abroad; technology enhanced collaborations; and glocal experiences.

## DEFINING GLOBALIZATION

The first part of this introduction is designed to provide an overview of different definitions of globalization and internationalization as they pertain to teacher education programs.

According to Fischman (2001):

> The number of articles, books and reports discussing the connection between globalization and education grew by leaps and bounds. Such prolific produc-

tion indicates a change in the scholarship about the teaching profession in
general. (p. 413)

In this book, we continue the conversation with a particular focus on
teacher education programs in the United States. More and more transnational and multilingual students are the mainstream of the U.S. classrooms. And
yet, teacher education programs continue to prepare teacher candidates and
support in-service teachers by providing parochial and insular experiences
related *only* to their U.S. context.

Therefore, this edited volume describes successful (and less successful)
attempts to internationalize teacher education programs. A recent McKinsey
report asserts that the persistence of educational achievement gaps between
and among underrepresented populations and their more advantaged counterparts imposes on the United States the economic equivalent of a "permanent
national recession" (McKinsey's emphasis). On an international level,

... The recurring annual economic cost of the international achievement gap is
substantially larger than the deep recession the United States is currently experiencing. (McKinsey, 2009, 5)

This book addresses this knowledge gap, particularly from the perspective of reconceptualizing the purpose of education to include the attainment
of global or cosmopolitan perspectives that can contribute to reducing educational gaps at both the high and low end of the achievement distribution. This
goal has important implications for how we not only educate today's students
but also how we prepare teachers to teach in a diverse and complex world in
which habits of perspective, inquiry, imagination, empathy, communication,
commitment, humility, integrity, and judgment increasingly resonate in importance (Darling-Hammond & Bransford, 2005; Sizer, 1992). The renewed
focus on these habits of mind is partially influenced by the idea that, on many
levels and regardless of family background (which is not destiny, as President Barack Obama reminds us), our students will increasingly have to think
creatively, analytically, practically, and regeneratively in efforts to address
recurring issues and challenges associated with global poverty, health epi-
demics, gender inequality, human mobility—both voluntary and involuntary,
trade, bioengineering, evolving technology, climate change, and income po-
larization that occur on local, national, and global scales (report from the
International Commission on Education for Sustainable Development Practice, 2008; Reimers, 2009).

Opportunities to collaborate, adapt, innovate, and create, inherent in the
above issues and challenges, suggest that students will increasingly need
access to not only a broad knowledge base, but also to adaptable strategies
and dispositions that will enable them to effectively participate with others

from different countries and cultures. There are growing concerns, however, that few practicing teachers in the United States are prepared to handle the demands of educating students for our changing global context (Levine, 2005); nor are teacher candidates acquiring a nuanced, global perspective with regard to their subject areas or the pedagogical strategies with which to eventually enable their students to consider multiple perspectives, think critically, or cultivate respect and tolerance for diverse peoples and cultures.

These dynamics undergird increased efforts to not only bring these issues to the fore, but also address them in thoughtful and deliberate ways. For example, the National Lieutenant Governor's Association (2008) supports the creation of a national policy on international education; the Council of Chief State School Officers' (2006) global education policy statement advocates the preparation of students for a global society in which they will both reside and shape; a recent conference organized by the National Education Association emphasized the importance of integrating global awareness in increasingly narrow curriculum; a recent report by the National Association of State Boards of Education (2006) urged institutions that prepare and train teachers to expose their candidates to global perspectives; and the Partnership for 21st Century Skills perceives global awareness as one of several competencies (including cognitive, metacognitive, financial/economic, business, and entrepreneurial and civic literacy) necessary for students to acquire (www.21stcenturyskills.org). Additionally, the National Research Council (2007), the Committee for Economic Development (2006), and the Asia Society (2008), advocate for and support the development of curriculum and instruction in world languages (particularly those that are less common) and sustained interventions that enable the cultivation of global competencies (which are equally important for teacher educators, charged with training teacher candidates, to also develop).

Growing consensus regarding the importance and utility of these strategies for promoting global competencies suggests the need for relevant frameworks that actively consider what global competence means within a particular institutional context and employing this knowledge to situate curriculum, instruction, and assessments within existing and new disciplines (potentially around global studies) (Longview Foundation, 2008). This book elaborates on this emerging framework and considers several challenges to its implementation, including issues inherent in learning to teach. The latent implications of these dynamics are also discussed.

## DEFINING GLOBAL COMPETENCE

The term global competence is not new and can be traced to Title VI of the National Defense Education Act (NDEA) of 1958 and the Fulbright-Hays Act of 1961, which served as the foundations for the internationalization of

U.S. higher education (National Research Council, 2007). Thus, for over five decades, some higher education officials and faculty have been concerned with not only how to develop deep understanding of world regions, diverse cultures, languages, economic and environmental systems, and global issues, but also the cultivation of certain habits of mind and ethical behaviors that value and encourage respect, integrity, and personal regard between and among diverse peoples (National Research Council, 2007; Reimers, 2009).

This focus however, has not effectively filtered to colleges and schools of education, which are among the least internationalized (Schneider, 2007). This is the case despite the pivotal roles these institutions, and by extension, their teacher preparation programs, can play in recognizing a context transformed by globalization; and in response, redefining their values and goals and increasing their capacities by developing faculty, for example, who can in turn prepare teacher candidates to eventually enable their own students to meaningfully participate in a globally connected environment (Rizvi & Lingard, 2009). Implicit in the foregoing is the idea that work needs to be initiated and integrated on many levels, including at the institutional, faculty, and student level. At the institutional level, for example, Quezada (2010) suggests that administrators and faculty can begin by focusing on several foundational questions, including assessing what globalization means for teacher education and how it informs conceptions of global competence in education, broadly conceived and specifically for globally competent teachers in the twenty-first century. Other questions include how colleges and schools of education can support their faculty in enabling teacher candidates to acquire the knowledge, skills, and dispositions that can promote effective teaching and learning in a global context. Still other questions can address the particular approaches, including a globalized curriculum, and the creation of global learning networks and new disciplines in global studies, that are necessary for promoting certain student experiences and outcomes (Longview Foundation, 2008).

Considered responses to these queries can contribute to an informed vision and a strategic plan that can reflect several goals, including consensus regarding institutional, departmental, and student outcomes; the careful use of scarce resources in targeted efforts at organizing, integrating, and implementing relevant activities campus-wide; and accountability for teaching and learning experiences and iterative assessments in meeting these goals. The Department of Teacher Education at Michigan State University's College of Education and San Diego's School of Leadership and Education Sciences provide several instances of institutions actively at work in internationalizing their programs vis-à-vis teaching, service, research, and outreach (Longview Foundation, 2008). Building on prior international work, both institutions recognized the increasing influence of globalization on the professional and personal lives of their target population and responded by identifying global competencies for their students and faculty. This foundational work enabled faculty to restructure courses within programs and at all levels to promote the competencies identified. In tandem with course redesign, faculty and administrators also crafted partnerships and networks abroad to support and reinforce faculty capacity, and restructured study-abroad programs.

Other examples include the Professional Development School Project of Ohio State University and the Global Awareness Project at Florida International University, which strongly emphasize international education in their teacher training programs (Merryfield, 1992; Tucker & Cistone, 1991). Additionally, a few institutions, such as Stanford University's International Studies Project, have taken the lead in assisting K–12 educators by offering curriculum and staff development services for these teachers statewide; and in the state of Wisconsin, efforts to integrate global perspectives and practices within K–16 curriculum, instruction, and assessments are promoted by a curriculum planning guide in international studies, teacher institutes, and state legislation. These institutions, at the forefront of globalizing their mission, vision, departments, and curriculum, are not the norm however.

Finally, three calls for action in the area of internationalizing teacher education are worth mentioning. Schneider (2007) discusses the interaction of international studies and teacher education programs and colleges in the United States. She talks about Teacher for a New Era (TNE) launched by the Carnegie Corporation of New York. Its intentions are to impact student learning by producing better classroom teachers with a global and social justice approach to teaching and learning.

Richardson (2001) is challenging all teacher educators to break the "virtual wall of silence" and to prepare student teachers for a global interdependent world. Richardson proposes to engage student teachers in international experiences and to integrate a global perspective in all aspects of the teacher education curriculum. Finally, a thorough rationale and a list of practical strategies for action to move their teacher education programs from parochial views to a twenty-first century view of teaching as a global endeavor are provided.

The third call for action comes from Shaklee & Baily (2012) in their edited volume. They contend that as students' transnational perspectives present in U.S. mainstream classrooms become commonplace, there is a disconnect between the skills teacher need and their training provided by colleges of education in their teacher preparation programs. They explain that there is a need to update the historic models of diversity and use a more global perspective on the topic. Teacher education should become a more international-minded profession that addresses the multinational challenges and opportunities facing American education in the twenty-first century.

That is, teacher education programs in general, and teacher candidates in particular, tend to have insular and parochial views of teaching and learning.

If big-picture conversations take place, they are mostly about the U.S. context. The intention of this book is to foster a more global, international, and cosmopolitan understanding of teaching and learning in general. Moreover, framing this global competency conversation within a social justice perspective is crucial to this volume. In this vein, we propose to showcase and understand the role of public schooling in the world and the initiatives already in place to further the achievement of racial, ethnic, socioeconomic, and linguistically diverse populations in the mainstream public school, another significant goal of this volume.

## DEFINING SOCIAL JUSTICE
## IN AN INTERNATIONAL FRAMEWORK

Social justice in teacher education has been used as a broad term to encompass a variety of different and distinct perspectives and practices (Adams, DeJong et al., 2008). Broad and encompassing terms sometimes are not very useful since they may lose their focus and usefulness. Therefore, in this book we are using the meta-analysis of two main characteristics of most social justice definitions as explained by Oyler (2011):

> In looking for the underlying commonalities across all the analyses and recommendations for social justice-oriented teacher education, two main themes emerge: (1) it is important for teachers to assume a capacity—rather than a deficit—orientation to young children, their families, and their communities; and (2) it is important for teachers to develop knowledge of oppression, a keen eye for inequity as it functions in schools, and a commitment to equity pedagogy. (p. 148)

Two early books on this topic as well as a critical review of them might shed some light on some of the challenges related to understanding social justice as a globalized phenomenon. Day et al. (2000) in his edited volume *The Life and Work of Teachers: International Perspectives in Changing Times* discusses some of the factors that have a crucial impact on students' learning opportunities around the world. Policy, school leadership, and teaching/teachers' lives seem to illustrate how similar these experiences are around the world. Moreover, it emphasizes how regional, national, and international mandates are affecting school leaders and teachers all over the world. Finally, it suggests that in spite of the circumstances they are exposed to on a regular basis—many times it is beyond their professional control and against their academic judgment.

Smyth et al. (2000) *Teacher's Work in a Globalizing Economy* addresses the impact of the global economy on teachers' work. It is based on two case studies in completely different settings to show how teachers are adapting and responding to significant changes in the way their professional work is defined. Moreover, it showcases similarities and differences in the way that they actively respond to these new forces and how they even participate in shaping these new processes to their advantage.

Fischman (2001) in his review of the books noted above argues that "neoliberal globalizers" are instituting new demands and policies on the teaching profession. These demands are another force that is de-professionalizing teachers and teacher educators interested in serious internationalization efforts for the profession. He proposes the nature of hope and the development of alternative proposals that are sensitive to teachers' lives and experiences instead of the current process of intensification of teachers' work. In this vein,

> . . . Hope in global times means that both teachers and students have no other possibility but to struggle to affirm themselves, it is up to them and to us as scholars and practitioners to imagine fruitful ways to identify the dangerous areas, the spaces for hope and extraordinary times in which collective action demonstrates that history is always in the making. (Fischman, p. 418)

Similarly, Wells (1998) reminds us that globalization for social justice is a very important force for educational change and a grand opportunity to revisit its definition. Wells also explains how the identity and independence of nation states and the construction of public education are being affected by economic and political globalization forces. Moreover, there is no clear agreement on how different globalization forces (from realist and critical theorists to liberal, neoliberal, and liberal, progressives theorists) have impacted the teaching profession. Finally, she critically analyzes some of the central aspects that have been impacted by global forces (privatization and decentralization of assessment; growing emphases on nationhood in the agendas of school reforms and educational markets) through the different approaches to globalization mentioned above.

It is interesting to note that Bigelow and Peterson (2002) have created a very useful and student-friendly anthology for teachers interested in teaching for justice in an unjust world. The book provides teachers with some strategies as well as some concrete readings and experiences to better understand globalization forces and their impact in an "increasingly complicated and scary world." This anthology provides different challenging situations that the world is facing from the destruction of the rain forest to global warming; from child labor to sweatshops, and so forth. Moreover, it also provides opportunities for students to read about successful experiences that regular people working in these unusual situation have created to "set things right." Their edited volume also provides several hands-on activities that include poetry, interviews, background readings, and role play among other interesting ways to make these abstract ideas practical and useful for students in the different grade levels.

## ORGANIZATION OF THE BOOK

After careful analysis of research efforts conducted on internationalization of teacher education programs, three basic experiences appear as the most usual ways to accomplish the task: study abroad, technology enhanced, and glocal experiences.

### Study-Abroad Section

This section details the development of a study-abroad experience for students in a teacher education program in order to internationalize their conceptualization of teaching and learning.

Study abroad is a well-known opportunity for universities interested in internationalizing their students' experiences. First we will present some study-abroad experiences that were develop to internationalize higher education in general followed by some research focused on teacher education experiences in particular.

Byram and Feng (2006) wrote a very interesting edited volume dedicated to the area of studying and living abroad for students in higher education. This book presents the experiences of international students studying in a place other than their native country (for example, Chinese students studying the UK, or Irish students in Japan). The chapters in this book research the need to adapt to a new education system while studying and living abroad even for short periods of time when students travel across the world to study. On the same venue, de Nooy and Hanna (2003) interviewed Australian university students returning from study in France. The study suggests that students' lack of French proficiency prevented them from accessing important information while studying in France. Therefore, students reproduced the stereotypical view of French administration as being inefficient. Implications of importance for implementing successful higher education students' experiences abroad are provided.

In terms of teacher education programs, according to Cushner (2007) cognitive orientations to cultural learning in schooling and teacher education are still the norm. Cultural differences are treated as an academic subject—students listen to speakers, observe classrooms, watch films, and read books in spite of the insights from research that suggests that firsthand experience is crucial to enhance intercultural development. Cushner (2007) further claims that the preparation of "internationally-minded" teachers has the potential to influence students in schools, but it needs to address "interpersonal and intercultural dimensions of communication, interaction and learning." It is important to mention that both international experiences in general but more focused student teaching experiences have the potential to foster a more "interculturally-sensitive approach to teaching as well as promote an "ethnorelative orientation" to schooling.

Palmer and Menard-Warwick (2012) detail a research project based on a study-abroad Second Language Acquisition class that was designed to develop multicultural awareness for bilingual teacher candidates. The study describes the life-changing experiences of eleven undergraduate student teachers from Texas in Cuernavaca, Mexico. For many of the students in the class, this was their first travel beyond Texas. Students engaged with local families, schools, and lecturers in order to improve their Spanish proficiency and to be able to facilitate and articulate a critical understanding and consciousness of the needs of immigrant children and second language learning in their future professional experiences. The authors define this critical consciousness as a global awareness about social justice issues that is influenced by the larger structures of power that influence the schooling experiences of immigrants both in Mexico and the United States. Moreover, they discuss the importance of a commitment to action as an intrinsic part of this new awareness based on this study-abroad experience. The authors found that dialogue journals were very useful in the creation of "interculturality" as a new construct that was a result of this study-abroad experience.

Brindley et al. (2009) also investigated the experiences of preservice teachers engaged in a month-long study-abroad internship in England. This study used the theoretical framework of consonance and dissonance for the study-abroad experience (Cochran-Smith, 1991). Findings from this research piece suggest that the study-abroad experience was very useful to compare and contrast the experiences of the student teachers as they related to the school context, the teacher's role, the learners, the buildings, and the community in a more comparative and social justice way. They also provide some concrete implications for planning and facilitating other student teacher experiences studying abroad.

Most recently, Marx and Moss (2011) wrote a very powerful piece on the experiences of preservice teachers in England as a way to help them develop their intercultural development. The study suggests that a faculty-led student teaching experience provided preservice students with a unique opportunity to confront their ethnocentric worldviews and begin to consider different ways in which language and culture influence teaching and learning. Marx and Moss (2011) found several important themes in their inquiry project: immersion in the culture, immersion in the school, and the role of the intercultural guide to promote reflective practices around issues of culture and self. These themes both challenged and supported intercultural development.

## Using Technology to Enhance the International Experience

This section details the development of technology-enhanced experiences for students in a teacher education program in order to internationalize their conceptualization of teaching and learning.

Technological gains during the last decade have increased the feasibility of technology-enhanced experiences with partners across the world. Gragert (2000) discusses the use of the Internet for international education. This piece deals with several important key issues that need to be taken into consideration while using technology to internationalize higher education. Among them, in an increasingly interdependent global society, there is a value to exploring global and cultural differences and similarities; the value of online collaborative project work; Internet-based global collaborations benefit skills development in different content areas, and so on.

Rogers (2011) extends to technology-enhanced experiences as transformational ones. The paper highlights that emerging technologies provide new opportunities in higher education to enable and support students from very different contexts to interact and collaborate with each other in a transformative way.

In terms of teacher education technology-enhanced experiences, Wilder et al. (2010) provide an exploratory classroom-based action research project of a successful field experience project between students in the United States and in Namibia. The findings suggest that this experience was very beneficial for both groups of students. Moreover, it provides practical applications and insights that could be useful for other teacher educators interested in internationalizing their teaching education programs in particular using technology-enhanced practices.

## Glocal

This section details the development of glocal experiences for students in a teacher education program in order to internationalize their conceptualization of teaching and learning.

Global/glocal—what is the difference?

According to Steger (2003), globalization is

> a multidimensional set of social processes that create, multiply, stretch, and intensify worldwide social interdependencies and exchanges while at the same time fostering in people a growing awareness of deepening connections between the local and the distant. (p. 13)

Today's world economies are clearly interdependent—however, our schooling systems and experiences are still parochial and very complex to navigate even when moving in the United States from one state to another. Kumaravadivelu (2003) adds to this discussion by stating,

> Life in this globalizing world carries with it a significant level of cultural flow. Most adolescent and adult students in urban areas . . . do not come to the classroom with a blank mental slate . . . they may be bringing to the classroom a much greater cultural awareness and adaptability than the language teaching profession has given them credit for. (Kumaravidelu, p. 179)

Therefore, our teacher education programs would benefit greatly from highlighting not only the challenges global local connections encompass, but also the opportunities they afford.

Glocalization is an important construct in order to better understand teacher education as an interconnected process. According to Kumaravadivelu (2008), glocalization is

> based on *dochakuka,* a Japanese word roughly meaning "global localization," which the Japanese business community often uses to refer to marketing issues, as in the popular slogan "think globally, act locally." (p. 45)

However, Pennycook (2003) has stated that the oversimplification of glocal—English language usage is for intercultural and global communication—and local languages for local identities does not fully represent the complexity of transnational realities. A very promising area of research that addresses the complexity of glocal, transnational, and multilingual realities is the research of hip-hop in international arenas. Androutsoppoulos (2009) also studied hip-hop artists who codeswitched using the local language/s for hip-hop singing while using English phrases to reference some more global ideas therefore,

> by relating them [hip-hop] to the notion of *glocalization* . . . I argue that English is a main resource for constructing "glocal" Hip Hop identities. (pp. 44–45)

In other words, the transnational hip-hop artist uses English and its cultural references as a purposeful resource to enhance his glocal linguistic flow. Because of this trend, more and more teacher educators are now challenged to face new discussions in their classrooms on issues related to social justice and democratic practices within their learning communities. As Blommaert (2003) stated:

> Part of linguistic inequality in any society—and consequently, part of much social inequality—depends on the incapacity of speakers to accurately perform

certain discourse functions on the basis of available resources. . . . Consequently, *differences* in the use of language are quickly, and quite systematical-
ly, translated into *inequalities* between speakers. (p. 615)

Another researcher who adds to this definition is Bhatia (2000), who uses
the term *glocalization* to refer to the hybridity in advertisements in rural
India where at least two linguistic systems are present. In his work, glocalization is paraphrased as "think and act both global and local at the same time"
(p. 161). In contrast, globalization is "thinking and acting globally" (i.e.,
advertising in English), while localization is "thinking locally and acting
locally" (i.e., advertising in the local regional language). For Bhatia, then,
multilingual advertisements in the rural India context are "glocal" by virtue
of being multilingual.

Glocalization is also a very political term. Bauman (2013) adds to this discussion by stating that globalization cuts both ways. Global forces sometimes
help local communities value their own cultural tribal sense. Geopolitical fragmentation provides opportunities to maneuver: it might reallocate poverty and its
stigma from "above" without even addressing the residual responsibility. Sometimes populations are reconceptualized as tourists and vagabonds. Therefore,
glocalization may end up reinforcing already existing patterns of domination.

Weber (2007) also discusses the evolution of the relationship between national and international development and educational change in the past decades.
He is concern about trends to compare and contrast teachers and teaching across
industrialized and developing countries. Therefore he seeks to make problematic
conventional understandings of globalization and glocal development, arguing
that these too should be revised given empirical data on teachers and teaching in
poor countries.

The past "neutral" teacher educator might become more and more a
breeding ground for the creation of "world-minded" teacher educators
(Zeichner, 2010) participating in an effort to view social justice in a comparative framework shaped by the tensions between the global and local forces
that shape their own realities.

According to Broadfoot (2000), in response to the glocal forces currently
influencing our society, a reconceptualization of Western education systems
and teacher education programs is needed. Comparative education has largely worked with the conventional delivery model and therefore has helped to
reinforce the status quo. In order to fulfill its promise, comparative education
studies must address the emerging new educational aspirations of the twenty-
first century. She proposes the term "comparative learnology" as the means
of understanding how individuals can be encouraged to engage successfully
with the many new forms of glocal learning opportunities that are likely to
characterize the third millennium.

Harth (2010) in his article also discusses how the technological advances in all areas of our lives have thickened the level of interactivity that binds us all. This new "glocal" reality should be the setting for new conversations about the goal of teaching and learning in this new interconnected reality. New question should be asked such as: What type of education do young citizens need in order to develop identities and connections to multiple communities? How can educators prepare them for this type of interconnectedness and dynamism? More specifically, what knowledge, skills, and perspectives will best enable them to thrive as glocal citizens? Educators should be able to prepare all their students for even more connected futures and to provide tools to lead in glocal communities of the near future.

In terms of glocalization as a way to internationalize preservice teacher education experiences, Merry Merryfield (1998) has been a pioneer. She believes that a good way to internationalize teacher education is not by sending students across the world to see other languages and cultures, but to create experiences in students' own communities where the glocal forces can be identified and developed. In her classes, she makes explicit connections between student teachers, linguistic and cultural identities with the linguistic and cultural identities present in their local communities. Merryfield argues that by helping students see firsthand the global local connections that are abundant in the United States in almost any community, they will be able to relate in a more personal way to glocal injustices and inequities. Finally, she talks about world-minded educators as the ones who have the habit of mind to think about how our local decisions affect people not only in our surrounding communities but across the world.

Some inspiring teachers (Stewart & Santiago, 2006) are creating experiences for their students in their classes that have implications for world-minded educators interested in developing a glocal understanding of language development. Stewart teaches Spanish as a foreign language in the affluent suburbs of Philadelphia. Santiago is a professor of ESL at the North Philadelphia campus; this program is for the non-traditional student and in a heavily Puerto Rican section of the city. By asking their students to create an autobiography that is in both English and Spanish for their students to share, the researchers found that this experience promoted a glocal understanding of students' lives and promoted serious discussions about equity and social justice among the participants. Finally, they also state that language teachers at any college or high school could find ways to use books and translated texts to engage their students in the world and the community around them: their glocal community while addressing the importance of world-minded educators interested in promoting social justice and democracy.

## CHARACTERISTICS OF THE BOOK

In this section we highlight some to the general characteristics of the book you are about to read followed by a more detailed section-by-section description.

Several aspects of the edited volume that are worth mentioning are:

1. The varied types of participants—some of the chapters present an experience with teachers at different points of their academic journey—from preservice to in-service; undergraduate and graduate; elementary and secondary certifications and different content areas (from generalists to science and social studies education, from monolingual teachers to bilingual and foreign language ones, etc.).
2. The varied locations of the experiences—the contexts range from Cambridge, England, to Costa Rica; from Namibia to the Philippines; from Israel to France, and so on. In the United States, from the New York metropolitan area to Utah and from Connecticut to Texas.
3. The varied perspectives on the internationalization efforts—most of the accounts are written from a U.S.-centered view of internationalization efforts, some are written as a result of a collaboration effort between a U.S. institution and an international one, and we also included a few chapters from an Italian and Israeli perspective.
4. Varied range of schooling contexts both in the United States and in the international setting—from international private school to urban public schools abroad; from suburban affluent public schools to urban poor schools in the United States.
5. The varied cutting-edge pedagogical approaches used to mediate the international collaboration—ranging from Problem Based Learning Task (PBLT) to constructivist hands-on data-driven science experiments; from a shared experience of watching a documentary across different settings to onsite museum visits.
6. The varied research methodologies used in the chapters range from reflective journey accounts to qualitative, mixed methods, and quantitative data-driven accounts, from a duoethnographic approach to theoretical proposals of the international collaborations.

Several aspects of the chapters in the study-abroad section are important to mention:

1. The varied duration of the study-abroad experience—some of the chapters present a short-term experience (two weeks), longer term (four weeks), and up to semester-long study-abroad projects.

2. The central importance of faculty-led programs in the study-abroad experience as a guarantee for students' engagement and debrief of their cross-cultural international experience.

The technology-enhanced section also has some poignant aspects worth mentioning:

1. The variety of platforms used in order to promote technology-enhanced collaborations ranging from Facebook to Ning, from Glogs to Skype.
2. The variety of types of collaborations—from asynchronous to a mix of synchronous and asynchronous experiences.

The glocal section also has a few shared viewpoints worth mentioning:

1. The varied conceptualizations of glocality ranging from an online hybrid third space to a hermeneutic journey of understanding and interpretations; from a creation of a set of course experiences to a space of struggle for democratic education across diverse contexts.
2. The central importance of utilizing local connections that are prevalent in the United States and elsewhere, and are global in nature (i.e., little Italy, Koreatown, little India, Chinatown) as an entry point to internationalizing teacher education programs. Yet, this option is often underutilized.

The final chapter of the edited volume is a conclusions chapter, in which the editors summarize the findings across the different initiatives and experiences. In addition, we detail future trends in the area of internationalizing teacher education programs.

## REFERENCES

Adams, M., K. DeJong, et al. (2008). "Review of the Year's Publication for 2007: Social Justice Education." *Equity & Excellence in Education* 41(4): 482–537.

Androutsopoulos, J. (2009). Language and the three spheres of hip hop. *Global linguistic flows: Hip hop cultures, youth identities, and the politics of language.* H. S. Alim, A. Ibrahim and A. Pennycook. New York: Routledge, 43–62.

Asia Society, *Going Global: Preparing Our Students for an Interconnected World.* New York: 2008.

Bauman, Z. (2013). "Glocalization and Hybridity," *Glocalism: Journal of Culture, Politics and Innovation* 1(1): 1–5.

Bhatia, S. (2000). "Language Socialisation and the Construction of Socio-moral Meanings." *Journal of Moral Education* 29(2): 149–166.

Bigelow, B. P. (2002). *Rethinking Globalization: Teaching for Justice in an Unjust World.* Milwaukee, WI, Rethinking schools.

Blommaert, J. (2003). "Commentary: A sociolinguistics of globalization." *Journal of Sociolinguistics* 7(4): 607–623.

Brindley, R., S. Quinn, et al. (2009). "Consonance and Dissonance in a Study Abroad Program as a Catalyst for Professional Development of Pre-Service Teachers." *Teaching and Teacher Education: An International Journal of Research and Studies* 25(3): 525–532.

Broadfoot, P. (2000). "Comparative Education for the 21st Century: Retrospect and Prospect." *Comparative Education* 36(3): 357–371.

Byram, M. and A. Feng (2006). *Living and studying abroad: research and practice.* Clevedon, England; Buffalo, NY: Multilingual Matters Ltd.

Cochran-Smith, M. (1991). "Learning to Teach against the Grain." *Harvard Educational Review* 61(3): 279–310.

Committee for Economic Development. *Education for Global Leadership.* Committee for Economic Development, Washington, DC: 2006. Available: www.ced.org/projects/educ_forlang.shtml.

Council of Chief State School Officers, *Global Education Policy Statement,* Washington, DC: 2006. Available: www.ccsso.org/content/pdfs/Global%20Education%20FINAL%20lowrez.pdf.

Cushner, K. (2007). "The Role of Experience in the Making of Internationally-Minded Teachers." *Teacher Education Quarterly* 34(1): 27–39.

Darling-Hammond, L., and J. Bransford (Eds.) (2005). *Preparing teachers for a changing world: What teachers should learn and be able to do.* San Francisco, CA: Jossey-Bass.

Day, C., A. Fernandez, et al. (2000). *The Life and Work of Teachers: International Perspectives in Changing Times.* Florence, KY: Taylor & Francis, Group, 288.

Fischman, G. E. (2001). "Teachers, Globalization, and Hope: Beyond the Narrative of Redemption." *Comparative Education Review* 45(3): 412–418.

Gragert, E. H. (2000). Expanding International Education through the Internet: No Longer Limited to the Global Studies and Language Curriculum. For full text: http://www.ed.gov/Technology/techconf/2000/edgragert.pdf., 14.

Harth, C. (2010). "Going Glocal: Adaptive Education for Local and Global Citizenship." *Independent School* 70(1).

Kumaravadivelu, B. (2003). "Problematizing cultural stereotypes in TESOL." *TESOL Quarterly* 37(4): 709–719.

Kumaravadivelu, B. (2008). *Cultural globalization and language education.* New Haven, Yale University Press.

Levine, M. H. (2005). (Progressive Policy Institute), *Putting the World into OurClassrooms: A New Vision for 31st Century Education,* April 2005.

Longview Foundation. (2008). *Teacher preparation for the global age: The imperative for change.* Retrieved from http://www.longviewfdn.org/files/44.pdf.

Marx, H. and D. M. Moss (2011). "Please Mind the Culture Gap: Intercultural Development during a Teacher Education Study Abroad Program." *Journal of Teacher Education* 62(1): 35–47.

Merryfield, M. (1992). Preparing social studies teachers for the twenty-first century: Perspectives on program effectiveness from a study of six exemplary teacher education programs in global education. *Theory and Research in Social Studies* 20:17–26.

Merryfield, M. M. (1998). "Pedagogy for Global Perspectives in Education: Studies of Teachers' Thinking and Practice." *Theory and Research in Social Education* 26(3): 342–379.

McKinsey & Company Social Sector Office. 2009. The economic impact of the achievement-gap in America's schools.

National Association of State Boards of Education. *Citizens for the 21st Century: Revitalizing the Civic Mission of Schools.* National Association of State Boards of Education, Alexandria, VA: 2006, 21.

National Lieutenant Governors Association (2008). Resolution in Support of Establishing a National International Education Policy. Available: www.nlga.us/web-content/Policy/Policy_List_2000_thru.html.

National Research Council. *International Education and Foreign Languages: Key to Securing America's Future.* Committee to Review Title VI and Fulbright Hays International Education Programs. Washington, DC: The National Academies Press, 2007.

Oyler, C. (2011). "Teacher Preparation for Inclusive and Critical (Special) Education." *Teacher Education and Special Education* 34(3): 201–218.

Palmer, D. K. and J. Menard-Warwick (2012). "Short-Term Study Abroad for Texas Preservice Teachers: On the Road from Empathy to Critical Awareness." *Multicultural Education* 19(3): 17–26.

Pennycook, A. (2003). "Global Englishes, Rip Slime and performativity." *Journal of Sociolinguistics* 7(4): 513–533.

Quezada, R. L. (2010). Internationalization of teacher education: Creating global competent teachers and teacher educators for the twenty-first century. Editorial, *Teaching Education* 21(1), 1–5. Special Issue: Internationalization of Teacher Education.

Reimers, F. M. (2009). Teaching for the 21st Century: Leading for Global Competency. *Educational leadership* 67(1).

Report from the International Commission on Education for Sustainable Development Practice (2008). The Earth Institute at Columbia University.

Richardson, V. and P. Placier (2001). "Teacher change." In V. Richardson (Ed.), *Handbook of research on teaching* (4th ed., pp. 905–947). Washington, DC: American Educational Research Association.

Rizvi, F. and B. Lingard (2009). *Globalizing Education Policy*. London: Routledge.

Rogers, P. C. (2011). "Shaping Global Citizens: Technology Enhanced Intercultural Collaboration and Transformation." *Educational Technology* 51(2): 47–52.

Schneider, A. I. (2007). *To Leave No Teacher Behind: Building International Competence into the Undergraduate Training of K–12 Teachers.* Washington, DC. Available: www.internationaledadvice.org.

Sizer, T. (1992). *Horace's School: Redesign of the American High School.* Boston: Houghton Mifflin Co.

Steger, M. B. (2003). *Globalization: A very short introduction.* Oxford; New York: Oxford University Press.

Stewart, J. A. and K. A. Santiago (2006). "Using the Literary Text to Engage Language Learners in a Multilingual Community." *Foreign Language Annals* 39(4): 683–696.

Tucker, J. L., and P. J. Cistone (1991). Global perspectives for teachers: An urgent priority. *Journal of Teacher Education* 42, 3–9.

Weber, E. (2007). "Globalization, "Glocal" Development, and Teachers' Work: A Research Agenda." *Review of Educational Research* 77(3): 279–309.

Wells, A. C., S. Sibyll, S. Carnochan, J. Allen Slayton, and A. Vasudeva (1998). "Globalization and Educational Change." In A. Hargreaves (Ed.), *International Handbook of Educational Change.* Dordrecht, Netherlands: Kluwer Academic Publishers, pp. 322–348.

Wilder, H., S. P. Ferris, et al. (2010). "Exploring International Multicultural Field Experiences in Educational Technology." *Multicultural Education & Technology Journal* 4(1): 30–42.

Zeichner, K. (2010). "Competition, economic rationalization, increased surveillance, and attacks on diversity: Neo-liberalism and the transformation of teacher education in the U.S." *Teaching & Teacher Education* 26(8): 1544–1552.

*I*

# Study Abroad

*Chapter One*

# International Student Teaching in Non-Western Cultures

*A Journey of Personal and Professional Transformation on the Road to Becoming a Globally Minded Teacher*

Leigh Martin

Vignette: In Jacey's first-day reflection, she described how her new home and country she was living in also impacted her hopes and future actions as an educator:

> In the short while that I have been in Singapore, including my first day at this school, I have learned that this is a very unique country; it's almost as if the country changes each person that lives or visits here into exemplary world citizens. From the locals to the vacationers, and finally the students, parents, and teachers at this school, Singapore is full of honest and accepting individuals from all different backgrounds. From what I've experienced so far, I plan on using this consistent message of honesty, trust and openness within my classroom not only during my student teaching, but also in my future classrooms. I will embody an accepting and trustworthy attitude with all my students and colleagues in order to portray the type of behavior that I expect in return.

One might expect that, upon arriving in a non-Western culture with language barriers and distinct traditions, these student teachers may have felt overwhelmed or even described elements of culture shock. Not one student teacher expressed any difficulties or frustrations as they assimilated into the new environment. Their first-day reflections depicted nothing but jubilation, acceptance, and a warm welcome into their new homes.

## STATEMENT OF PURPOSE

This chapter explores how five first-year teachers describe the intercultural development that occurred while student teaching in a non-Western culture and how those experiences influenced their personal and professional outlook on teaching and social justice in their home culture. This study attempts to bridge the gap between current research focusing on student teaching experiences in Western cultures by adding the voices of student teachers in non-Western cultures. For the purposes of this study, non-Western is defined as cultures that have adopted cultural values, beliefs, and traditions not commonly associated with Western Europe.

Nationwide, teacher education faculty are repeating such phrases as "connect with students," "make learning meaningful," and "build upon the student's prior knowledge." With a gaping disconnect between the cultural backgrounds and life experiences of the teacher and the students, it is difficult to fathom how these expectations might be achievable. Research has clearly indicated that those who enter the teaching profession are predominantly white, middle-class American women possessing little understanding of their own culture, let alone that of others and the role that culture plays in teaching and learning (Gay, 2000; Marsh et al., 2011; Marx, 2008; Sleeter & Grant, 2007). An ethnocentric worldview of a teacher who lacks intercultural experiences, having never experienced being the "other," raises valid concern for the ability to make learning meaningful for the diversity in today's schools and the global scene that they should be preparing students for.

As universities strive to internationalize teacher education programs, it is crucial that their graduates enter the teaching field possessing not only the competencies but also the confidence necessary to teach all students, including non-Western immigrants that comprise a majority of the foreign-born population in the United States today. For this reason, this study focused specifically on student teaching experiences in non-Western cultures as it more closely resembles the immigrant population in U.S. schools. Several publications and dissertations have focused on the impact of international student teaching experiences; however, they have been situated predominantly in Western cultures (Cushner & Mahon, 2003; Marx, 2008; Stachowski, Richardson, & Henderson, 2003). As the diversity in U.S. schools continues to increase, it is of the utmost importance that our educators exhibit the intercultural skills necessary to make learning meaningful for all students. Although the ethnic backgrounds of teachers in the United States are not as culturally diverse as the students whom they teach, intercultural development is attainable when one reaches beyond the comforts of their home communities and experiences life as the "other." While practice teaching in an international environment, the student teacher typically lives in the local community among the local community members. In doing so, the student teacher often experiences an existence as a minority in relation to language, race, ethnicity, and religion. Research has suggested that student teaching in multicultural classrooms while living as an outsider in a foreign community can cause preservice teachers to critically examine their own cultural identities and beliefs as well as those of their students, making intercultural sensitivity possible in ways not achievable in domestic placements.

## DESCRIPTION OF SETTING

This study was predicated on the belief that student teaching in an American international school, in a non-Western culture, can serve as a catalyst for preservice teachers to simultaneously gain cultural sensitivity while deepening their understanding of teaching and learning. These schools are held to the rigorous international and U.S. standards as mandated by the entities that accredit them. Most American international schools are accredited by the same accrediting bodies as schools in the United States but are additionally held accountable for international and host country standards as well. It is not uncommon for graduates of American international schools to earn one, two, or three diplomas at the time of graduation. Whereas a U.S. diploma is standard, it is possible the graduate will also earn an international baccalaureate degree and a diploma from the host national curriculum as well.

The students who attend American international schools typically come from privileged families and are from diverse family backgrounds. As later described by each of the participants in this study, it is common for the student body to be comprised of host country nationals and other expatriate families living overseas for diplomatic or international business-related purposes. Although the social capital of these students provides privileges not commonly found among the more diverse population in U.S. schools, the students in American international schools do bring their own unique set of challenges. These challenges include: unique cultural values and traditions; limited English skills; parents who may be routinely away for business, extravagant travel, or, in some cases, living elsewhere while the student lives on the school campus; and a host of other challenges. In some cases the students may be living in a dichotomy of two cultures, where their school day operates predominantly on U.S. norms but their home life is rooted in non-Western traditions. While this may seem easily dismissible, this dichotomy impacts such issues as arrival and ending times of school, which may differ greatly from the student's neighbors or other family members.

Although the students at American international schools typically do enjoy great social capital outside of school, the conglomeration of these unique characteristics is part of the culture of the school and the student body that the teachers and student teachers take into account when building relationships and constructing academic learning. As evidenced in this study, the value gained through a student teaching experience in a non-Western culture is not diminished because of the privilege the student's experience. The daily interactions that the student teachers experienced with multiple nationalities inside the school day, and the rich cultural experiences while living in the host culture outside of the school, provided interactions with a variety of cultures and increased not only the ability to empathize with one culture, but a host of cultures, while recognizing that each is similar and unique in its own way.

## METHODOLOGY

### Research Design

Qualitative research was the most appropriate methodology applied in this study as I examined the lived experiences of student teachers as they began their teaching careers and reflected upon their student teaching experiences in non-Western cultures. Eisner (1998) described qualitative considerations in human affairs as a "ubiquitous part of life and manifest themselves whenever we experience the qualities of the environment" (p. 21). He further explained that "experience is what we achieve as those qualities come to be known. It is through qualitative inquiry, the intelligent apprehension of the qualitative world, that we *make sense*" (p. 21).

Qualitative research is interested in gaining a deep understanding of a small number of specified cases. When conducting qualitative research, there is greater interest in depth than in breadth, as the intent is not to produce generalizable results that can be applied to a larger population. According to Creswell (1998), the participants must "be individuals who have experienced the phenomenon being explored and can articulate their conscious experiences" (p. 111).

### Data Collection

Qualitative methodology was employed as a framework for this study. Data-gathering methods included: (a) a demographic survey of participants; (b) in-depth interviews pertaining to their experiences abroad and teaching practices; (c) in-depth follow-up discussion questions that further investigate the strands that arose from the initial interview; (d) artifacts, including lesson plans and curricular documents; and (e) a semi-structured blog kept throughout their first year of teaching.

## Data Analysis

Sharing the stories of student teachers provided an opportunity for them to simultaneously make meaning of their experiences as the knowledge gained abroad influenced their current teaching practices. As the primary instrument for data collection and analysis, it was my hope that I would encourage rich description by being adaptive and responsive as the participants described in-depth accounts of their experiences.

The essence of qualitative research is to allow meaning to be socially constructed and interpreted as individuals interact with their world. The meaning can have multiple interpretations and is not fixed, but rather, can change over time (Merriam, 2002). The researcher serves as the primary instrument for data collection and must try to understand the meaning of social events in context while considering the subjectivity of human partici-pants as well as the subjectivity of the researcher herself (Esterberg, 2002). The inductive nature of this qualitative research provided an avenue to gather data and to build concepts and themes that might emerge from the data. The method of allowing a situation to speak for itself was described by Eisner (1998) as an emergent focus. In such a situation, the researcher focuses on selected common themes, which become the major object of the researcher's attention.

## Research Questions

This study attempted to add to existing literature. Specifically, this study intended to bridge the gap between current research focusing on student teaching experiences in Western cultures by adding the voice of those who student teach in non-Western cultures. The following research questions guided this study.

1. How do first-year teachers describe the intercultural development that occurs while student teaching in a non-Western culture?
2. How has student teaching abroad influenced your mind-set (as a teacher or in general)?
3. What unique skills have you gained while student teaching abroad?
4. How has student teaching abroad influenced you personally?

## The Participants

The participants were purposefully selected to take part in this study. Through purposive sampling participants were selected according to two criteria. Each participant was required to have student taught in a non-West-ern culture in the year prior to this study being conducted. The participants were also required to serve as first-year teachers at the time the study was being conducted. Below is a demographic depiction of the participants before and during student teaching. Pseudonyms were used to provide confidentiality and anonymity regarding the participants.

## Alissa

Alissa was raised in what she described as a "bedroom community" to a university town of fewer than 60,000 people. The town itself had no stoplights and was surrounded by farmland. When asked to describe the diversity that existed within her community, there was little to speak of with the exception of two foreign exchange students in her high school whom she befriended. College exposed her to an increasingly diverse student population, although the university she attended was also attended predominantly by white students.

Alissa first began to consider study abroad programs during her freshman year. She described her interest as stemming from a desire to "really experience another culture, beyond just traveling through it." With the understanding that her college offered international student teaching, she initially expressed interest in student teaching in an English-speaking country. However, having had several friends in college who spoke highly of their own travels throughout South America, she chose to student teach in Brazil. Alissa completed her student teaching in a privately operated prekindergarten through twelfth grade school located in the capital city of Brasilia. The school catered to the needs of Americans, Brazilians, and students from multiple other nationalities. Over half of the students at the school were Brazilian nationals; less than 20 percent were American students, while the remaining students represented approximately forty-five different nationalities. Alissa student taught in both first- and second-grade classrooms. She is now teaching third grade in a public school in the Midwest of the United States.

## Amanda

Although her family moved several times throughout her schooling, all of Amanda's childhood was spent in rural communities within the same Midwestern state. Amanda described the schools as "not extremely diverse in terms of race or religion." She went on to say, "I know there's a lot of ways to measure diversity, but my schools were predominantly Caucasian students. I could count on my hands the other ethnicities. Students were from the same Christian belief background. So quite a bit of continuity in the schools I grew up in." However, even with the little diversity that existed, Amanda contended that she had interacted with people from a more diverse background. She attributed these interactions to teams that she played on and also her interest in learning Spanish, beginning in high school and accelerating in college when Spanish became a passion.

While in college, Amanda found herself involved in several diverse student groups on campus, namely with Saudi Arabian students. Amanda illuminated her interest in the Saudi culture by explaining,

> "I wanted to get to know where they were from. I was good friends with a lot of them and I wanted to see how they grew up, and what made them who they were. I was really curious to learn about Islam, to be honest. In the States, there is such a negative perception toward that part of the world. I kind of wanted to go to see for myself." She continued, "I was just really craving that experience . . . hands-on, eyewitness kind of experience."

Although her first choice was to student teach in Saudi Arabia, Amanda's student teaching coordinator encouraged her to consider Egypt instead, as the university had a long-standing relationship with several schools there. With a major in art education, Amanda completed her student teaching in Cairo, Egypt, at an independent coeducational day school that offered an education program for prekindergarten through grade twelve. The school had a strong fine arts program, which particularly appealed to Amanda. Among an enrollment of approximately 1,400 students, nearly half were U.S. citizens. The remaining students were Egyptian nationals or other nationalities. Amanda shared her time between the elementary, middle level, and high school art teachers. She is currently teaching intermediate level art in a private American school in Mumbai, India, and recently married a man of Indian descent whom she met in India.

*Darci*

Like the other participants, Darci described her hometown as small, rural, and lacking in diversity, "with only a handful of students who were non-white." After high school, she studied at a small liberal arts college that had greater cultural diversity, although her interactions with diverse groups were limited. An educational excursion to the Caribbean during her sophomore year sparked an interest in various cultures. During her graduate studies, Darci became involved with a non-profit organization as she tutored immigrants who were preparing for the U.S. Citizen and Immigration Services (USCIS) test to become citizens and practicing conversational English with English language learners at the university.

Having heard numerous positive reports from her peers who had studied abroad during their college years, Darci never wavered in her dreams to student teach abroad. She student taught in Thailand where nearly one hundred boarding students lived on campus and over four hundred students attended school each day. Slightly less than half of the students were full or part Thai, with the remaining comprised of thirty-five other nationalities. Darci is now teaching high school biology in a large metropolitan school district in the Midwestern United States.

## Jacey

Jacey was raised in a town of fewer than 3,000 people. She described religious affiliations to be the extent of the diversity in the community in which she was raised, stating that there were "essentially three big churches in town: Lutheran, Methodist, and Catholic. It was basically a farming community where everybody knows everybody." Her surroundings changed slightly when she went to college, as she described: "I visually saw more diversity in terms of different races, but in terms of who I actually hung out with and talked to and who I interacted with. . . . No, there was not that big of a difference in college."

She was initially attracted to this university because of its vast study abroad program; however, as a college athlete, it was challenging to commit to a semester away from her team and training. Therefore, Jacey considered international student teaching as the perfect opportunity to combine study abroad with a required semester of coursework. She had long dreamed of seeing more of the world, but, more importantly, she considered study abroad as an opportunity to prepare for her upcoming career as an educator. Jacey remarked, "What caught my attention was the diversity that I would be faced with in the classroom. And that's something that obviously, I hadn't really had." Describing herself as a firm believer in multicultural education, she went on to describe a passion for exposing students to different points of views: "I teach English, so I enjoy different authors from different backgrounds, cultures and what not. Now that I think of it, perhaps I had that desire because I wasn't given that as a kid."

Jacey credited one small unit in her high school AP English class for exposing her to authors from different cultures. As she recalled this awakening, Jacey stated, "I never considered that there was literature outside of white American male and a few female authors that I read in high school. And in that one unit, I was like 'oh my gosh, how small town am I?' and it got me hooked."

Jacey completed her student teaching in a high school English classroom, in the city-state of Singapore. This private school is one of the largest American international schools in the world, and serves a diverse learning community of more than 3,800 students from more than fifty countries in grades prekindergarten through grade twelve. Jacey was hired as an English teacher at the same school where she student taught.

*Janelle*

Janelle grew up in a rural, farming community and graduated in a class of thirty-seven students. With the exception of an occasional foreign exchange student and two students with African ancestry, Janelle had very few interactions with diverse groups of people until she entered college. While in college, she lived in a dormitory that also housed the international students, allowing her the opportunity to meet several students from other countries although she still described her college years as being surrounded by mostly Caucasian students.

Janelle's passion for international travel was ignited when she participated in a university program as a summer camp counselor on a military base in Okinawa, Japan. Through this summer camp she realized that her dream was to teach overseas, and the best road to pursuing that dream was to student-teach overseas. Like Alissa, Janelle student taught at the same privately operated prekindergarten through twelfth grade school located in the capital city of Brasilia, Brazil. Janelle spent the first half of her student teaching experience working with elementary art students and the second half with secondary art students. Her experience student teaching with the international baccalaureate (IB) curriculum in Brazil contributed significantly to Janelle being hired as an IB art teacher in the only IB school located in her home state in the Midwestern United States.

## FINDINGS

The findings below illuminate the student teachers' responses to three primary research questions. The questions included: (1) How has student teaching abroad influenced your mind-set, as a teacher or in general? (2) What unique skills have you gained while student teaching abroad? (3) How has student teaching abroad influenced you personally? Responses were collated according to recurring themes.

For the first question, two themes became apparent as the participants discussed the influences of student teaching abroad on their mind-set. Those two themes were (1) professional relationships and collaboration and (2) enthusiasm for teaching.

### Professional Relationships and Collaboration

All five participants mentioned professional relationships in some capacity. Amanda described the professionally minded faculty with years of experience as important factors contributing to her growth as an educator, while Jacey portrayed an environment rich with collaboration as an incentive to take more risks in the classroom. Janelle described collaboration as a source of encouragement to provide a better education for her students. Jacey celebrates the impact that the experiences has had on her mind-set, not only for the immediate semester, but for the future as well:

> During my student teaching semester [abroad] I have grown both personally and professionally. From the endless collaboration with colleagues to the many opportunities for reflection through talks with my cooperating teacher, I have developed into the educator I've always wanted to be. Working with the faculty, as well as the students has changed the way I view teaching. This school provided me with an environment where learning and taking risks in the classroom is not only accepted, but celebrated.

The collaboration and professional relationships mentioned were not limited only to the cooperating teachers assigned to mentor them, but was extended to include school faculty, colleagues and people from outside of the school walls as well.

## Enthusiasm for Teaching

Enthusiasm for teaching was expressed explicitly by four of the five participants. While one confirmed that she had, indeed, made the right decision in choosing the teaching profession, another described the experience as incredible and expressed excitement for the opportunity to be exposed to various cultures and teaching diverse populations of students.

After a year of anticipation, Amanda recalled how much she appreciated working with children:

> Being at the university immersed in classes and textbooks for four years can really tend to surround you and submerge you but this experience helped me break back into the joy of teaching, the hands on, face to face interactions that I as an educator thrive on.

Additionally, Jacey discussed her excitement for teaching in the context of both student teaching and her upcoming career as a teacher. When noting the location of her student teaching and the diversity within the student body, her enthusiasm was not only for the profession, but for the values that she hoped to instill in her students. She stated, "My experience with student teaching has only made me more enthusiastic about helping my future students to become life-long learners who are constantly striving to stretch their knowledge and perspective of the world around them."

Question 2: What unique skills have you gained while student teaching abroad?

Overwhelmingly, the participants responded to this question with a new level of appreciation for diversity. Although Amanda had an extensive travel history prior to student teaching, she summarized the impressions of the diverse student body by stating, "Working at an international school has shown me a whole new definition of diversity."

*Exposure to multiple nationalities and unique perspectives*

Exposure to multiple nationalities was unparalleled to anything that the participants had experienced in their home state. One participant remarked, "Never in [my home state] had I worked with a group of sixteen students representing nine separate nationalities," while another participant reiterated this point, stating the following: "Now, depending on where one teaches in the United States, this could be part of life already, but as far as my experience goes, this is the first time that I have taught this many students in one class speaking English as a second language."

Jacey, who admittedly had limited experiences with diverse cultures prior to student teaching, discussed the overwhelming impact that this new view has offered her:

> During my semester abroad I encountered a lot of different perspectives in each of my classes as well as in my social life. All the different cultures and worldviews my students brought to each class really opened my eyes to the different points of view that students from all around the world may have. In any given class I would have questions thrown at me that I had never really considered because I was unaware of that perspective.

She further addressed the unique perspective this experience provided with the following description:

> This is unique to my experience teaching in Singapore because had I stayed in [my home state] I would have been in classes full of students with similar worldviews as myself. However, in saying this I'm not implying that those worldviews are necessarily narrow or close-minded, just that a student from India sharing their insights and perspectives in class will have a very different approach than a student from a small town in the U.S.

When reflecting on the various cultures, languages, social classes, and other various dynamics impacting any diverse classroom, Alissa made a valuable point: "As the classroom teacher, I had to find a way to lead all these students into a cohesive classroom community. Whether I am in Brasilia or Iowa, these are challenges that all schools face."

An interesting final point in relation to exposure to diverse cultures was an increased cognizance of this worldview and its impact on personal judgments. As one participant became more aware of her previously limited scope of the world, she recognized that her judgments of situations may have also been limited in scope. She expressed that in future interactions she will be differently able to assess a situation based on increased life experiences.

## Second language speakers necessitated differentiated instruction

Participants gave extensive responses that revealed an increased ability to embrace and teach to diverse student needs within the classroom setting. They disclosed acquiring a wider set of skills to accommodate the varying needs of their students. Amanda elaborated on the impact that such a diverse student population had on the culture of the classroom: "I have seen (and admire) the use of multiple languages in a classroom and many of the students have a very global perspective of the world due to their third culture upbringing. ESL students were very common, and it really helped me to improve my communication by using multiple ways to describe one item or process for the students to better understand, as well as visuals."

While some participants expressed a new ability to incorporate multiple points of view due to the wide range of cultures represented in the classroom, others discussed visual representations to accommodate second language learners. Although Janelle student taught on a different continent, her experience was remarkably similar to Amanda's. Janelle described the impact that the multilingual students had on classroom dynamics as well as the modes of instruction:

> I have gained the ability to alter the delivery of my speech to different students and different classes due to language barriers. In any one of the classes I taught, one could hear at least three different languages being spoken at one time. All students know English, but some students hold it as a second or third language, so altering the delivery of my lessons was a useful tool to capture the attention and allow for understanding of all students. I used many visuals and developed handouts to aid this. I showed the steps to every lesson I did, as part of producing visuals.

Darci expressed the importance of vocabulary when teaching students who do not speak English as a native language. With an increased attention to language, Darci learned that there is a vast difference between asking a question which elicits a one-word response versus an open-ended question which requires a student to define or describe an idea or issue. This firsthand experience enabled her to recognize the confusion that can exist when using different dialects of the English language or when conversing with those who speak another primary language. This caused her to focus additional attention on vocabulary acquisition as a basis for understanding content knowledge.

Living in a foreign community, as well as teaching students of varying cultures, necessitates an ability to assimilate. This held true in the neighborhoods in which these participants lived as well as in the schools where they were student teaching. In addition to varying instructional techniques, participants also discussed not only a need but also a desire to adapt to the other cultures in unpredictable or unexpected situations:

Along with the readiness to accept all new things comes the ability to adapt quickly to your surroundings. Because of my teaching overseas I have developed the ability to learn my environment and take the necessary steps to assimilate quickly. In terms of my school life and the teaching skills I've gained through this, I am now much more equipped to jump into a teaching team or curriculum, which may be new to me, and be successful in implementing myself as a part of the group.

When comparing her home culture and upbringing with the student teaching location, Jacey explained her new perspective: "While this may be the case in all new schools or teams I join, I feel that being in Singapore has taught me how to do this successfully without putting labels on the experience (e.g., "good" or "bad"). Therefore, in my teaching this has helped me to look at new methods and strategies as different, not any better or worse than what I learned in college or in my field experiences."

Ultimately, the participants had direct contact and built meaningful relationships with students and colleagues from various cultures while expanding their understanding not only of the world but also of teaching. Amanda summed up her experience by stating, "I would say I learned just as much about the world from my students as they did from me."

Question 3: How has student teaching abroad influenced you personally?

The theme throughout these responses depicts a newfound awareness or a new lens through which the participants are able to view themselves. As they were introduced to an outsider's perspective, the participants recognized new views on their home culture, personal value, and characteristics. Additionally, daily interactions in the non-Western cultures resulted in a surprising awareness of their own biases, preferences, stereotypes, and assumptions. Because each participant specifically elaborated on the personal growth and awareness, this question will be broken down as elaborated upon by each participant.

## Self-awareness

### Amanda

Perhaps Amanda's description of herself as an Egyptian was the most revealing sign of how intimately she immersed herself into the culture during her student teaching experience. She answered this question in Arabic, stating, "*Ana Masria*" [I am Egyptian]. She gave an elaborate explanation of the significance of this phrase:

> While this statement is incredibly inaccurate, it conveys how I feel personally here. I have developed a life in Cairo that includes very dear friends and families. I worked hard at picking up the Arabic language and that challenge

alone of learning a new language (without instruction) (while student teaching) (in a completely new country), had a profound effect on me personally.

In addition to gaining a new culture, Amanda also came to appreciate her own native culture by stepping away from it: "Being in Egypt specifically has enabled me to reflect on home and the things I love (and miss) such as clean air and green grass, but also see the value in living in the midst of such an ancient civilization. It has opened my eyes to this half of the world too, literally."

Amanda also came to the humbling realization that, although she perceived herself as well traveled with a global view of the world, there were many cultures that she had not yet experienced:

> I believe I came into this experience with a fairly worldly, conscientious view of humanity but it was such an incredible experience just to meet my students and the other teachers who have seen so many other countries and lived in so many other cultures that showed me that I'm just at the tip of the iceberg when it comes to understanding this whole world.

Additionally, she opened her mind to the idea of visiting places that had not previously intrigued her: "Before this trip I had little interest in living or working in Asia, but now (perhaps that I am closer, or have met others who loved their time in Asia) I see it as a viable option for my future. It has definitely continued to open my eyes to the world and learn to embrace differences with joy."

## Janelle

Janelle described personal and individual growth in both her thoughts and perceptions of the world. She spoke about her previous travels and the culminating effects that each foreign culture had on her development. More importantly, she discussed the personal traits that had impacted her, such as her ability to adapt, reflect, analyze, and keep adapting. She described her place in life: "As a young person, getting ready to graduate, I know I'm still finding myself and this experience has both justified my thoughts on who I am as well as shaken them to their core" while she continued to illustrate her place in the world; "In the big picture I am a part of the world or nation and who I am as an individual will hold a small part in it." Like Amanda, Janelle gained access to an outsider's perspective of her home culture as well and recognized the varying views of the United States, often unrecognized from the homeland:

> My thoughts on how others view the United States seem to change with every country I live in. Perceptions and ideas of the U.S. weigh greatly on how the U.S. is presented to the people in the news, in conversation, and through their

own government. I have learned that every country will have supporters as well as haters of the United States. It's interesting to find that many Brazilians, like many other cultures, love U.S. entertainment. The rest is pretty split, depending on who you talk to.

Additionally, Janelle recognized characteristics of the Brazilian culture that she had chosen to incorporate into her own life: "My thoughts have been further justified, in that people are the most important thing in life." She explained that each time she traveled she gained a new perspective on other cultures as well as increased self-awareness. She commented about the high priority that Brazilians placed on family and relationships while opening their homes to others and making her feel comfortable while there.

## Jacey

Numerous factors played a role in the personal growth that Jacey experienced while student teaching in Singapore; namely, living with a new family and being surrounded by people who did not relate to her on a daily basis. "Singapore has challenged me and how I react to new people and places. While I've always considered myself to be an open and accepting individual, my experience overseas has taught me to control my immediate reactions a bit more carefully."

Jacey described her initial reactions during her first weeks, as she found herself immersed in cultural diversity like she had not previously experienced: "When I first arrived in Singapore and started meeting all of my colleagues, I was quick to be surprised or shocked at certain things people did or said; these reactions were never meant to be hurtful or narrow-minded they were simply my genuine reactions to the things people said or even the things people claimed never to have heard of or experienced."

Having lived all of her life in one state, Jacey had not been exposed to the array of diversity that she was amid during her student teaching. Through this experience, she recognized that her thoughts, reactions, and opinions were not necessarily commonly shared when the people around her came from various cultural backgrounds. Living with a host family exposed Jacey to the inside perspective of a new family environment. Moreover, spending most of her days with people who did not necessarily relate to her small-town up-bringing challenged her to examine how she reacted to new people and places. While her perceived self-image was one of acceptance and honoring differences, Jacey quickly recognized when her opinions were in the minority.

After her first month in Singapore, Jacey noticed that people seemed to feel uncomfortable around her or hesitant to share certain information with her. Upon reflection, she attributed this to what she described as her immediate reaction and facial expression that seemed to create a disconnect between her and the people she met. She explained, "While I may feel connected to other people, that doesn't necessarily mean they will understand the things I've been through or I'll understand the things they've experienced."

While reflecting on her personal growth throughout the semester of student teaching, Jacey explained that through her increased interaction with a diverse population, her self-awareness was elevated as she recognized a need to absorb and reflect on each encounter while making a conscious effort to be humble in an effort to ensure that the persons with whom she was interacting felt comfortable and willing to share their ideas. She also recognized that through this enculturation process, she would continue to grow in her own personal understanding of cultural differences. She shared this new awareness in her final reflection: "In the end, the different experiences and opinions people hold shouldn't act as something that shocks me; it should act as something that intrigues me and pushes me to learn more."

### Alissa

Alissa described the experience of student teaching abroad as one that stretched her personally. The extensive lived experiences in a non-Western culture enabled Alissa to dwell among various cultures "in language, culture, mindset and pace of life." Through this "indescribable experience," she moved beyond culture shock and learned to embrace her new environment. Being placed in another culture so vastly different from her own enabled her to reflect on her own presumptions and background while recognizing these differences.

### Darci

When asked about personal growth during student teaching, Darci revealed new insights into her own travel preferences and inner strength. Since her experience was completely on her own, Darci learned that she preferred having someone with whom to share her experiences, but, at the same time, she commented that "sometimes it is nice to start off alone and just meet and travel with new people."

> I learned how to be open to new experiences and renewed my excitement in trying everything once. I am more confident in approaching new people—this has given me the opportunity to share experiences with people from all over the world.

## COMMONALITIES AMONG PARTICIPANTS

The themes throughout these responses depicted a newfound awareness, or a new lens through which the participants were able to view themselves. As they were introduced to an outsider's perspective they recognized that they gained new views on their home culture, and their personal value and characteristics. Additionally, daily interactions in the non-Western cultures brought about a surprising awareness of their own biases, preferences, stereotypes, and assumptions.

## Implications for Teaching and Social Justice

The greater majority of U.S.-educated teachers have European ancestry; therefore, in a non-Western culture, the abounding cultural differences serve to further increase the intercultural relations and competencies gained by those living within such cultures. For example, there are certainly unique differences that a person must acclimate to within a foreign but Western culture; however, these differences are not as encompassing as the comprehensiveness of a non-Western culture. Whereas there may be unique language, customs, and religious practices encountered on an individual basis within Western cultures, a person living in a non-Western culture is often inundated simultaneously with these differences, and without reprieve. For the duration of the time spent living in a non-Western culture, one must live within that culture, and with the inability to retreat into customs that are known and comfortable.

The analysis of the participants revealed that a clear distinction exists between the participants in this study and a majority of U.S. teachers with a more limited scope of experiences. That distinction lies in how individuals view differences. Hammer and Bennett (2003) described individuals in the ethnocentric stages as avoiders of differences, whereas those in the ethnorelative stages as seekers of differences. Cushner (2011) asserted, "There is every indication to suggest that today's classroom teachers and teacher education students are stuck in the ethnocentric side of this scale and may not have the requisite disposition to be effective intercultural educators nor possess the skills necessary to guide young people to develop intercultural competence" (p. 604).

Cushner further illuminated numerous relevant studies that also used Bennett's framework as a reliable instrument to examine the intercultural sensitivity of both classroom teachers and students in those classrooms. These studies indicate that 84 percent to 91 percent of the U.S. classroom teachers participating in these studies fell at the minimization stage or below (Bayles, 2009; Mahon, 2006, 2009; Pappamihiel, 2004). Two additional studies (Pedersen, 1998; Straffon, 2003) looked at the intercultural sensitivity of the school-age students and found data that contrasted from that of the classroom teachers, suggesting that the students are better prepared to embrace diversity than many of their teachers. Cushner (2012) summarized these studies with the assertion that "the greater amount of exposure to difference (urban vs.

suburban and rural schools in the Pedersen study and the amount of time in international schools in the Straffon study), the higher level of intercultural sensitivity. As this chapter unfolds, this statement by Cushner becomes crucial and central to the analysis of the current study.

These aforementioned assertions ignite the necessity for teacher education candidates to awaken their breadth and depth of experiences to enable them to relate to students from diverse backgrounds. Without intentionally interrupting cultural hegemony, prevailing cultural norms are inevitably imposed by the predominantly white, middle class, and monolingual teaching force in U.S. schools. Beliefs about teaching and learning go unchallenged when misconceptions about diverse children's lives and cultures are socially reproduced by abounding stereotypes. The National Center for Educational Statistics (2009) attested that, during the 2006 to 2007 academic year, more than four out of ten students in U.S. schools were from underrepresented groups. This being the case, the participants' experiences in non-Western cultures were substantial, timely, and relevant as there is further indication that this ratio will continue to rise, with 20 percent of U.S. public school enrollment now being comprised of students with Hispanic ancestry. The participants in this study revealed that their experiences in non-Western cultures disrupted their previously deficient paradigms and replaced them, thus increasing their ability and desire to coalesce into a diverse, yet harmonious, society.

The non-Western focus of this study illuminated the lived experiences of the participants during their student teaching experiences, where they often coexisted as constituents of the societies while they were living abroad. For these participants, the closest resemblance to their home culture was found within the school hours, where the language of instruction was English and the school structure mostly resembled a U.S. school day. However, even within the confines of the school campus, multiple languages could be heard among both students and staff, and the cultural diversity in the classrooms was far more apparent than is typical in U.S. schools. Although it is likely that the participants were inadvertently granted some social privileges by the sheer nature of being U.S. Americans, they undoubtedly found themselves submerged in a sea of language barriers, diverse religious practices, and cultural norms. Through their daily routines of interacting within the communities in a foreign language, the participants gained firsthand experiences with the accompanying challenges while trying to assimilate into a society. In their attempts to assimilate, their obvious accents or inability to speak the language was just one characteristic that made full assimilation impossible.

In addition to the language barriers, the participants also described numerous other encounters where they had to readjust their habits or lifestyles to meet the expectations of the cultures in which they were living. Ranging from culturally different methods of greeting new friends, to the timeliness of one's arrival and deviating routes home to avoid interrupting public prayer time, the participants provided copious examples of lived experiences that altered their thinking and behavior both personally and professionally. Additional challenges came when attempting to buy groceries, reading labels not only in a different language, but in some case, even in a different alphabet, making attempted pronunciation impossible as well. One participant spoke of her experiences with daily prayer calls and the need to coordinate taxi rides, shopping trips, and other routine activities to accommodate prayer times throughout the day. Other participants told of needing to differentiate between black market sales and legal sales in an effort to remain within the laws of the country, or bartering for better prices and in some cases not being taken seriously because of their female gender. The participants recognized the limits that societies imposed on them when they demonstrated insufficient language skills or cultural deficiencies. When these challenges became personal experiences, the participants felt the frustrations as limited language or cultural abilities were misinterpreted as lacking ability or intelligence.

The participants' social equilibrium was disrupted when the dominant culture in which they were living held distinctly unique beliefs and perceptions from what the participants perceived to be true about social engagements and interactions. Although the social equilibriums will likely be re-balanced upon returning to their home culture, these participants have enhanced their awareness of others through their own lived experiences, thus bringing new empathy to their teaching and to the students whom they will teach. This empathy is depicted by Bennett and Bennett (2001) within the adaptation stage of the Developmental Model for Intercultural Sensitivity (DMIS). Through the extended period living in such a diverse culture, and without the ability to withdraw from the diverse setting, the participants' level of cultural sensitivity actually advanced beyond the superficial recognition and acceptance of cultural differences. Most teachers who have never lived outside of their home culture for any extended period of time often place emphasis on the commonalities of all people, ethnocentrically expressing such ideas as, *"Deep down we are all the same,"* or *"When you really get to know them, they're pretty much like us."* However, even as the participants move back into their home cultures, they will carry with them the ethno-relevant self-awareness as well as the awareness of others, accepting cultural differences as viable alternative method for interacting, both in their personal and professional lives.

Whereas it is possible to have had similar experiences in Western cultures, the inundation with vast differences in a non-Western culture was all encompassing for the participants in this study. As Cushner (2012) suggested, the extended period of time in a diverse environment enabled the participants to move from the comfortable stage of minimization into the advanced stage of adaptation, where they began to recognize that differences are important and worthy to embrace, not only in their classrooms but their communities as well. This study augments Cushner's recommendation for teachers to extend beyond their inherently narrow-minded perspectives and environments and provides evidence of participants exhibiting transformational intercultural interactions, as based on their experiences specifically in non-Western cultures. Being from European ancestry and commonly upheld Western traditions, the participants found that living in a non-Western culture altered almost every aspect of their lives, causing them to deal with the discomfort often experienced by students who comprise an increasingly larger percentage of U.S. classrooms and communities. Through this disequilibrium, the participants gained empathy and cultural sensitivity found in the adaptation stage, which can also be characterized as "intentionality" and "authenticity" and "typically occurs when casual contact with other cultures becomes more intense," such as when living abroad for a significant amount of time (Bennett & Bennett, 2001).

## CONCLUSION

Throughout this qualitative study, the stories of the participants are not intended to be generalized across larger groups of students. However, the details of their experiences are rich with evidence of personal and professional growth. When looked at individually, their experiences illuminate the possibilities as teacher educators, teachers, and student teachers continue this journey of becoming culturally sensitive community members and educators while providing culturally relevant teaching to best meet the needs of all students.

## MY STORY

For over a decade I have supervised nearly twenty student teachers per semester in Western and non-Western cultures; each semester I have the good fortune of reading their reflections, similar to those used in this study. In reading these reflections, I recognize that the experiences the student teachers are living out and the lessons that they are learning are predictable in many ways; however, it is the details of their stories that add richness to those lessons. Although I could tell them my stories, it is not until they personally engage in their own lived experiences that those lessons become meaningful and begin to transform their lives, as it did mine. My desire to specifically focus on non-Western cultures stemmed from several professional conversations where I often sensed that the experiences in American international schools were discounted by the sheer nature of the familiar curriculum, regardless of the diversity that existed within the school or outside its campus. In reflecting upon my own experiences, I questioned this thinking, recalling countless scenarios from my own experiences in Japan, Egypt, and Brazil in which I remembered feeling as much, if not more, inundated with cultural, religious, economic, and language diversity than what some of my student teachers in Western cultures wrote of in their reflections. Such was the impetus for my interest in exploring the impact of international student teaching in non-Western cultures.

When I unbracketed my own experiences and I listened to the stories of the participants in this study, I was immediately lost in memories of Cairo, where I student taught. Although it was an American school, I was living in a culture more unfamiliar to me than I had ever imagined. I recalled my arrival and the overwhelming sound of the Arabic language, with shouts and guttural sounds resembling aggression in my own language, yet resulting in hugs in the unfamiliar land; I recalled two days of answering my telephone every time the doorbell rang, as the sound of the doorbell resembled what I knew to be a telephone; the constant, never ending clamor and commotion of the city, giving new definition to the term *noise pollution*; waking to prayer call at the crack of dawn each day of my three years there; and the drummer boy who proudly pounded on my door in the middle of the night during Ramadan, reminding me to wake up so as to not miss my chance to eat before the sun was up, and expecting *baksheesh* for his good work. I recalled choosing my meat by pointing to my desired portion of the skinned cow that hung by its tail outside of the butcher; I recalled needing to rely on my husband to be firm in bartering when I couldn't be taken seriously as a woman; searching for anything that resembled a Christmas tree in December and trying to explain at the produce market that a gourd just wasn't the same as a pumpkin in October; and the donkey carts on the streets, side by side with the Mercedes and BMWs.

I recalled the *bowab* and his family of five living on my doorstep who were granted the rights to live there in exchange for opening doors, carrying groceries, and watering the plants. And the embarrassing moment when I learned one of my most valuable lessons ever from that man: *Different is not wrong*, as he rejected my gift of an empty hair-spray bottle to mist the plants before polishing the leaves. Assuming he didn't know how to use it, I demonstrated the proper spraying techniques rather than accepting his practice of blowing water from his mouth through pursed lips. As I attempted to enforce upon him my Western customs and privileges granted to me as an American, I neglected to recognize that his home, my doorstep, provided no place to store such an item, and thus his mouth served the same purpose and was far more convenient.

I recalled the Egyptian aide in the school who outwardly critiqued me, and the pride I took in cleaning my own apartment rather than hiring a cleaning lady. My culture had taught me to scoff at people who hired out work that they could do themselves; yet, in that moment, I was being judged for not providing work for someone in need. *"You Americans are so greedy with your riches,"* she exclaimed in the teacher's lounge. *Different is not wrong.*

These encounters outside of the school taught me more than any textbook or teacher education course could possible attempt to emulate. Through these experiences, interacting daily within a diverse culture, I learned that culture is everything. Culture is not only the language we speak, the food we eat, or the holidays we celebrate as it is often reduced to in U.S. schools. Culture is everything we say and do. It is how we interact; it is the tone of voice we use, the words we choose, the way we structure our days, the items we surround ourselves with, and the space we feel comfortable within. It is all-encompassing. Our culture defines us and cannot be dismissed in classroom settings.

In this study, the emphasis on first-year teachers grew out of the question I am repeatedly asked: *"Will student teaching abroad make me a better teacher?"* While I have been inclined to affirm that it does, I was challenged to find literature to support such evidence, especially when the student teaching experience was situated in a non-Western culture. Throughout this study, I listened to the participants' stories, knowing that their experiences outside of their home culture had transformed them personally, and I found myself eager to discern the ways in which that transformation would manifest into classroom practices as they began their careers.

## REFERENCES

Bayles, P. (2009). "Assessing the intercultural sensitivity of elementary teachers in bilingual schools in a Texas school district" (Unpublished doctoral dissertation). University of Minnesota, MN. Retrieved from http://conservancy.umn.edu/bitstream/49152/1/Bayles_umn_0130E_10245.pdf.

Bennett, J. M., & Bennett, M. J. (2001, June). Developing intercultural sensitivity: An integral approach to global and domestic diversity. In *The Diversity Symposium, 2001* [electronic version]. Symposium conducted at the Bentley Campus in Waltham, MA. Retrieved from http://www.diversitycollegium.org/pdf2001/2001Bennettspaper.pdf.

Creswell, J. W. (1998). *Qualitative inquiry and research design choosing among five traditions.* Thousand Oaks, CA: Sage.

Cushner, K. (2011). Intercultural research in teacher education: an essential intersection in the preparation of globally competent teachers. *Action in Teacher Education, 33*:5–6, 601–614.

Cushner, K., & Mahon, J. (2002). Overseas student teaching: affecting personal, professional, and global competencies in an age of globalization. *Journal of Studies in International Education, 6*, 44–58.

Eisner, E. W. (1998). *The enlightened eye: qualitative inquiry and the enhancement of educational practice.* Upper Saddle River, NJ: Merrill.

Gay, G. (2000). *Culturally responsive teaching: Theory, research, & practice.* New York: Teachers College Press.

Hammer, M. R., & Bennett, M. J. (2003). Measuring intercultural sensitivity: The Intercultural Development Inventory. *International Journal for Intercultural Relations, 27*(4), 403–419.

Mahon, J. (2006). Under the invisible cloak: Teacher understanding of cultural differences. *Intercultural Education, 17*(4), 391–405.

Mahon, J. (2009). Conflict style and cultural understanding among teachers in the western United States. *International Journal of Intercultural Relations, 33*(1), 46–56.

Marsh, T., Hollingworth, L., Hale, S., & Gillon, K. (2011). *Organization and administration of Iowa public and private schools*. Dubuque, IA: Kendall Hunt.

Marx, H. A. (2008). Learning about self far from home: A preservice teacher's intercultural development during an international program. *NERA Conference Proceedings 2008.* Paper 34. Retrieved from http://digitalcommons.uconn.edu/nera_2008/34.

Merriam, S., & Associates. (2002). *Qualitative research in Practice: Examples for discussion and analysis.* San Francisco, CA: Jossey-Bass.

Pappamihiel, N.E. (2004). Hugs and Smiles: Demonstrating caring in a multicultural early childhood classroom. *Early Child Development and Care, 174*(6), 539–548.

Pedersen, P. (1998). Intercultural sensitivity and the early adolescent. *Dissertation Abstracts International*, 9826849.

Sleeter, C. E., & Grant, C. A. (2007). *Making choices for multicultural education: five approaches to race, class, and gender* (5th ed.). Danvers, MA: John Wiley & Sons, Inc.

Stachowski, L. L., Richardson, J. W., & Henderson, M. (2003). Student teachers report on the influence of cultural values on classroom practice and community involvement: perspectives from the Navajo reservation and from abroad. *The Teacher Education, 39*(1), 52–63.

Straffon, D. A. (2003). Assessing the intercultural sensitivity of high school students attending an international school. *International Journal of Intercultural Relations, 27*(4), 487–501.

*Chapter Two*

# Over There

*Exploring a WWII-Themed Short-Duration Study-Abroad Program for Preservice Teachers*

## David M. Moss and Alan S. Marcus

### INTRODUCTION

Under an overcast sky, it was a cool late spring morning as the waves crashed on to the beaches of Normandy, France, and a group of Americans made their way through the sand. Nearly seven decades since D-Day on June 6, 1944, this group of visiting Americans were not soldiers but preservice teachers. They were not here to liberate but to learn—by participating in a two-week study-abroad program with visits to WWII historic sites and museums in Europe. At their home institution of the University of Connecticut, the preservice teachers explored World War II through textbooks, film, photographs, and soldiers' letters. They would continue to analyze and evaluate the events of the war following this study-abroad program, but little had prepared them for the power of this moment. Reverent silence fell upon this small cohort of teachers in training as they recognized the importance of visiting places of historical significance such as this. On this beach the blood of soldiers stained the sand, and the tide of the war turned. The power of *place* was repeated at the Anne Frank House in the Netherlands and Buchenwald concentration camp in Germany. The preservice teachers would never be the same, and countless numbers of their future students would benefit from their participation in this experiential international program.

This chapter explores the planning, goals, implementation, and outcomes of a short-duration study-abroad program, coupled with a full-semester course, designed to bring to life the mission of preparing globally competent teachers at the Neag School of Education at the University of Connecticut. This international experience and related course work advance this aim by preparing preservice teachers to deeply consider issues of history and how it is represented and commemorated across cultures, and is designed to enhance preservice teachers' understanding of global perspectives and their ability to effectively help the middle and high school students they will teach to be productive members of a global society. Fostering global perspectives through direct international experiences with WWII historic sites and museums in Great Britain, France, the Netherlands, and Germany to explore European perspectives of the war, participants analyze how these sites tell the story of WWII within the context of their various national narratives. The World War II focus emphasizes the development of historical empathy, and particularly the understanding of multiple global perspectives. Student participants, from an integrated bachelors/masters teacher preparation program, take on the roles of professional historians to examine the possibilities and perils of films and museums/historic sites as ways of knowing about the past, enhancing their ability to think historically and to consider issues of social justice. Additionally, students took on the role of professional educators to explore the classroom implications of movies and museums/historic sites for everyday history instruction.

The many challenges and opportunities of this program are addressed through the description of planning and program activities, discussion of student journals and course work to document the impact of the program on the participants, and the presentation of instructional aims for key aspects of this program to highlight crucial elements. In this vein, contrasting the purposeful outcomes of a short-duration experience with traditional semester-long study-abroad programs will encourage readers to think strategically about program design and perhaps increase opportunities for preservice teachers to study abroad as part of their formal professional preparation through the development of faculty-led programs as described and discussed below.

## STUDY ABROAD AND TEACHER EDUCATION

The vast majority of teachers in U.S. schools are European-American and monolingual in English, and thus culturally different from many of the students they teach. These teachers often hold ethnocentric beliefs that may negatively influence the educational experiences of their diverse students (Gay, 2000). Marx and Moss (2011) note that teacher educators must challenge teachers' ethnocentric worldviews and prepare them to successfully teach culturally diverse student populations. To these ends, teacher education programs typically include a combination of multicultural course work and clinical placements within schools that serve such culturally diverse student populations. However, research cautions that without guided reflection these experiences may reinforce existing beliefs, confirm stereotypes, and hinder preservice teachers' ability to seek alternative ways of teaching (Irvine, 2003; Sleeter, 2001).

Moving beyond domestic school placements and course work, the literature describes teacher education study-abroad programs that afford candidates an opportunity to immerse themselves in an international school setting but also with the primary aim of participation in a teaching practicum (Cushner & Mahon, 2002). Advocates for such teacher education study-abroad experiences suggest that the opportunity to live and work in a foreign culture serves as a catalyst for transforming preservice teachers' ethnocentric worldviews and moving them toward a path of culturally responsive teaching (Cushner & Brennan, 2007). Although we strongly support such international programs and aims, we contend that the primary design of cross-cultural study-abroad work in teacher education need not be limited to experiences that involve practice teaching. There are other ways to promote important aspects of culturally responsive pedagogies in our next generation of teachers.

One such approach is faculty-led, short-duration study-tour programs that immerse preservice candidates in experiential programming coupled with more traditional course work back at the home institution. While the focus of the often full-semester study-abroad programs designed around classroom experiences involve all of the learning inherent in such student teaching practicum in combination with cultural immersion, short-duration programs have different aims. Hutchings et al. (2002) describe study tours as having the potential to expand global horizons for both students and faculty as they are a platform to build links with institutions abroad. Already common to academic and professional programs across the university, such as in business and literature, they offer significant potential for teacher education as well. Faculty-led short-duration study-abroad programs—frequently known as study tours—allow faculty and students to travel together in an intensive learning and living context. In that sense, study-tour programs are *experiential* focused-learning opportunities (Braskamp et al., 2009). But this intensive learning does not occur in a vacuum. Porth (1997) describes the essence of an international study tour as involving both traditional classroom learning and experiential learning opportunities abroad with a three-phase model: (a) predeparture/classroom phase; (b) abroad (on-site) phase; and (c) return to campus (re-entry) phase.

A significant advantage of faculty-led, short-duration study-tour programs is that individuals may sojourn outside the footprint of the standard academic year. Additionally, such experiences are typically more affordable due to the confined duration of the time abroad and thus may offer greater opportunity for participation by teacher education candidates. Preservice teachers are an underrepresented group in study abroad. According to a recent report (Open Doors, 2012), only about 4 percent of all students studying abroad from the United States are education majors (out of over a quarter of a million students who study abroad each year). With a pressing need to produce teachers who are on the path to an ethnorelative worldview, and thus in an ideal position to develop as culturally responsive practitioners, well-designed short-duration programs can offer significant potential to respond to this urgent call.

In the following section we address the aims of the Integrated Bachelors/ Masters teacher education program at the University of Connecticut, contrast this WWII short-duration study-tour program with the semester-long international internship program at the university, and establish the specific aims of the secondary social studies program of study as the context for the program design and implementation features discussed later.

## PROGRAM CONTEXT

The core tenets of the University of Connecticut's Integrated Bachelors/ Masters (IBM) program include a strong liberal arts background, the development of general and subject-specific pedagogical knowledge, and high-quality clinical placements. Study-abroad programs within the Neag School are developed with these underlying principles in mind. Prior to admission to this upper-division professional preparation program, freshman and sophomores are typically regarded as pre-education majors. Admission to the IBM program is highly competitive, keeping with the program goals of preparing outstanding educators to be decision makers, leaders, and innovators. As noted in Howard, Levine, and Moss (2014):

> The program is organized around three themes—student as learner, student as teacher, teacher as leader—that require progressively more complex and demanding coursework and clinic placements. Each cohort takes three years to complete their program; during each of six semesters, students complete course work, clinic placements, and a seminar that fosters reflection on and learning from clinic placements. The full-time student teaching occurs in the senior year (second year in the program as they are admitted as juniors). The final year of study (often referred to as the fifth year because it adds one year to the typical four-year undergraduate experience) is when students engage in graduate-level course work and a yearlong internship.
>
> It is in this fifth and final year of the program that the semester-long international internship program in London, England is housed. Consistent with the teacher as leader theme for that year, internships—whether domestic or abroad—are designed to build upon student teaching and afford students direct experiences as leaders-in-training. For example, internships directly in-

volve 5th year interns in school reform projects such as large-scale curriculum development or the planning and implementation of special initiatives such as "History Day." Internships are often school-based as opposed to tied to an individual classroom, and are associated with a graduate-level research project involving timely and relevant questions that encourage students to pursue formal inquiry as a teacher-researcher.

For the London, England, internship site, this leadership lens is layered onto a cultural immersion experience. All program requirements for this international experience are essentially identical to the domestic options, except that students going abroad in the fall term of the fifth year are required to initiate their research project earlier and study intercultural learning and development in the summer term prior to their departure. In that sense, the so-called full-semester London-based program is actually a whole calendar year program beginning in the summer term with a research methods and cultural theory course. It continues as they travel abroad for the fall term and intern in schools, take graduate-level classes, and conduct the research project. Finally, the experience extends into the re-entry spring semester where students are required to take a seminar that both supports their intercultural reflection and the completion of their research project. Although this teacher education model is non-traditional in the sense that it extends the preservice experience to an internship year beyond student teaching, similar to student teaching international programs, the school-based work is the hallmark of the program while abroad. In the case of this program, interns are immersed in the culture of high-performing urban schools in London. Cultural immersion and reflection are the keys to this program. Supported by significant opportunities for reflection, this program is designed to help preservice teachers develop ethnorelative perspectives in support of culturally responsive teaching (Marx & Moss, 2011).

In contrast, the WWII short-duration study-tour program is not designed to be a classroom-based cultural immersion program, as students are only abroad for a matter of several weeks, but does afford a different pathway to develop as a global educator—and ultimately a culturally responsive teacher. For this WWII-focused museum and historical site experience, the means by which global competence is defined and fostered is consistent with the aims of the secondary social studies program.

The social studies education program, known among students as "Team Social Studies," follows the framework of the larger teacher education program as described earlier while adding goals specific to the discipline. We strive to have our preservice social studies candidates teach all facets of social studies in authentic and meaningful ways that will encourage their students to be lifelong learners and will help their students to engage in their civic community. We expect our graduates to serve as change agents in their schools and in society, providing leadership and compassion. We achieve this through several social studies-specific goals that mentor preservice teachers who:

- Understand and incorporate global perspectives and dispositions into their teaching.
- Practice and promote the habits of historical thinking including asking compelling questions, developing historical empathy, connecting the past and present, and evaluating sources of evidence.
- Actively collaborate in a community of professional educators.
- Model and promote civic engagement.

First, we ask preservice teachers to be both historians and teachers from a global perspective. Studying world cultures and history is already a part of the social studies curriculum. The shift we ask preservice teachers to make as part of this program is to consider culture and history from the point of view of non-American cultures. This shift does not exclude American views, but adds to and enhances them and helps preservice social studies teachers to see through and use multiple lenses in their teaching. For example, with WWII we ask teachers to consider how the British, French, Germans, and Russians experienced the war and how their cultures remember and commemorate the war today.

Second, we work with preservice teachers to practice and promote the habits of historical thinking. Historical thinking involves deep content knowledge that is integrated with specific skills. First, the preservice teachers must practice these habits themselves as "historians." Inquiry—asking questions, researching, evaluating sources, using evidence to make claims, and taking informed action—is a core component to historical thinking (NCSS, 2013). In addition, the ability to develop K–12 students' historical empathy, particularly the ability to recognize others' perspectives, is an essential element to our social studies education program. Recognizing other perspectives is directly connected to the goal of learning about and understanding global perspectives. One project the preservice teachers completed to meet this goal is to design and create a museum exhibit on how weather and geography impacted WWII. They developed questions, conducted research, located and evaluated sources, used evidence to support claims, and did all of this while considering multiple perspectives on the war.

Third, we provide opportunities for preservice teachers to actively collaborate in a community of professional educators including their preservice peers, teachers and administrator in local schools, museum educators, and university faculty. This learning community provides intellectual and emotional support for its members while also preparing them to productively collaborate and communicate as professionals. The preservice teachers are also exposed to new ways of thinking and multiple models of professional practice.

Finally, we model and promote issues of civic engagement. We strive to encourage teachers to practice civic engagement and to help their students do so as well. Civically engaged citizens are aware of and understand contemporary issues—local, regional, national, and international—can weigh evidence and analyze other points of view, and can communicate and act upon what they learn in order to promote the common good. The content and skills promoted in a rigorous social studies curriculum are critical to promote civic engagement and maintain democracy.

All of these goals promote and encourage teachers who value and actively consider issues of social justice in their teaching and in the education community more broadly. Issues of social justice are important beyond the borders of the social studies classroom but also hold a particular relevance as we can explore these issues through the social studies content covered in class.

It is important to note that the two study-abroad programs—full-semester London internship and WWII study tour—are designed around a similar model: required predeparture, study abroad, and re-entry experiences. In both the planning and execution of each distinct program, the outcomes are clearly articulated and experiences are designed to promote such aims. For the London program, cultural immersion and reflection in an internship is paramount (and thus a full semester is mandated); and for the WWII program, preparing globally competent teachers is accomplished via the consideration of historical thinking, development of the habits of historical inquiry, understanding and incorporating global perspectives into the development of curriculum and museum exhibits, developing connections with institutions abroad, and actively collaborating in a community of globally minded professionals. As will be addressed in the final section of this chapter, the notion of global competence is broad (Longview Foundation, 2008), and a key message of this chapter is that there is more than one way to design and implement study-abroad programs specifically designed for preservice teachers.

In the following section we will address the specific aims of the WWII study-tour program, including key design and implementation features.

## PROGRAM DESIGN AND FEATURES

### Background

The study-abroad program is part of a University of Connecticut-based course titled "Teaching World War II: Multiple Perspectives on the War in Europe." It is designed for preservice secondary social studies teachers to enhance their understanding of global perspectives and their ability to effectively help the middle and high school students they teach to be productive global citizens. The preservice teachers complete two days of preparation work (twelve hours total) followed by travel to WWII-focused historic sites and museums in Great Britain, France, the Netherlands, and Germany where they learn about European perspectives of WWII, analyze how these museums tell the story of WWII within the context of their own national narrative, and interview museum staff. The pre-departure class time and travel occur in May after the customary academic year is complete. The following fall the students complete a full semester of coursework that includes fieldwork at museums in Washington, DC.

The students who enroll in the course are all preservice social studies teachers. Prior to going abroad and taking the re-entry course, as a routine element of their program they all complete a full semester of social studies methods. The methods course is required for all students regardless of participation in the study-abroad program and is instrumental in introducing key concepts and practices related to history education, museum education, global perspectives, and empathy. As part of the methods course the preservice teachers engage in a series of online communications with preservice teachers from the University of Nottingham in England. They exchange essays and PowerPoint presentations as well as engage in discussions around critical issues in history education and specifically about WWII and the Holocaust. Subsequently, those students who participate in the study tour meet their preservice counterparts from Nottingham during the visit to London and experience museums and sites together. Both the online exchanges and in-person museum experiences offer direct interactions with international peers around issues of WWII through a global lens.

Studying abroad affords students opportunities to interact with history and culture, thus fostering global perspectives through direct international experiences. Students thoroughly investigate their own experiences as students of World War II with two purposes. First, they take on the roles of professional historians to examine the possibilities and perils of films and museums/historic sites as ways of knowing about the past. Students enhance their ability to think historically, particularly to analyze and evaluate films and museums/historic sites. Second, students take on the role of professional educators to explore the classroom advantages and disadvantages of movies and museums/historic sites for everyday historical instruction. Together these two aims support the development of global competence by enhancing the preservice teachers' exposure to global perspectives while also reinforcing the notion of teaching for social justice by encouraging a critical examination of sources of information, by expanding their experiences to better see how others view and experience the world, and by reflecting on the advantages and limitations of their own experiences and privilege as Americans and college students.

The focus on World War II emphasizes the development of historical empathy, particularly understanding multiple global perspectives of WWII and the impact of the war on soldiers and civilians, with the specific goal of developing the ability to be productive global citizens. Hence, the films, museums/historic sites, and readings concentrate on exploring American, British, French, Dutch, German, and other perspectives of both soldiers and other victims and survivors.

The fostering of teachers with global perspectives requires *direct* international experiences, and this program affords students opportunities to interact with history and culture in a way that cannot be accomplished by only studying in the United States.

## Course Objectives and Guiding Questions

A set of overall objectives and guiding questions steers the course, including the study-abroad component. The three objectives include:

1. Students will know and be able to skillfully analyze, interpret, and evaluate films and museums in order to understand the past.
2. Students will know and be able to effectively develop lessons for secondary students that incorporate films and museums into their social studies curriculum.
3. Students will know and be able to explore their role as global citizens and strengthen their capacity to participate in a global community.

In addition there are several learning outcomes specifically for the study-abroad component of the course. These outcomes are:

Students will:

- Investigate key events and people from WWII in order to identify turning points in the war and determine cause and effect for various elements of the war from the perspective of multiple participants.
- Explore the human experience during war and the features that shape human activities during war.
- Cultivate an appreciation for teaching about the past in ways that provide multiple international perspectives, develop historical empathy, and stimulate student inquiry.
- Analyze and critique WWII museums/historic sites and consider whether they are an effective means for teaching about the war.
- Evaluate the role of museums in depicting the past and in the development of students' historical understanding.

- Consider how to prepare students for participation as citizens in a global community with ethnorelative perspectives beyond that of the United States.

Finally, there are four guiding questions that direct all course activities and assessments. These are:

1. Was World War II a "good" war?
2. How can we use WWII films and museums as effective teaching tools, particularly to understand multiple perspectives? What opportunities do they create? What dangers do they pose?
3. How do films and museums enable us to engage the past? What avenues do they open up and what avenues do they close down?
4. What is the relationship of film and museums to other ways of knowing the past? How do they serve as evidence and as representations of the past in comparison to other primary and secondary documents?

## Study-Abroad Experiences

Prior to visiting each site the students provide an overview/preview and lead a discussion (students are preassigned sites and conduct research as part of the previsit preparation). At each site the preservice teachers have some time to tour on their own and some time meeting with museum staff to discuss museum education, history education, and global perspectives on WWII. After each visit the students self-lead debriefs of each site. As noted, in 2013 our London visits also included collaboration with preservice social studies teachers from the University of Nottingham.

The Europe visit runs for about two weeks. The 2013 trip (most recent at the time of publication) included the following experiences:

### Duxford Air Base, Duxford, England

Duxford is the site of a former WWII airbase. There are multiple exhibits each in a separate hangar, memorials, and dozens of planes and other vehicles. The museum provides the British perspective of WWII with a heavy emphasis on the Battle of Britain and the role of airpower. The preservice teachers learn about just how differently the average British citizen experienced the war compared to Americans. There is also a hangar and memorial dedicated to the Americans, which provides the opportunity to evaluate how the British view American involvement in the war—something unique to the preservice teachers.

*Green's Park WWII Memorials*

Green's Park in London has several WWII memorials including a general memorial, a memorial for the British airmen who served during the war, as well as memorials for New Zealand, Australia, and those who served from Africa. The memorials show a British perspective while emphasizing the importance of the commonwealth and bonds with other (non-American) nations. These memorials reinforce the point that the dominant American viewpoint taught in the United States is not the only way to learn about WWII or other events. This tour, as well as to the HMS *Belfast* and Churchill War Rooms, included students from the University of Nottingham.

*HMS Belfast, Churchill's Cabinet War Rooms*

The HMS *Belfast* is a British navy ship from WWII based in the Thames River in London. The Churchill War Rooms is the underground bunker where the British government functioned during the war. Both emphasize the British role in the war and show a focus on Churchill (rather than FDR) and the impact of the war in London.

*Mémorial de la Shoah, Paris*

This museum is France's major Holocaust museum. Viewing the Holocaust via a French perspective added an important dimension both in terms of considering the French experience and also analyzing how a French museum chose to remember these events.

*Normandy beaches/Pont-du-hoc/American Cemetery*

The preservice teachers visited several of the Normandy beaches including Pont-du-hoc and the American Cemetery. Here students developed strong emotional connections to the past and viewed American perspectives alongside European ones. These sites also emphasized the power of place—the feeling of awe in being at the location of significant events.

*Musée de l 'Armee, Paris*

The military museum in Paris provides a uniquely French narrative covering all eras of French history. The mostly one-dimensional perspective affords a wonderful opportunity to see how museum can convey a narrow view of the past. The story of the U.S. role in both WWI and WWII is shown as limited, a real revelation to the preservice teachers.

*The Jewish History Museum/Old Jewish Neighborhood Tour/Portuguese Synagogue, Amsterdam*

The visit to Amsterdam includes a visit to the Jewish History Museum, and varying by year, a tour of the old Jewish neighborhood or the Portuguese synagogue. This site provides Jewish cultural background, adding context to the students' understanding of WWII and the Holocaust. It also provides a Dutch perspective.

*Anne Frank House, Amsterdam*

Similar to the Normandy beaches, the power of place is overwhelming when walking into the Anne Frank House. Once again the preservice teachers deepened their emotional bonds to the past. They especially appreciated exposure to the perspectives of Anne's father, Otto, as well as other people who helped hide or hid with Anne. This expands the perspective beyond just that of Anne, which they know from reading her diary prior to the trip.

*Holocaust Memorial, Berlin*

The focus of the visit to the Holocaust Memorial in Berlin, Germany was consideration of how the Germans are choosing to remember and honor victims. Larger issues of memorialization play an important role in the discussions.

*Buchenwald Concentration Camp, Germany*

Buchenwald was the third site that emphasized the power of place and helped the preservice teachers establish strong emotional bonds with the past. They also explored how the site is preserved and how the Germans chose to present it in modern society.

*Jewish Museum, Berlin*

Berlin's Jewish Museum provided a German-Jewish perspective and a fascinating forum to examine the use of evidence in creating historical narratives. It also offered a way to evaluate how a museum can create balance between its educational and memorializing missions.

*Topography of Terror Museum, Berlin*

This relatively new museum, which opened in 2010, delivers a uniquely German perspective, distinctly different from the allies. Two specific issues emerge from the visit. First, why do they focus primarily on the Third Reich and not many of the more brutal aspects of the war? Second, why do they rely primarily on photographs to tell the story?

Table 2.1 illustrates an overview of the WWII study-abroad program for preservice secondary social studies teachers.

In the following section we will discuss the assessments and overall impact of the program on the preservice teacher participants.

## PROGRAM IMPACT

### Major Assessments

The students are required to complete five major assignments and multiple smaller assignments as a means of assessing their growth and learning. All of these assessments are directly related to the study-abroad experience. First, students must maintain a reflective journal throughout the study-abroad experience and class sessions to record their experiences and critical reflections. Second, working as a group, students are required to create a museum exhibit in collaboration with a local museum. Third, students write and present a grant proposal to help facilitate the integration of WWII museums/

**Table 2.1.**

|  | **Key Components** | **Assessments** |
|---|---|---|
| **Pre-Visit** | Two days of coursework | Informal |
|  | • Readings prior to class<br>• Content preparation<br>• Intercultural understanding and communication training<br>• Team building<br>• Museum education preparation |  |
|  | Multiple museum visits through previous coursework |  |
|  | Online collaboration with preservice social studies students from the University of Nottingham, England |  |
| **During Visit** | Visits to museums and historic sites in England, France, the Netherlands, Germany (two weeks). | Presentation/orientation of museums to peers |
| **Post-Visit** | Full-semester course |  |
|  | • Mini-teaching<br>• Monument visits<br>• Museum visits in Washington, DC<br>• Readings<br>• Film viewings<br>• Small group projects | 1. Reflective journal<br>2. Teaching of World War II film<br>3. Monuments/memorials project<br>4. Museum exhibit creation<br>5. Grant proposal |

historic sites and film into the social studies/history curriculum. Fourth, students complete a mini-teaching lesson based on a film viewed by the class. Fifth, students must visit and present about monuments and memorials in the United States. See appendix A ("Key Elements from Course Syllabus") for an overview of the assignments and appendix B ("Selected Course Assessments") for a full description of select assessments.

## Student Development

Overall, the preservice teachers demonstrated clear evidence of growth in their understanding of history as having multiple perspectives and narratives, in their ability to develop lessons that present more global perspectives, and in their interest in continuing to pursue international opportunities and thus further mature as global citizens. Across all journals the preservice teachers reflected on how the visits to museums across Europe changed how they viewed WWII and opened their eyes to new ways of thinking about history, increasing empathy, and providing ideas for teaching. Representative of this shift is one participant who wrote in her journal (referring to a group of French students at the American Cemetery in Normandy): "This really got me thinking about learning history from multiple perspectives. How would this French group be studying WWII compared to American students? How would they see their role in something like D-Day compared to the U.S. perspective?"

The preservice teachers also demonstrated their growth through lessons they created, which were more likely to include additional perspectives when compared to units created the year before. The preservice teachers also showed an ability to be civically engaged in the creation of an exhibit on the impact of weather and geography on WWII that was installed at a local museum near the university. Finally, the participants became much more eager to travel and work abroad. Several decided to teach abroad, including in Thailand, Spain, and South Africa. Several others went back to Europe for further short-term international experiences. We even received multiple comments from department chairs and principals that the preservice teachers' study-abroad experiences played a prominent role in the hiring process and helped to distinguish them as candidates, particularly because they could speak from experience about empathy and global citizenship. Examples of student products can be seen at:

- Website for student-created tour book (from 2011 trip), https://sites. google.com/a/uconn.edu/wwii-tour-book/home
- Website for student-created museum exhibit (from 2013 trip), www. ww2weathergeography.weebly.com

# CONCLUSIONS

A key aim for this chapter was to present and discuss central elements of a short-duration WWII study-tour program as means for preparing globally competent teachers. In summary, participants in this program take on the roles of professional historians and educators to examine the possibilities and perils of films and museums/historic sites as ways of knowing about the past through a global lens. The development of global competence is explicitly promoted by enhancing preservice teachers' exposure to global perspectives while also reinforcing the notion of teaching for social justice by encouraging a critical examination of sources of information, by promoting experiences to better see how others view and experience the world, and by reflecting on the advantages and limitations of their own experiences and privilege as Americans.

It is important to recall that the two study-abroad programs discussed within this chapter—full-semester London internship and WWII study tour—are both designed around the predeparture, study abroad, and re-entry model. We assert that such a model is necessary to achieve our aims for promoting global competency as operationalized for each distinct program. For the London program, cultural immersion and reflection in an internship supported by a teacher-as-researcher project is foremost; in contrast, the WWII program preparing globally competent teachers is accomplished via the development of the habits of historical inquiry, understanding and incorporating global perspectives into curriculum and museum exhibit planning, fostering connections with institutions abroad, and actively collaborating in a community of globally minded professionals. The construct of global competence is broad, and the key message of this chapter is that there are multiple ways to design and implement study-abroad programs specifically for preservice teachers—it depends upon which aspects of global competence you prioritize and it is likely that no single program can meet all the various aims. Although many successful programs involve student teaching or other school-based activities, faculty-led short-duration study-tour programs offer a viable option to help the next generation of teachers develop as globally competent professionals.

To conclude this chapter, we would like to briefly address the ongoing teacher education internationalization efforts at the Neag School at the University of Connecticut as it offers important lessons learned for programs engaged in such work. Although the WWII program is only several years old, the full-semester London-based internship has been running for approximately two decades. Yet, both programs remain a work in progress. Partnerships with the Office of Global Affairs at our university, especially education abroad, have been instrumental in assisting with the logistical design and execution of each program. Similarly, the academic component of each program evolves along with the literature in the fields of intercultural studies, study abroad, and teacher education—to name but a few. Key faculty hold the primary responsibility for each program, and since the pre and post model of both programs involves substantial faculty involvement, our programs would not be possible without both significant faculty effort and institutional support. For example, the re-entry seminar as part of the London program and post-study-abroad course in the WWII program are assigned to faculty as routine elements of their teaching load. In that way, the Neag School has institutionalized both programs by supporting faculty in all aspects of its implementation.

At the time of the development of this chapter, as a teacher education program at our university we find ourselves in program-wide discussions regarding the further internationalization of our programs to enhance our ability to foster globally competent teachers who implement culturally and linguistically best practices in their classrooms. In a recently developed internal report at our university titled, "Rationale for the implementation of expanded cultural immersion experience programs" (Moss et al., 2014), we address the motivation for expanding our study-abroad programs in teacher education and echo a point made earlier in this chapter that an ethnorelative worldview is a key element of the broader construct of global competence and, for educators, globally competent teaching. As such, we advocate that teacher education candidates should pursue the purposeful development of knowledge, skills, and beliefs that promote global competence. Bennett (2004) describes an ethnorelative worldview as one that allows for "the experience of one's own beliefs and behaviors as just one organization of reality among many viable possibilities" (p. 62). The ethnorelative developmental stages are "ways of *seeking cultural difference*, either by accepting its importance, by adapting perspective to take it into account, or by integrating the whole concept into a definition of identity" (2004, p. 63, italics in original). Seeking difference is a core notion underpinning the pursuit of social justice, and encouraging ever greater numbers of preservice teachers to seek such difference through direct international experiential opportunities will help serve the elusive aim of promoting equity across the American educational system today.

## ACKNOWLEDGMENTS

Developing and implementing high-quality study-abroad programs requires involvement from across the university. Drs. Kevin Brennan and Dorothea Hast, along with Cheryl Blain and the entire professional staff in the Office of Education Abroad at the University of Connecticut, enable such programs as described within the chapter to not merely exist—but to thrive. We'd also like to acknowledge the dean's office at the Neag School of Education at the University of Connecticut for their long-standing support of the internationalization of teacher education. Deans Richard Schwab and Thomas DeFranco, along with Drs. Tim Weinland as department head in the early years of development and Mary Anne Doyle today, have steadfastly supported our international work. Finally, financial support in the form of scholarships to WWII participants was provided through the UConn Foundation via a gift from the Dunn Family Fund as well as from the Connecticut Museum of Natural History through the Goodwin Fund.

## APPENDIX A: KEY ELEMENTS FROM COURSE SYLLABUS

### Course Overview

This course brings together two undertakings: the study of the past and the development of effective ways of teaching history. Its historical focus will be World War II, and we shall endeavor to comprehend this complex and consequential conflict as deeply and as rigorously as would a class devoted solely to the history of this war. We shall do this principally through the study of films, museum displays, historic sites, and memorials.

We will thoroughly investigate our own experiences as students of World War II with two purposes. First, we will take on the roles of professional historians to examine the possibilities and perils of films and museums/historic sites as ways of knowing about the past. You will enhance your own ability to think historically, particularly to analyze and evaluate films and museums/historic sites. Second, we will take on the role of professional educators to explore the classroom advantages and disadvantages of movies and museums/historic sites for everyday historical instruction.

Our focus on World War II will emphasize the development of historical empathy, particularly understanding multiple global perspectives of WWII and the impact of the war on soldiers and civilians, with the specific goal of developing our ability to be productive global citizens. Hence, our films, museums/historic sites, and readings will concentrate on exploring American, British, French, German, and other European perspectives of both soldiers and other victims and survivors.

A significant component of the course includes field site visits. During the first half of the course we will journey to Europe to witness firsthand the location and artifacts of many critical moments during World War II. The second half of the course includes the viewing and analysis of numerous World War II films and a visit to the United States Holocaust Memorial Museum in Washington, DC.

Essential Questions for the Course:

1. Was World War II a "good" war?
2. How can we use WWII films and museums as effective teaching tools, particularly to understand multiple perspectives? What opportunities do they create? What dangers do they pose?
3. How do films and museums enable us to engage the past? What avenues do they open up and what avenues do they close down?
4. What is the relationship of film and museums to other ways of knowing the past? How do they serve as evidence and as representations of the past in comparison to other primary and secondary documents?

## Goals and Objectives

Enduring Understandings/Objectives:

1. Students will know and be able to skillfully analyze, interpret, and evaluate films and museums in order to understand the past.
2. Students will know and be able to effectively develop lessons for secondary students that incorporate films and museums into their social studies curriculum.
3. Students will know and be able to explore their role as global citizens and strengthen their capacity to participate in a global community.

As part of the enduring understandings above, students will know and be able to:

- investigate key events and people from WWII in order to identify turning points in the war and determine cause and effect for various elements of the war from the perspective of multiple participants
- explore the human experience (civilians and soldiers) during war and the features that shape human activities during war
- continue to evolve a personal philosophy of learning and teaching social studies
- cultivate an appreciation for teaching about the past in ways that provide multiple perspectives, develop historical empathy, and stimulate student inquiry
- consider how to prepare their students for participation as citizens in a global community by "learning" history/social studies throughout their adult lives
- analyze and critique WWII films and museums and consider whether they are an effective means for teaching about the war

- evaluate the role of film and museums in depicting the past and in the development of students' historical understanding
- demonstrate the skills and knowledge to effectively use film to teach history and to effectively incorporate trips to museums into the curriculum

Readings:

- *History on Trial*, Deborah Lipstadt (2005)
- *Night*, Elie Weisel (2008)
- *Alan's War*, Emmanuel Guibert (2008)
- *Preserving Memory: The Struggle to Create America's Holocaust Museum*, Edward T. Linenthal (2001)
- *In the Garden of Beasts*, Erik Larson (2011)
- *Freedom From Fear*, David Kennedy
- *Diary of Anne Frank*
- "Teaching History with Film," Marcus, Metzger, Paxton, Stoddard
- *War and Genocide: A Concise History of the Holocaust*, Doris Bergen (2009, second edition)

Required Films to View (some may be viewed in class):

- *Schindler's List* (1993)
- *Europa Europa* (1990)
- *The Pianist* (2002)
- *The Shop on Main Street* (1965)
- *Defiance* (2008)
- *Life is Beautiful* (1997)
- *Saving Private Ryan* (1998)
- *Patton* (1970)
- *A Bridge Too Far* (1977)
- *The Longest Day* (1962)
- *Band of Brothers* (2001)
- *Swing Kids* (1993)
- *The Bridge* (1959)
- *Sarah's Key* (2010)
- *Amen* (2002)
- *The Counterfeiters* (2007)
- *Train of Life* (1998)
- *Black Book* (2006)
- *Miracle at Santa Anna* (2008)
- *A Film Unfinished* (2010)

**Projects/Assignments**

There will be five (5) major products expected from each student. In addition, there are several smaller assignments that support the larger products and various in-class assignments. The five major products are:

1. Reflective journal
2. Teaching of World War II film
3. Monuments/memorials project
4. Museum exhibit creation—how weather and geography impacted WWII
5. Grant proposal

Additional Resources—Websites—World War II:

- Imperial War Museum (United Kingdom): http://www.iwm.org.uk/
- Normandy (Dday): http://www.normandie-tourisme.fr/normandy-tourism-109-2.html; http://www.normandiememoire.com/NM60Anglais/nmeh/accueil.php
- Museum of Jewish Art and History (France): http://www.mahj.org/
- Museum (France): http://www.invalides.org/
- KL-Natzweiler concentration camp and museum (France): http://www.struthof.fr/index.php?id=1&L=1
- Anne Frank House (Amsterdam): www.annefrank.org
- The Jewish Museum of Deportation and Resistance (JMDR), Mechelen, Belgium: http://www.cicb.be/en/home_en.htm
- Battle of the Bulge—Bastogne: http://www.criba.be/; http://www.bastognehistoricalcenter.be/index2.php?sm=bastogne_en-1
- U.S. Holocaust Memorial Museum: www.ushmm.org
- Holocaust Denial on Trial: http://www.hdot.org/
- United States WWII Memorial (Washington, DC): http://www.wwiimemorial.com/

## APPENDIX B: SELECTED COURSE ASSESSMENTS

Reflective Journal:

The purpose of the journal is to help you record what you are learning (about WWII, about teaching with film and museums/historic sites, about analyzing historical sources, and about global citizenship) and how you are reacting to that learning (emotional reactions, ideas for teaching, reflections on the nature of history, etc.). Your journal entries may help you in the completion of your other projects while also allowing me a window into your growth and development during the semester. It is expected that you will candidly record in this journal your reflections as a student of history aspiring to teach history and social studies.

There are required entries for each of the readings, films, and museums/historic sites. In addition you are required to include at least five (5) other entries at any time during the semester as well as a short introduction/overview to the journal and a final summary entry. The final summary entry should highlight your key reflections from during the semester and, drawing from the journal, must explicitly address the course's essential questions.

Each page of the journal will have two columns. The first column is for information or ideas that you are learning from a reading, film, museum/historic site, class session, and so on. The second column is for your personal thoughts, reflections, ideas, feelings, and so forth. in reaction to or in addition to what is in the first column. For your second column keep in mind the course's essential questions.

1. Was World War II a good war?
2. How can we use WWII films and museums/historic sites as effective teaching tools? What opportunities do they create? What dangers do they pose?
3. How do films and museums/historic sites enable us to engage the past? What avenues do they open up and what avenues do they close?
4. What is the relationship of film and museums/historic sites to other ways of knowing the past? How do they serve as evidence and as representations of the past in comparison to other primary and secondary documents?

Other variations of the two columns are okay (e.g., different colors) as long as you have notes and meta sections. In summary:

- An entry is required for each reading, film, and museum/historic site—you already have these for Europe. (You can do one entry for a set of assignments due a particular day as long as you include reflections on all of the readings/films). Be sure to include a date with each entry.
- You must complete at least five (5) additional entries.
- Include an introduction or overview of the journal that previews the journal for the reader.
- Provide a summary entry with overall thoughts and reflections and that addresses the course's essential questions.
- Each page (and thus entry) must have two columns—one for what you are learning and one for your thoughts, reflections, ideas, and feelings.

Museum Exhibit Assignment:

Working as one large group, we will collaborate with the Connecticut Museum of Natural History to plan, design, and build a museum exhibit focused on how weather and geography impacted the European theater of WWII. We will learn about all phases of museum exhibit design and apply our studies to a real museum project. The exhibit will culminate in hosting a grand opening for the community. Website for final product: www. ww2weathergeography.weebly.com.

Monument follow-up assignment:

Monuments and memorials are an important way our society remembers the past. Our collective memory of past people and events is expressed, in part, through the monuments and memorials in towns and cities throughout the United States.

Our goal is to explore how World War II and other historical events, are remembered through monuments here in Connecticut and the region and to consider how we might use monuments in our teaching.

In pairs you will research, visit, and present local monuments and memorials about WWII and another topic of your choice. Please complete the following tasks:

With your partner, research background information on local monuments and memorials including:

• WWII monuments/memorials
• Another topic or location or theme of your choice (e.g., you could decide to go to the CT State House and explore all monuments there across multiple events, or you could choose a specific event like 9/11, or you could choose a theme like women/women's history).
• Some towns may have multiple monuments while others may have few. There is no restriction on which towns or how many towns you cover. Visiting monuments in your hometown where you teach is always a good option but may not be enough to complete the assignment.

Questions to consider for your research include:

• When was the monument/memorial built?
• Who funded the monument/memorial?
• Who sponsored/promoted/proposed/championed the monument/memorial?
• What controversies arose in planning or building the monument/memorial?
• What is the purpose, function, and/or goal of the monument/memorial?

- Has the monument/memorial been changed in any way?
- Take photos of each monument/memorial. You will use the photos to describe the monument/memorials to your colleagues during presentations in class.

With your group, visit the monuments/memorials you researched. During your visit complete the following:

Answer the following questions:

- What is the history/background of your monument (funding, who proposed/designed it, controversies, location, etc.)?
- What is your first impression of this monument?
- What is the monument's primary message about WWII (or another event/person)?
- How does the monument make you feel?
- How does the monument make use of words, light, architecture, materials, sound, symbols, and other aesthetics to convey its message, establish a mood, impact a visitor, and so on?
- Whose values and perspectives are best represented, and whose values/perspectives are left out?
- How does this monument compare to the others you have visited?
- What does the monument portray in a positive way? What does it portray in a negative way?

Back in class you will discuss your monuments/memorials as part of an interactive gallery walk.

On a laptop you will present your monument/memorial. The format of the presentations (e.g., PowerPoint, wiki, prezi, and so on, is up to you). The presentation should include images and text.

One person from each team will present while the other team member rotates to see the other presentations. The process then repeats with presenters and audience switching roles.

When presenting your monument/memorial you must provide copies of a one-page handout with background information, analysis, and resources (Alan can make copies for you if provided at least a week prior to the presentations).

Lessons for WWII Film Assignment:

For this assignment students will work in small groups. Each group will be assigned the film(s) for one day of class and will be responsible for developing lessons for using the film(s) for teaching with secondary students. You will present the lessons to the class, and at least in part, teach the lessons. The activities are an opportunity to practice developing lessons for films and to receive colleague feedback lessons and teaching.

Your responsibilities include:

- Develop the lessons and submit them for review, along with your plan for presenting them, two weeks prior to teaching.

    The lessons should include recommendations for use of the film in secondary history classrooms—when and how to use and a list of resources that might accompany the film. Be sure to include primary and secondary sources.

- Teach/present the lesson to the class (twenty-five-minute lesson).

    You are welcome to include PowerPoints, handouts, and so on. I can help with copying of materials if they are submitted in a timely manner (at least one week prior to the lesson).

- Participate in a "meta" session about your lesson.

## Simulated Grant Proposal

Grant Proposal Paper:
    You and a colleague are applying for a grant of up to $2,500 to use in your school district to help facilitate the integration of film *or* museums into the social studies/history curriculum. The ultimate goal is to demonstrate your skills in developing effective lessons for film or museums. A secondary goal is to give you practice at applying for funding. As part of the grant application, you must create, and present (informally in class) a component of a unit for WWII or another topic of your choice that employs film and/or site visits to museums/historic sites as its central pedagogical tool(s). You are to submit your project in a narrative of no more than twelve pages.
    The narrative should begin with an opening section that provides an overview of your application (what is your topic/project, how will the funds be used, the strengths of your project) and then must answer the following questions:

- What are the student objectives and guiding questions for this unit?
- What educational purpose does your unit serve?
- What materials provide background for you as the curriculum developer and what materials are included as part of the classroom practices in your unit?
- What is your rationale for choosing your specific topic and for choosing these materials?

- What are the activities for the unit? How do these activities meet your objectives?

Setting for unit: The school context for your unit is a class (or multiple classes) with high school students who are of mixed ability levels (non-tracked), represent a diverse range of racial and ethnic backgrounds, and come from a wide range of income levels. Technology and general resources are readily available, and the administration and parents are supportive of your efforts. You may choose whether the course is world history (ninth/tenth grade) or United States history (eleventh grade).

The committee reviewing the grant applications is comprised of teachers and historians.

Suggested format for proposal:

- Overview of project (two pages).

  1. What is your topic/project?
  2. How will the funds be used (an overview—the actual budget goes in appendix A)?
  3. The strengths of your project.

- Rationale for choosing your specific topic and for choosing the materials (two pages).
- Overview/outline of the lesson including guiding questions/objectives and a one-page calendar outline of lesson (one to two pages).
- Information about all of the films and/or museums used in the lesson including detailed descriptions, rationale for including, a brief analysis of each (historical accuracy, perspectives included and left out, strengths and weaknesses, etc.) (three to four pages, may vary depending on number of films/museums). Supplemental information could be included in an appendix.
- An outline of activities for the unit. This should be a day by day lesson plan. You do *not* need to include accompanying materials/handouts/rubric, and so on. You *do* need to discuss how you are assessing within and across the lessons. There is no minimum or maximum length (number of days) of the lesson (three to four pages).

Include: Proposed budget; a list of all resources used for the proposal both for yourself and for the lessons; and a self-evaluation of the proposal using the rubric.

# REFERENCES

Bennett, M. J. (2004). Becoming interculturally competent. In J. Wurzel (Ed.), *Toward multi-culturalism: A reader in multicultural education* (pp. 62–77). Newton, MA: Intercultural Resource Corporation.

Braskamp, L. A., Braskamp, D. C., & Merrill, K. C. (2009). Assessing programs in global learning and development of students with education abroad experiences. *Frontiers: The interdisciplinary journal of study abroad, 18*, 101–118.

Cushner, K., & Brennan, S. (2007). The value of learning to teach in another culture. In K. Cushner & S. Brennan (Eds.), *Intercultural student teaching: A bridge to global competence* (pp. 1–12). Lanham, MD: Rowman & Littlefield Education.

Cushner, K., & Mahon, J. (2002). Overseas student teaching: Affecting personal, professional, and global competencies in an age of globalization. *Journal of Studies in International Education, 6*(1), 44–58.

Gay, G. (2000). *Culturally responsive teaching: Theory, research, and practice*. New York: Teachers College Press.

Howard, E. R., Levine, T. H., & Moss, D. M. (2014). The urgency of preparing teachers for second language learners. In E. R. Howard, T. H. Levine, & D. M. Moss (Eds.), *Preparing classroom teachers to succeed with second language learners: Lessons from a faculty learning community*. New York: Routledge.

Hutchings, K., Jackson, P., & McEllister, R. (2002). Exploiting the Links between Theory and Practice: Developing Students' Cross-cultural Understanding through an International Study Tour to China, *Higher Education Research & Development, 21*(1), 55–71.

Irvine, J. J. (2003). *Educating teachers for diversity: Seeing with a cultural eye*. New York: Teachers College Press.

Longview Foundation. (2008). *Teacher preparation for the global age: The imperative for change*. Silver Spring, MD: Author.

Marx, H., & Moss D. M. (2011). Please mind the culture gap: Intercultural development during a teacher education study abroad program. *Journal of Teacher Education, 62*(1), 35–47.

Moss, D. M., Kaufman, D., Rojas, E., Roselle, R. and Wagner, M. (2014). Rationale for the implementation of expanded cultural immersion experience programs. Unpublished report, University of Connecticut, Storrs, CT.

National Council for the Social Studies (2013). College, Career, and Civic Life: C3 Framework for State Social Studies Standards. Silver Spring, MD.

Open Doors. (2012). *Open Doors 2012 Fast Facts*. New York: Institute for International Education.

Porth, S. J. (1997). Management education goes international: A model for designing and teaching a study tour course. *Journal of Management Education, 21*(2), 190–199.

Sleeter, C. E. (2001). Preparing teachers for culturally diverse schools: Research and the overwhelming presence of whiteness. *Journal of Teacher Education, 52*(2), 94–106.

## Chapter Three

# Culture and Class

*Latina Preservice Teachers in Costa Rica*

## Mary Petrón and Burcu Ates

### INTRODUCTION

I feel now that I tried that I can't just come back and teach in Houston . . . I would be stuck, but there is so much to see. I feel like this is Costa Rica, imagine the other countries, how their system works, maybe I'll find better methods, you know? So I just want to learn more and more. (Yadira, interview, March 6, 2014)

These thoughts are from Yadira, a preservice teacher of Mexican descent who participated in a study-abroad program in Costa Rica where she taught content area lessons in Spanish and English to public elementary school children. It was taken from an interview with her conducted ten months after she returned from the study abroad. She has been changed by the experience and developed the ability to view education from an international perspective, recognizing the wealth of knowledge that exists beyond the confines of the United States.

Internationalization of higher education has been a common theme and an educational goal for administrators, faculty, and researchers not only in U.S. institutions, but also in other countries (Thomas, 2006; Kabilan, 2013). There are various rationales (i.e., political, academic, cultural/social, and economic) for internationalizing higher education (Kreber, 2009). From the academic point of view, it is "the goal of achieving international standards for both teaching and research" (Kreber, 2009, p. 3); and from a cultural/social point of view, it involves "understanding foreign languages and cultures, the preservation of national culture, and respect for diversity" (Kreber, 2009, pp.

3–4). Although a high degree of attention is given to internationalization within institutions of higher education in general, teacher preparation remains among the least internationalized functions of U.S. campuses (Stewart, 2013).

Many colleges and universities in the United States continue to promote internationalization on and off campus through various activities and programs. One of the most common programs is the study abroad. Colleges of education have responded, albeit more slowly, to the need for internationalization or international education through field experiences in other countries (Alfaro, 2008). Teacher candidates' understanding of internationalization and/or globalization is imperative. Yet, as Stewart (2013, p. 84) stated, "Few teachers today are prepared with the knowledge and skills to educate students for the new global reality. To facilitate their students' learning, teachers themselves need to become globally competent individuals." Our work abroad suggests that study-abroad programs may have the potential to enhance this competency. State and national accreditation agencies such as the National Council for the Accreditation of Teacher Education (NCATE) also support the initiatives of multicultural and global perspectives (Alfaro, 2008), which are highlighted under the Diversity Standard 4:

> One of the goals of this standard is the development of educators who can help all students learn or support their learning through their professional roles in schools. This goal requires educators who can reflect *multicultural and global perspectives* that draw on the histories, experiences, and representations of students and families from diverse populations. (NCATE, 2008)

Thus, teacher preparation programs need to provide opportunities for preservice teachers to develop their multicultural and global knowledge and skills. As Armstrong (2008) noted, "As part of the educational system, teacher preparation is integral to addressing the need for a teacher workforce prepared to meet the demands of a global society" (p. 492).

This case study explores how bilingual Latina preservice teachers made sense of their experiences in a four-week study-abroad program in Costa Rica. We observed and documented their journey in Costa Rican classrooms and analyzed the connections they made to U.S. classrooms at various levels, from their commitment to social justice to their cultural analysis of classroom management. Most studies focus on the experiences of predominantly white students (e.g., Guadino, Moss, & Wilson, 2012; Phillion & Malewski, 2011, Zhao, Meyers, & Meyer, 2009; Stachowski, Viscounti, & Dimmett, 2000; Jiang & DeVillar, 2011; Sharma, Rahatzad, & Phillion, 2012). By focusing on Latina participants, an underrepresented population, this study fills a gap in the literature on study-abroad programs in teacher preparation.

## LITERATURE REVIEW

Phillion, Malewski, Sharma, and Wang (2009) stated, "Study abroad in teacher education remains under-researched, under-theorized and under-evaluated. In particular, there is little emphasis placed on researching the development of preservice teachers' understanding of multicultural issues during study abroad programs" (p. 325). In teacher education, one of the common goals of such programs is developing the cultural competence of preservice teachers, which may enable them to work effectively with diverse students (Phillion & Malewski, 2011). As Armstrong (2008) stated, "Because of America's increasingly diverse student profiles, attention to cultural differences is no longer a question—rather, it is an imperative" (p. 492). Several studies include preservice teachers' journey during study-abroad programs. Most of the studies report on how preservice teachers increased their ability to navigate in unfamiliar cultures, improved or became aware of new languages, and critically examined the differences and similarities between the United States and the host country (Phillion, Malewski, Sharma, & Wang, 2009; Sumka, 2005; Wilson & Flournoy, 2007; Brindley, Quinn, & Morton, 2009).

Stachowski and Sparks (2007) examined the data and reports amassed during thirty years of Indiana University's Overseas Project. The Overseas Project has served over 2,000 preservice teachers in field experiences in twelve different countries ranging from Australia to India. The goals of the Overseas Project are as follows:

> (1) developing a broader understanding of the pluralistic world in which we live and of the mutual influence of nation upon nation; (2) providing intercultural teaching and community involvement experiences in overseas nations—experiences which offer realistic, in-depth exposure to other ways of life and schooling; and (3) facilitating professional and personal growth through increased self-confidence and self-esteem, greater adaptability, and acquisition of new and different teaching methods, ideas, and philosophies. (p. 119)

According to Stachowski and Sparks, the evidence is clear that the participants in the Overseas Project benefited greatly from the experience and that the project's goals of enhancing understanding of a global perspective, increasing intercultural awareness, and personal/professional growth of participants have been met.

Phillion, Malewski, Sharma, and Wang (2009) reported on the experiences of fifty-four predominantly white preservice teachers during a three-week summer program in Honduras who had little or no previous international travel or cross-cultural experiences. The preservice teachers were enrolled in multicultural and introductory teacher education courses. Teacher candidates completed autobiographical reflections and journal entries during the study. The results revealed that preservice teachers gained understanding of cultural practices and differences. Furthermore, they demonstrated a commitment to work on the barriers which exist between white teachers and diverse student populations.

Leigh (2012) studied five white female first year teachers who had completed their student teaching at American international schools in non-Western countries. Using data collected from participants' reflection and interviews, she found that they had been influenced on both personal and professional levels including increased self-awareness, collaborative skills, ability to address the needs of second language learners, and appreciation of diverse perspectives. Her participants demonstrated an advanced level of cultural sensitivity falling into the category of Adaptation as measured by Bennett's Developmental Mode of Intercultural Sensitivity (1993).

Richardson (2012) conducted a retrospective mixed-methods study using a combination of questionnaires and interviews to study teacher education students from the United States and Canada who had participated in study-abroad programs over a fifteen-year period. Students reported positive benefits including exposure to a different educational and cultural system. They also reported challenges such as homesickness and working extended school days. All in all, they believed they were better prepared to address the needs of culturally diverse learners.

Palmer and Menard-Warwick (2012) reported on their study-abroad program in which they offered a course in second language acquisition in Mexico. The eleven undergraduate preservice teachers who participated in the study also had minimal international travel experience. The goal of the program was "to facilitate preservice teachers' ability to articulate a critical understanding of the needs of immigrant and second language learning students in their future public school classrooms" (p. 17). The data included preservice teachers' course assignments, pre- and post-surveys, follow-up interviews, and dialogue journals. The results indicated that preservice teachers began to develop empathy for their future diverse students as well as critical consciousness regarding bias and the imbalance of power (Palmer & Menard-Warwick, 2012).

Jiang and Devillar (2011) examined the experiences of thirteen white student teachers (twelve female) who spent a semester student teaching in Belize, China, and Mexico. The objective of the study was to compare the student teachers' reflections and experiences. The data included weekly student e-journals, an open-ended questionnaire administered upon their return from study abroad, and researchers' on-site observations. Out of many positive results of the international student-teaching program, preservice teachers noted the appreciation and understanding they gained toward linguistic diversity in the instructional setting and importance of modifying the instructional pedagogies to meet the needs of linguistically diverse students.

Alfaro (2008) in her study examined the nine-month experiences of four (one Latino, one Latina, one white female, and one white male) elementary education biliteracy (Spanish and English) preservice teachers in Mexico. The purpose of the study was to analyze preservice teachers' self-reflection related to teaching in an international setting and examine "cultural and inter-cultural experiences of difference from a global perspective" (p. 21). The data sources included journal entries and interview data. Alfaro concluded that this international teaching experience offered an opportunity for preservice teachers to self-reflect, learn about their own cultural identities, improve their instructional practices, and demonstrate a commitment to implementing culturally relevant pedagogy in order to meet the needs of all students.

It appears that the influence that teaching abroad has on preservice teachers is similar in the case of in-service educators. Thomas (2006) analyzed survey data, interviews, and classroom observations of licensed teachers who taught first in the United States, then abroad for at least one year and had returned to the United States to teach. Her participants included inexperienced teachers (less than three years) as well as experienced (four or more years). Her findings were similar to those of studies of preservice teachers in that teaching abroad influenced the development of a global perspective (Bryan & Sprague, 1997; Kissock, 1997; Stachowski & Sparks, 2007) and cultural empathy (Malewski, Sharma, & Phillion, 2012). In addition, she found a strong connection between teaching abroad, culturally responsive pedagogy, and curricular choices, as well as personal growth (Merryfield, 2000; Razanno, 1996).

Finally, in one of the few studies that specifically addressed the issue of how the racial diversity of participants influences how they make sense of their experiences while teaching abroad, Trilokekar and Kukar (2011) studied five diverse Canadian preservice teachers (one Chinese, one white, two South Asian, and one Afro-Canadian). Using a framework of transformative learning theory (Mezirow, 1978), four conceptual categories emerged from the in-depth interviews of the participants: experiencing racial dynamics, experiencing "outsider" status, engaging in risk-taking/experiencing new identities, and recognizing privilege and power relations (p. 1144). The researchers found that race shaped the process of meaning-making. They stated that the study-abroad literature "must begin to describe and explain how differences among students—through their race, gender, class, status, and power—and their diverse personal experiences" (p. 1149) shape their study-abroad experiences.

For the most part, the success of study-abroad programs at the institutional level is often measured by the number of students who participated in the study-abroad programs rather than what students did and learned during this experience (Coryell, Spencer, & Sehin, 2014). Numerous institutions have developed study-abroad programs for teacher candidates; yet, these activities "remain isolated events rather than part of an overall strategy to promote their graduates' global competence" (Stewart, 2013, p. 85). Discussing similar concerns, Armstrong (2008) asked very crucial questions: "How should universities and colleges best prepare teachers, who will in turn prepare children for realities of a globalized future? What should teacher education in a global society look like?" (p. 493). In teacher education and specifically in ESL education, we believe that the preparation of teacher candidates should not only be about teaching ESL methods and pedagogical strategies. Teachers need to go beyond "just good teaching" (DeJong & Harper, 2005) and being "nice" (Nieto, 2010, p. 264). We believe preservice teachers and inservice teachers need to understand issues related to social class, immigration, culture, and language learning at a deep level. Pereira (2013) also noted,

> Teachers' professional practice involves not only teaching methods and pedagogical strategies, but also teachers' beliefs and representations about their work, their perspectives on the social world and the socio-cultural and human diversity, and their ethical commitment and attitude toward educational and social inequalities. (pp. 166–167)

When preservice teachers attend study-abroad programs, through the guidance and instruction of their professors they should begin to view their context and education setting with critical eyes. Well-structured short-term study-abroad programs which are more accessible to a larger and more diverse pool of preservice teachers (Spenser & Tuma, 2002) provide some of the same goals as long-term programs (Donnelly-Smith, 2009). Yet, the skills learned in such programs should not be limited to the celebration of adapting to a new culture and language. Dooly and Villanueva (2006) state, "students must develop more than mere 'intercultural communicative competence.' They must be made aware of cultures (own and others) and be made aware of how this will help them interpret and understand others" (p. 226). We believe teaching which includes issues of social justice will allow such interpretation and dialogue. As Lemley (2014) notes, "By taking on social justice pedagogy, each individual is challenged to understand what it means to create classroom communities with access, equity, quality, and opportunity to learn as a fundamental goal" (p. 27). In order to ensure that preservice teachers have the opportunity to experience, interpret, and reflect upon issues of social justice, it is critical to include situations in which these issues arise. This was a priority as we set up the study abroad.

# THE STUDY

## Context

A four-week study-abroad program in Costa Rica was organized by the researchers in the college of education at a regional university in the south central United States. Eight undergraduate and three graduate students went to Costa Rica accompanied by two researchers. Two weeks were spent in an urban area in central Costa Rica and two weeks were spent in a semi-urban area in western Costa Rica. Preservice teachers stayed with Costa Rican host families. In central Costa Rica, all study participants were placed at the same public elementary school and taught content area lessons in Spanish. In western Costa Rica, they were assigned to two different public elementary schools. At both schools they taught English and content area lessons in Spanish. All four schools served children from low-income families. Working at low-income public schools was an important element in the structure of the study-abroad experience. As organizers, we believed that these field experiences in Costa Rican public schools would better represent the schooling of the majority of Costa Rican children. Furthermore, we believed that opportunities to engage fully with issues of social justice were more likely to occur in a public school setting. For this same reason, we also were careful to choose schools in each area which served significant numbers of children of Nicaraguan immigrants. In addition to teaching and observing at these schools, all study participants visited three other schools in central Costa Rica.

## Methodology

Since we sought to examine how these Latinas made sense of the study-abroad experience and how they connected it to their personal and professional lives, a qualitative case study approach was chosen. According to Merriam (2007), "The case offers a means of investigating complex social units consisting of multiple variables of potential importance in understanding the phenomenon. Anchored in real-life situations, the case study results in a rich and holistic account of the phenomenon" (p. 41). This study is interpretive in nature because we are "interested in (1) how people interpret their experiences (2) how they construct their worlds and (3) what meaning they attribute to their experiences" (Merriam, 2002, p. 23). Certainly, all qualitative research is concerned with meaning construction; however, interpretivism focuses on how individuals make sense of reality and come to understand their experiences.

The study was conducted in two phases. The first took place during the study-abroad experience. During their stay in Costa Rica, the preservice teachers wrote daily journal entry reflections on their experiences in the school and community, as well as interactions they had with various locals (from teachers to administrators in K–12 settings to their host families). The prompt was very open-ended. Students were instructed to reflect on anything that they thought was critical, interesting, valuable, or meaningful. As organizers of the study abroad, we were participant observers of the experience. The data also included our own field notes and reflective journals recorded during the study abroad. The field notes were recorded during participant observation experiences in both social contexts such as going to the beach and academic contexts such when as the preservice teachers gave lessons in the Costa Rican schools. As Marshall and Rossman (2006) suggested: "Immersion in the setting permits the researcher to hear, to see, and to begin to experience reality as the participants do" (p. 100).

The second phase of the study involved in-depth interviews (Marshall & Rossman, 2006) of the participants about the study-abroad experience ten months after they returned. The interviews were semi-structured in nature. Esterberg (2002) asserted that semi-structured interviews enable the researchers to "move beyond our own experiences and ideas and really understand the other person's point of view" (p. 87). A bilingual Latina graduate assistant conducted the interviews because we believed that the preservice teachers would express their thoughts freely to a peer rather than feel intimidated talking to former study-abroad professors. The interviews were conducted almost a year later because we wanted to examine how the participants made sense of the experience after the initial excitement of study abroad had faded and they had returned to working in U.S. schools. In this way, we hoped to capture the essence of the long-term connections they made rather than just those which occurred in the moment.

## Participants

Four of the six Latina undergraduates who attended a four-week Costa Rican study-abroad program participated in the study. It was a sample of convenience. Although all six agreed to participate, difficulties in scheduling limited the number to four. All four were studying to be elementary bilingual education teachers. There was a more expensive study-abroad program in Spain that summer as well. All four noted that their decision to participate in the Costa Rican trip was based primarily on cost. Laura, Sandra, Yadira, and Karla (pseudonyms) are in their early twenties and are first-generation college students. All of their parents came to the United States as teens or adults. Laura's parents are from El Salvador, as are Karla's. Both young women had visited El Salvador on several occasions but had never traveled to any other country. Yadira's parents came from Mexico. She visits there approximately twice a year but has never been to any other country. Sandra's parents are from Colombia. She has visited Colombia and Mexico on numerous occasions.

In the literature much attention has been given to white monolingual English-speaking preservice teachers predominantly from middle-class families. While we recognize that the majority of preservice teachers in the United States continue to come from white, middle-class English-speaking backgrounds (Gollnick & Chinn, 2013), the absence of research on study-abroad programs from the perspective of minority participants serves to reify the lack of diversity in education. To fill a gap in the research on teacher education study-abroad programs and address the issue from a culturally and linguistically diverse perspective, this study explores the experiences of four Latina bilingual education preservice teachers who are the U.S.-born children of working-class immigrant parents.

The following general research questions guided our inquiry: How do bilingual Latina preservice teachers connect their experiences in Costa Rican schools to their own cultural backgrounds? How do bilingual preservice teachers connect their experiences in Costa Rican schools to their practice as future teachers in the U.S. classrooms?

## Data Analysis

Thematic analysis (Boyatzis, 1998) was used to find common threads that emerged from the preservice teachers' reflections in Costa Rica and later follow-up interviews, which were transcribed verbatim. In our analysis, the reflections and interview transcripts were divided into segments that related to a distinct concept. Each text segment was then coded into a topical category. Themes were formed by grouping the common responses of the participants under relevant categories. The field notes and reflective journals of the authors were coded in a similar fashion. However, since the emphasis was on the perceptions of the preservice teachers, we coded our field notes and reflective journals after completing the coding on the preservice teachers' texts. We used a variety of strategies to triangulate the data (Denzin, 1970). First, we used multiple sources of data and compared the different data sets. In addition, each author coded all data independently. We discussed any discrepancies between our coding until we reached "plausible explanations about the phenomena being studied" (Mathison, 1988, p. 17). Finally, we engaged in member checking with the participants (Merriam, 2002) in order to discuss our interpretations. The themes that were most salient in the data related to issues of social justice, including immigrant populations, as well as the school atmosphere with respect to discipline and children's overall maturity and happiness.

FINDINGS

## Commitment to Social Justice

One of the most prominent themes to emerge from the data related to the preservice teachers' commitment to teach in underserved areas in the United States. The interviews and reflections of all four participants included extensive analysis of social class as it relates to schooling. According to our own reflective journals, this was also a frequent topic of their conversations. They referenced specific schools as they engaged in making sense of their experiences. They spent one morning touring Red River, an elite private school in central Costa Rica, which the children of top governmental officials and leaders of national and international corporations attended. Red River has many teachers from the United States, and the medium of instruction is English. The director spoke with the students about the possibility of applying to teach there in the future. Members of the administration had completed advanced degrees in the United States. The school was outfitted with the latest technology and air conditioning. The library was well-stocked, and the arts program included instruction by well-known artists. Sandra described the school: "There was one school that was super nice and it compared a lot to the American schools here, the Red River school . . . they have iPads in every classroom and all these like things."

The next day the preservice teachers visited a preschool that served primarily Nicaraguan families. The school was located in a *ciudad perdida* or shantytown settled by undocumented Nicaraguan and other Central American squatters fleeing civil war and economic deprivation. In general, Costa Ricans spoke of the town and its inhabitants in disparaging terms. The town has over 36,000 inhabitants; services like running water and electricity to some areas are a product of the recent past. Water initially had to be carried from a stream located below the town. The school began as a result of the efforts of a volunteer from the United States and a single mother from Nicaragua. The preschool children had to walk from a general meeting room to their classroom some distance away. Sandra described the area and the school:

> We literally walked like I think four blocks or something on a road, like through the houses, you know. It's not nice. It's like a dirt road and rocks and pebbles and you have to walk through that to get to your school and then the class that they went in was like this small building. It was upstairs and it was so hot, so hot and it was a very small area.

The juxtaposition between the schools that the affluent attended and those that the poor attended made an impact on these Latina preservice teachers. It served as the impetus both during and after the trip for declarations of their commitment to work in low-income schools. During the interview, Sandra reflected on how her experience in Costa Rican schools influenced the type of school she wants to work at in the United States.

> For example, right now I'm at a school that has a lot of high resources and they are very well off . . . so I was thinking about it, if my teacher asked me back for the student teaching, I would probably say no, not because I didn't enjoy the kids and stuff, just because I felt like I don't know, there was no challenge to me. . . . Because me before it [study abroad] was like "oh, I'm going to get a job, where I can get a job, and I'm going to teach," but now it's like I want to teach in a school where I know that I can make a higher impact.

Every participant commented on wanting to work where they could make a difference. Their commitment to social justice as teachers connected Costa Rica to their initial decision to become bilingual educators and to their personal educational experiences as students in low-income schools in the United States. Yadira stated,

> Like I grew up with nothing in a Hispanic school . . . I guess it [study abroad] just emphasized what I wanted to do before, cause I always wanted to obviously work in bilingual cause I was bilingual, it just made me wanting to do it even more . . . I don't know, cause some kids don't always make it, but I did; so I want to help someone I guess, get to as far as I got or even better.

As they reflected on their international teaching experience, they focused on social justice and the distinction between social classes in contrast to most other studies in which understanding cultural differences (Phillion, Malewski, Sharma, & Wang, 2009) or developing empathy for culturally and linguistically diverse learners (Thomas, 2006; Palmer & Menard-Warwick, 2012; Jiang & Devillar, 2011) proved to be more salient. Certainly, the fact that these preservice teachers were bilingual and from cultural backgrounds with much in common with those in Costa Rican is an important one. At the same time, these individuals had limited experiences outside of the United States and had only attended school there. Yet, the global perspective they displayed focused on the intersection of social class and education both at home and abroad.

## Immigration

We found no studies in which the participants made any reference to the intersection of globalization and immigration. A global perspective on immigration was almost absent from our study as well. As much as they were able to affirm their commitment to social justice in schooling and their desire to work with marginalized children, for the most part their power of analysis fell short of seeing parallels between home and abroad. However, despite the fact that only one of the four appeared to make direct connections between the plight of undocumented immigrants to the United States and to Costa Rica, the topic of immigration emerged as an important theme. They all noted that many Costa Ricans spoke negatively about Nicaraguan immigrants to the country, as is evident in this excerpt from Laura: "I don't know if they like people from Nicaragua. . . . The poor schools have kids from Nicaragua. So yeah, I would say they probably don't like Nicaraguans." However, only Yadira compared treatment of Nicaraguans in Costa Rica to that of Mexicans or Hispanics in general in the United States.

> They talk about people from Nicaragua like people from here talk about Mexicans. So I feel that was so, like where am I, because at the end of the day I am used to everyone here feeling a certain way against Hispanic people as a whole, not just Mexican and then we go to Costa Rica and they feel kind of elitist toward people from Nicaragua and they just say it like nothing. . . . So I thought that was not great . . . it is just uncomfortable . . . their attitude, I feel is not any better than people here against Mexicans.

Clearly, Yadira was able to view the immigration issue more globally than were the other participants.

Interestingly, Yadira has a dark complexion, whereas the other participants were light-skinned, like many Costa Ricans. As Trilokekar and Kukar (2011) found, the color of one's skin affected the study-abroad experience. Yadira noted that skin color was a factor when Costa Rican police boarded a bus to ask for identification in an effort to apprehend undocumented Nicaraguan immigrants. Darker individuals appeared to be singled out, including one of the author's own children. She stated, "I think they asked her [author's daughter] because she is like darker . . . I think they choose just if you looked like you are from Nicaragua and they are mostly darker than Costa Ricans." She also noted that color was present in the way she was viewed as well, as is evident in the following quote, "They expected some blonde, blue-eyed girl coming from the United States . . . 'cause then they were like . . . oh you are from Mexico, right?" None of the other participants mentioned skin color at all as it related to immigration or their own treatment in Costa Rica. Her experiences as being dark-skinned Latina may have indeed influenced her perceptions. Skin color prejudice within the Latino community has been documented (Chavez-Dueñas, Adames, & Organista, 2013). Furthermore, dark-skinned Latinos in the United States have lower incomes, lower educational attainment, and self-report higher levels of perceived discrimination than do light-skinned Latinos (Arce, Murgia, & Frisbie, 1987). Yadira immediately noticed the color line in Costa Rica because of her own personal experiences in the United States. She may also have been more attuned to the immigration issue due to the fact that she is of Mexican descent. Anti-immigrant discourse in the United States tends to be framed as a Mexican problem, not a Salvadoran or Colombian problem (Kingsolver, 2010).

## Happy Children vs. Disciplined Children

Numerous studies have referenced that study-abroad participants benefited from exposure to a different education system (Richardson, 2012; Stachowski & Sparks, 2007; Phillion, Malewski, Sharma, & Wang, 2009; Kabilan, 2013). However, these Latina preservice teachers made connections between Costa Rican schools and their Latino cultural backgrounds. The study-abroad experience led preservice teacher to re-examine what was considered commonplace in the United States through a Latino cultural lens. Many of their reflections focused on the policing of children that they viewed as ever present in the U.S. schools in contrast to Costa Rica. In the following excerpt from the interview, Karla is comparing and contrasting recess in both countries:

> I remember the bell ringing and then their recess, they just ran out [in Costa Rica]; there is nobody, cause at recess here [in the United States] people patrol them, there wasn't really anyone patrolling them, it was just them and their own time. . . . It is more relaxed with discipline.

Initially they struggled with the noise as they viewed classrooms solely through the lens of their educational experiences as children in U.S. schools. Ultimately, however, these Latina preservice teachers accepted this relaxed discipline as liberating and contributing to what they called children's maturity and independence. Interdependence, rather than independence, would have been a more accurate term based on the way the preservice teachers described what they meant. In their discussions, interviews, and reflections, they referenced an emphasis on interpersonal relatedness, relationships, and mutual respect, which has been well-documented in the literature on Latino culture (Dixon, Graber, & Brooks-Gunn, 2008). Children working together and being responsible for other children is commonplace. Laura described the difference in this way:

> They [Costa Rican children] acted more mature than what their age is, than over here. I feel like over here [United States] they're babied a lot. . . . Over there [Costa Rica] there's more independence and they grow up a lot faster . . . they're very social [Costa Rica children]. The teacher lets them talk, like when these kids were like fighting and the teacher lets them argue, but because they resolve it themselves and then the teacher just keeps teaching; but over here it's like . . . okay you have to be quiet in the classroom.

As is evident in this excerpt, Laura viewed the interdependence among the children, as well as the freedom to talk given to Costa Rican children, as contributing to their maturity. Children were allowed to roam free at recess and had to settle their own disputes, as opposed to adult intervention. In other words, developing and maintaining social relationships is part of education in Costa Rican schools. In this way, it encompasses the Spanish definition of *educación*, which includes more than academics (Reese, Balzano, Gallimore, & Goldenberg, 1995). It includes, among other things, having appropriate social skills.

Instead of only viewing Costa Rican classrooms through a U.S. lens, they began to make connections between what they saw in Costa Rican classrooms and their own family cultural background. This was particularly evident when they considered conversational patterns. Overlapping in turn-taking and interrupting are common features in conversations among Spanish-speakers, both of which are generally not acceptable among English-speakers (Ardila, 2004). Participants mentioned feeling comfortable with this style of interaction, which they saw as typical of their own families. Sandra commented on the conversational patterns in a Costa Rican classroom:

> You know here [United States] students have to raise their hand, like you get in trouble if you don't raise your hand . . . and if you are shouting then you are not following directions but there [Costa Rica], you don't have to raise your hand, you just, the ideas are just bouncing off the walls everywhere. . . . I really liked it cause having dinner with my family is like that, it's open conversation, and it's loud, and it doesn't mean that nobody is listening to each other and nothing is getting done, it's just how you are interacting a lot. I like that and that's what it reminded me of, like a big family and that is how I would like my classroom to be.

This connection between their family background and the Costa Rican classroom extended to the relationships between teachers and students. The participants believed that teachers behaved more like mothers and that the classrooms resembled families. They perceived the family atmosphere as a Latino characteristic and that it represented what they wanted to foster in their own classroom. Considering the fact that these preservice teachers will be bilingual teachers working primarily with Latino children, the family atmosphere in the classroom represents culturally relevant pedagogy. Teachers are often seen as an extension of the family structure in Latino cultures. Mothers entrust them with their children and expect them to play the role of parent during school hours (Reese, Balzano, Gallimore, & Goldenberg, 1995).

The difference in the amount of control exerted over children by teachers in the United States and Costa Rica was a major preoccupation of these preservice teachers. It was mentioned frequently in their reflections and interviews and was often phrased as happy children versus disciplined children. These Latina preservice teachers believed that the relaxed atmosphere of the educational setting contributed to the overall happiness of the children and their enjoyment of school. Laura offered a comparison between the United States and Costa Rica with respect to the attitude toward schooling:

> I just feel like sometimes it is just too much focus on trying to get the children to always be perfect, to always be quiet, always be in line [in the United States], cause over there the kids are just happy. I never really see them not wanting to be at school; I never heard a kid saying, "Oh, I don't want to be here" . . . I think it is cause they have so much more freedom . . . I'm guessing here they are just trying to make sure everyone always behaves . . . less discipline would be good.

Every participant mentioned how happy children were in Costa Rica and how much they enjoyed school. In contrast in the United States, they viewed children constantly being controlled, which led to negative attitudes toward school. We have not been able to find any international studies which correlate school discipline with children's happiness. However, according to Programme for International Assessment (PISA) surveys, a higher percentage of Costa Rican children report being happy at school than U.S. children (Organisation for Economic Co-operation and Development, 2013, p. 24). Costa Rica is significantly above average on the percentage of children reporting happiness at school while the United States is below (p. 24). Furthermore, a higher percentage of Costa Rican children than U.S. children attend schools where there is a consensus among teachers and administrators on the importance of the social and emotional development of students (p. 23).

In general, the participants expressed the tension as a dichotomy between a U.S. sense of individualism and order and a Latino sense of the collectivism (Hofstede, 1983; Triandis, McCusker, & Hui, 1990). As a whole, they sought to strike a balance between the two, which reflected their own backgrounds as Latinas raised in U.S. society. Yadira described the epiphany she had with respect to the classroom in the United States after the Costa Rican experience.

> I just changed the way I approach them [the children] and what to allow and what not allow in the classroom, so I don't focus so much on what I said before structure, more like allowing them to learn and grow socially not just academically.

Yadira's conclusion that she needed to focus on more than academic growth in the classroom is in line with the literature. Zins, Bloodworth, Weissberg, and Walberg (2004) argue that importance of social and emotional learning is often lost in this age of accountability and its emphasis on academic test scores. Adelman and Taylor (2000) assert that if schools only emphasize academic instruction and school management in order to push children to reach academic success they are not likely to succeed. Consequently, the international perspective on classrooms that came as a result of the study-abroad experience enabled these participants to identify areas of need in the U.S. classroom.

## IMPLICATIONS AND CHALLENGES

As organizers of the study-abroad program we had an intentional social justice vision. As Miller and Sylayeva (2013) stated, "Study-abroad programs can also be specifically tailored to expose prospective teachers to racial and socioeconomic diversity" (p. 14). Since this was one of the goals of our program, it dictated the specific sites we chose. Arranging preservice teachers' field experience in low-income communities, in less privileged schools was difficult, but purposeful, as was the visit to an elite, private school. As a result, they had the opportunity to critically compare the resources and opportunities available to diverse social classes. This enhanced their desire to work in high-need, low-income communities. Although others may disagree, we believe sending preservice teachers to American schools abroad defeats the purpose of international education.

A commitmnent to social justice also includes a focus on culturally responsive teaching (Rahatzad, Ware, & Haugen, 2013). These preservice teachers connected Latino culture and schooling in ways they may not have been able to do without the study abroad. As stated previously, they had only attended U.S. schools. Therefore, while they had prior experience with *educación* in the home, academic skills reign supreme in U.S. schools. The fact that they asserted their intention to create a similar family atmosphere in their own classrooms and include a strong focus on social development demonstrated professional growth in the area of culturally responsive teaching.

Finally, we would like to address the importance of providing access to study-abroad experiences to all preservice teachers. Armstrong (2008) states, "Today's students will live and work in a global society where international knowledge and skills are imperative, not solely for a growing number of jobs and professions, but also for one's social, emotional, and psychological well-being" (p. 493). All four participants stated that they chose the Costa Rican study-abroad program because it was less expensive than the other program being offered. In Sivakumaran, Sutton, Todd, and Garcia's (2011) study, among teacher education program students who were surveyed, 55.2 percent stated the reason they were not able to participate in a study abroad was the financial cost of such programs. Ideally, although we believe longer-term study-abroad programs will be more successful in enhancing an understanding of issues of social justice, lack of financial resources definitely limits the number of students in such programs. If cost prohibits individuals like the Latina bilingual preservice teachers from participating, we are reproducing the status quo and promoting further marginalization of diverse populations. Therefore, study-abroad program organizers need to create programs that are affordable for all students and not accessible to only a few. Furthermore, university administration must commit to providing grants, scholarships, and financial aid packages to students.

## CONCLUSION

In this study we investigated how Latina preservice teachers reflected on their experiences in Costa Rica and the comparisons they have made between the two countries. The study-abroad experience enhanced the preservice teachers, commitment to issues related to social justice in education. It confirms the significance of study-abroad programs in teacher education programs for the development of a global perspective. The Latina bilingual preservice teachers critically reflected on issues related to education, immigration, and social justice through an international lens. As noted before, we believe successful study-abroad programs in teacher education need to focus on issues related to language, culture, race, and diversity at a deep level as teacher educators may not be able to address such issues adequately in mainstream teacher education programs or curriculum. As Rahatzad, Ware, and Haugen (2013) stated:

> Teacher preparation should move beyond "cuddly" acknowledgments of multiculturalism and engage within other cultures, such as language and geographic location. A required second-language proficiency and immersive study-abroad experience are need for all teacher education programs. Such a requirement would also attract a more diverse group of teacher candidates, specifically those willing to experience other cultures directly and not simply experience the world through prepackaged cultural curriculum. (p. 49)

We hope this call for accessible study-abroad programs is realized by many teacher education programs both in the United States and internationally.

## REFERENCES

Adelman, H. S. & Taylor, L. (2000). Shaping the future of mental health in schools. *Psychology in the Schools, 37*, 49–60.

Alfaro, C. (2008). Global student teaching experiences: Stories bridging cultural and intercultural difference. *Multicultural Education, 15*(4), 20–26.

Ardila, J. A. (2004). Transition relevance places and overlapping in (Spanish-English) conversational etiquette. *Modern Language Review, 99*(3), 635–650.

Bodur, Y. (2012). Impact of course and fieldwork on multicultural beliefs and attitudes. *Educational Forum, 76*(1), 41–56.

Boyatzis, R. E. (1998). *Transforming qualitative information: Thematic analysis and code development.* Thousand Oaks, CA: Sage Publications.

Brindley, R., Quinn, S., & Morton, M. L. Consonance and dissonance in a study abroad program as a catalyst for professional development of preservice teachers. *Teaching and Teacher Education, 25*, 525–532.

Bryan, S. L., & Sprague, M. M. (1997). The effect of overseas internships on early teaching experiences. *The Clearing House, 70*, 199–201.

Coryell, J. E., Spencer, B. J., & Sehin, O. (2014). Cosmopolitan adult education and global citizenship: Perceptions from a European itinerant graduate professional study abroad program. *Adult Education Quarterly, 64*(2), 145–164.

Denzin, N. K. (1970). *The research act: A theoretical introduction to sociological methods.* New York: McGraw-Hill.

Dixon, S. V., Graber, J. A., & Brooks-Gunn, J. (2008). The roles of respect for parental authority and parenting practices in parent–child conflict among African American, Latino, and European American families. *Journal of Family Psychology, 22*(1), 1–10.

Donnelly-Smith, L. (2009). Global learning through short-term study abroad. *Peer Review, 11*(4), 12–15.

Dooly, M., & Villanueva, M. (2006). Internationalisation as a key dimension to teacher education. *European Journal of Teacher Education, 29*(2), 223–240.

Esterberg, K. (2002). *Qualitative methods in social research.* New York: McGraw-Hill.

Gaudino, A., Moss, D., & Wilson, E. (2012). Key issues in an international clinical experience for graduate students in education: Implications for policy and practice. *Journal of International Education and Leadership, 2*(3), 1–16.

Gollnick, D. M., & Chinn, P. C. (2013). *Multicultural education in a pluralistic society* (9th ed.). Boston, MA: Pearson.

Hofstede, G. (1983). Dimensions of national cultures in fifty countries and three regions. In J. Deregowski et al. (Eds.) *Explications in cross-cultural psychology.* Lisse, the Netherlands: Swets and Zeitlinger.

Jiang, B., & DeVillar, R. A. (2011). Effects of school and cultural contexts on student teaching abroad outcomes: Insights from U.S. student teachers in Belize, China and Mexico. *Action in Teacher Education, 33*(1), 47–62.

Kabilan, M. K. (2013). A phenomenological study of an international teaching practicum: Preservice teachers' experiences of professional development. *Teaching and Teacher Education, 36*, 198–209.

Kingsolver, A. (2010). Talk of 'broken borders' and stone wall: Anti-immigrant discourse and legislation from California to South Carolina. *Southern Anthropologist, 35*(1), 21–40.

Kissock, C. (1997). Student teaching overseas. In M. Merryfield, E. Jarchow, & S. Pickert (Eds.) *Preparing teachers to teach global perspectives: A handbook for teacher educators* (pp. 123–142). Thousand Oaks, CA: Corwin Press, Inc.

Kreber, C. (2009). Different perspectives on internationalization in higher education. *New Directions for Teaching and Learning, 118*, 1–14.

Leigh, M. (2012). *International student teaching in non-Western cultures: Impact on first year teachers* (Doctoral dissertation, Iowa State University). Retrieved from http://lib.dr.iastate.edu/cgi/viewcontent.cgi?article=3406&context=etd.

Lemley, C. K. (2014). Social justice in teacher education: Naming discrimination to promote transformative action. *Critical Questions in Education, 5*(1), 26–51.

Malewski, E., Sharma, S., & Phillion, J. (2012). How international field experiences promote cross-cultural awareness in preservice teachers through experiential learning: Findings from a six-year collective case study. *Teachers College Record, 114*(8), 1–44.

Marshall, C., & Rossman, G. B. (2006). *Designing qualitative research* (4th ed.). Thousand Oaks, CA: Sage.

Mathison, S. (1988). Why triangulation? *Educational Researcher, 17*, 13–17.

Merriam, S. (2002). *Qualitative research in practice: Examples for discussion and practice.* San Francisco, CA: Jossey-Bass.

Merriam, S. (2007). *Qualitative research and case study applications in education* (2nd ed.). San Francisco, CA: Jossey-Bass.

Merryfield, M. M. (2000). Why aren't teachers being prepared to teach for diversity, equity and global interconnectedness? A study of the lived experiences in the making of multicultural and global educators. *Teaching and Teacher Education, 16*, 429–443.

Mezirow, J. (1978). Perspective transformation. *Adult Education, 28*, 100–110.

Miller, G., & Sylayeva, L. (2013). Socially just teaching through the eyes of Russian immigrants. In G. Miller & L. De Oliveira (Eds.), *Teacher education for social justice: Perspectives and lessons learned* (pp. 11–22). Charlotte: Information Age Publishing Inc.

National Council for the Accreditation of Teacher Education. (2008). Experiences working with diverse students in P–12 schools. Retrieved from http://www.ncate.org/Standards/Unit-Standards/UnitStandardsineffect2008/tabid/476/Default.aspx.

Nieto, S. (2010). *Language, culture, and teaching. Critical perspectives* (2nd ed.). New York: Routledge.

Organisation for Economic Co-operation and Development, (2013). *PISA 2012 results: Ready to learn: Students' engagement, drive and self-beliefs* (Vol. III). Paris: OECD Publishing.

Palmer, D., & Menard-Warwick, J. (2012). Short-term study abroad for Texas preservice teachers: On the road from empathy to critical awareness. *Multicultural Education, 19*(3), 17–26.

Pereira, F. (2013). Initial teacher education for social justice and teaching work in urban schools: An (im)pertinent reflection. *Alberta Journal of Educational Research, 59*(2), 162–180.

Phillion, J., & Malewski, E. (2011). Study abroad in teacher education: Delving into cultural diversity and developing cultural competence. *Action in Teacher Education, 33*(5–6), 643–657.

Phillion, J., Malewski, E., Sharma, S., & Wang, Y. (2009). Reimagining the curriculum in study abroad: Globalizing multiculturalism to prepare future teachers. *Frontiers: The Interdisciplinary Journal of Study Abroad, 18*, 323–339.

Rahatzad, J., Ware, J., & Haugen, M. (2013). Chocolate-covered twinkies: Social justice and superficial aims in teacher education. In G. Miller & L. De Oliveira (Eds.), *Teacher education for social justice: Perspectives and lessons learned* (pp. 35–52). Charlotte: Information Age Publishing Inc.

Razzano, E. (1996). The overseas route to multicultural and international education. *The Clearing House, 69*(5), 268–270.

Reese, L., Balzano, S., Gallimore, R., & Goldenberg, C. (1995). The concept of *Educación*: Latino family values and American schooling. *International Journal of Educational Research, 23*(1), 57–81.

Richardson, P. (2012). *Study abroad teacher education programme: Student perspectives on professional and personal development* (doctoral dissertation, University of Sheffield). Retrieved from http://www.eltap.org/resources.aspx.

Sharma, S., Rahatzad, J., & Phillion, J. (2012). How preservice teachers engage in the process of (de)colonization from an international field experience in Honduras. *Interchange, 43*(4), 363–377.

Sivakumaran, T., Sutton, J., Todd, T., & Garcia, K. N. (2011). Transcending classroom borders: Determining student perceptions of study abroad programs in a teacher education program. *National Teacher Education Journal, 4*(2), 19–22.

Spenser, S. E., & Tuma, K. (Eds.). (2002). *The guide to successful short-term programs abroad.* Retrieved from http://www.nafsa.org/uploadedFiles/guide_to_successful_short-term.pdf?n=3985.

Stachowski, L. L., & Sparks, T. (2007) Thirty years and 2,000 student teachers later: An overseas student teaching project that is popular, successful, and replicable. *Teacher Education Quarterly, 34*, 115–132.

Stachowski, L. L., Visconti, V. A., & Dimmett, D. L. (2000). U.S. student teachers on overseas youth culture: Observations, reflections and implications for teaching practice. *International Education, 30*(1), 5–16.

Stewart, V. (2013). Succeeding globally: Transforming the teaching profession. *International Educator, 22*(3), 82–87.

Sumka, S. (2005). The impact of study abroad: Educational travel as a model for responsible tourism. *Transitions Abroad* [online]. Retrieved from www.transitionsabroad.com/listings/study/articles/studymay1.shtml.

Thomas, P. (2006). Preservice practicum teaching in Central Asia: A positive experience for both worlds. *Journal of Social Studies Research, 3*(1), 21–25.

Triandis, H. C., McCusker, C., & Hui, C. M. (1990). Multimethod probes of individualism and collectivism. *Journal of Personality and Social Psychology, 29,* 1006–1020.

Trilokekar, R. D., & Kukar, P. (2011). Disorienting experiences during study abroad: Reflections of preservice teacher candidates. *Teaching and Teacher Education, 27,* 1141–1150.

Wilson, A., and Flournoy, M. (2007). Preparatory courses for student teaching abroad. In K. Cushner and S. Brennan (Eds.), *Intercultural student teaching: A bridge to global competence* (pp. 34–56). Lanham, MD: Rowman & Littlefield.

Zhao, Y., Meyers, L., & Meyer, B. (2009). Cross-cultural immersion in China: Preparing preservice elementary teachers to work with diverse student populations in the United States. *Asia-Pacific Journal of Teacher Education, 37*(3), 295–317.

Zins, J. E., Bloodworth, M. R., Weissberg, R. P., & Walberg, H. J. (2004). The scientific base linking social and emotional learning to school success. In J. Zins, R. Weissberg, M. Wang, & H. J. Walberg (Eds.), *Building academic success on social and emotional learning: What does the research say?* (pp. 3–22). New York: Teachers College Press.

*Chapter Four*

# International Teaching

*Bringing Home Global Perspectives*

Sarah Thomas

INTRODUCTION

I think you need to challenge kids to see things differently because the only way we're going to have peace in this world is if they are willing to try to see things from another person's perspective.

—Mary, study participant who taught in Brazil

Like Mary, I have spent time teaching abroad and agree that one way to internationalize American classrooms and enable the goals of social justice is to bring another perspective to the table. This includes immersing oneself in another culture, and teaching abroad is perhaps the most authentic way this can be done. There may be no better way for teachers to learn about another culture and to think more deeply about their own cultures than by working and living in another country.

Since at least 1808, U.S. teachers have been working in international capacities. Current international teaching experiences have their origins in the schools and programs that were created after World War II (Crossley and Watson 2003). These schools include independent international schools, United States Department of Defense Dependent Schools, and United States Department of State Affiliated Schools for Teaching Overseas. Other ways teachers have gone overseas include teacher exchanges and Peace Corps appointments. While the type of overseas experience will certainly differ in length and intensity (i.e., living in the outskirts of Dakar, Senegal, is very different from joining an expatriate community in Paris, France), living in another culture does change individuals (Quezada and Alfaro 2007; Sta-chowski et al. 2003; Sussman 2002). While abroad, each teacher has a unique experience that transforms his or her teaching, and the influence of this transformation or the gaining of a global perspective often appears when teachers return to practice in their home countries.

Wang (2005) maintained that educating from a global perspective stimu-lates both students and teachers to think critically about their place in the world, challenge stereotypes, and empathize with the worldviews of people from other countries. Research (Malweski et al. 2012; Pope and Wilder 2005; Villegas and Lucas 2002; Quezada and Alfaro 2007; Stachowski et al. 2003; Sussman 2002) has shown that in order for teachers to prepare their students to become citizens of the world, teachers must develop a keen understanding of their own global perspectives and cultural empathy (defined as the ability to accept another cultural point of view), and a good way to do this is through interaction with individuals who are not from the United States. This overseas experience enables global perspectives that teachers can bring to the classroom, and simultaneously thrusts the idea of social justice to the forefront.

In *Preparing Teachers to Teach Global Perspective* (1997), Kissock maintains that providing opportunities for student teachers to teach overseas, or work in a community different from that which they are familiar, prepares future teachers for their work in the global world. He suggests that these opportunities help students expand their worldview and increase their cultu-ral empathy, both dispositions that are necessary in a twenty-first century classroom. Bryan and Sprague's (1997) report corroborates Kissock's anec-dotal evidence and supports his inferences that teaching abroad provides "life lessons" in teaching abilities, understanding the role of education in society, and expanding their worldviews.

The purpose of this study was to examine the influence, if any, of an overseas teaching experience on teaching decisions when: (1) teachers return to their home country; and (2) how those decisions can serve to international-ize American classrooms, thereby enabling practices that promote social jus-tice. Teaching decisions include but are not limited to the following areas of decision making: curriculum, classroom management, and instructional be-haviors.

## Research Methods

I became interested in the influence of an overseas teaching experience when I returned to the United States after living in Brussels, Belgium, for six years. Given my growing awareness of differences in cultures, I wanted to examine the changes in perspectives that teachers with similar experiences developed.

This led to a phenomenological study where teachers self-reported changes in their understanding via an online questionnaire and individual interviews.

## Participants

Thirty-eight individuals who taught overseas and were teaching in their home country at the time of the research completed an online questionnaire. Subsequently, a convenience sampling approach (Patton 2002) was used to select four individuals for the qualitative portion of the study. The four individuals were interviewed, and three of the four were observed in their classrooms, which included study of the displays and other materials in the classrooms.

Since there are gaps in the literature on this population of teachers (Cornell 2003; Wang 2005) the focus in this study is on teachers who first taught in the United States, then taught overseas, and eventually returned to teach in the United States. Thus, student teachers and preservice teachers were not part of this study. Additionally, participants had to have a minimum of one-year teaching experience in the United States prior to teaching overseas. For this study, a less experienced teacher was defined as one who had one to three years' teaching experience, had switched disciplines or grades (for example, elementary school to high school or science to physical education) or was a career switcher (for example doctor to middle school science teacher). Experienced teachers were defined as those who had four or more years' experience. In addition to having taught in the United States a minimum of one year, participants must have taught overseas for a minimum of one year.

Thirty (30) percent male and 70 percent female participants completed the questionnaire. Of those who answered the race question, seven were non-white and 28 were white. Ninety-seven percent of the teachers were native English speakers, and 72 percent could speak a language other than English at the basic or proficient level. Teachers taught at both public and private schools overseas.

Sixty-seven percent of the teaching institutions were located in urban areas, 16 percent in suburban areas, and 16 percent in rural areas. During the duration of the study, 48 percent of teachers were teaching at public institutions in the United States, and 52 percent reported being employed by private or parochial schools. Thirty-three teachers answered the question about teaching experience, with twenty-one reporting being experienced teachers. The time teachers spent overseas varied from one year to twenty-plus years. Teachers taught in a number of capacities, including prekindergarten, elementary school, middle school, high school, and university. Subjects taught included English to speakers of other languages, mathematics, English, history, theater, music, physical education, biology, chemistry, art, and information technology. The same teachers covered the globe teaching in the follow-

**Table 4.1.  Overseas Teaching Experience**

| Overseas Teaching Experience | Response Percentage |
|---|---|
| Independent International School | 64.9% |
| Department of Defense Dependents School | .05% |
| U.S. Department of State Affiliated School For Teaching Overseas | .03% |
| Local School | 27.0% |
| Peace Corps Placement | .03% |
| Other (please specify) | 8% |

ing places: South America, Europe, Asia, Australia, the Middle East, and Africa.

A tool for the quantitative aspect of the study was derived from McKiernan (1980), and permission was obtained for its adaptation.

The questionnaire was tailored to address whether and how overseas teaching experiences influenced teachers' attitudes, beliefs, and behaviors about instruction and curriculum. The questionnaire was divided into four parts: preplanning, travel, and friendship; curriculum and instruction; personal growth; and cross-cultural understanding, and used a five-point Likert scale. In addition to the Likert scale questions, the questionnaire included two open-ended questions and a demographics section.

One open-ended question asked participants to fill in the blanks: Before I taught overseas I _____ and now I _____. The first question aimed at determining whether teachers can identify the changes the overseas teaching experience brought to their thinking. The second open-ended question asked, In what ways is your teaching different than your colleagues who have not taught overseas? This question was included because it aimed to identify specific instruction or curricular changes that occurred because of the overseas teaching experience. Twenty-four of the participants elected to respond to the first question and thirty-one participants answered the second question.

In addition to the questionnaire, a qualitative component contributed to the data sources. Of the participants who completed the survey, a convenience sampling approach (Patton 2002) was used to interview four individuals in the qualitative study. Interview participants were selected based on location and their willingness to be interviewed, to be observed, and to share curriculum. The participants were all located in southeastern Massachusetts. Three of the participants were interviewed in their classrooms; two were interviewed after school, and one was interviewed during his preparatory period. One participant is presently not teaching and was interviewed at her home. All interviews lasted between forty-five minutes and an hour and a half. One participant was interviewed two times; the first interview was one hour, and the second interview lasted forty-five minutes. The participants included two men and two women, all considered experienced teachers.

The interview questions were based on those developed by Bryan and Sprague (1997) given the similarity of focus. In the course of the study, however, other questions emerged from participants' responses, therefore making the interview loosely structured. Once all the material was transcribed, I initially used the Atlas TI program but later reverted to coding the interviews offline as it enabled greater responsiveness to the data. I read and reread the interviews in an effort to isolate data that highlight not only the prevalence (Creswell 1998) of particular themes, but also whether certain codes could be combined, modified, or eliminated.

The final part of the qualitative research was the teaching observations of three of the four interview participants. Observations were conducted to determine if the teachers actually engaged in the activities in which they self-reported. Each teacher was visited once for a full class period. During the observations careful notes of the classroom set up were taken, and I sat in the back of the classrooms. I did not participate in the conversations (unless I

Table 4.2. Interview Participants

| Participants | Teaching experience | Overseas placement | Current position |
|---|---|---|---|
| Mary | Experienced 10+ years | Feedback School in Rio de Janeiro and Modern American Institute in Belo Horizonte, one and one-half years; American school of Belo Horizonte, three years | English teacher at a suburban public school in Massachusetts |
| Martha | Experienced 9+ years | Leysin American School, Leysin, Switzerland, two years; Anglo-American School, Moscow, Russia, two years | Art director for an urban nonprofit organization in Massachusetts |
| Matthew | Experienced 10+ years | Peace Corps in Poland, two years; University of Warsaw Poland, one year; American School in Warsaw, three years | English teacher at a suburban public school in Massachusetts |
| Mark | Experienced 5+ years | All-boys boarding school in Sydney, Australia, one year | English teacher at a private school in Massachusetts |

was explicitly asked something). I employed a teacher observation method of writing what I saw, heard, and thought.

Since three of the four interview participants were teaching during the study, only three classes were observed. Two classes were observed for a ninety-minute block and one class was observed for thirty minutes. While observing the three participants, I used a scripted format in order to have a "reality" check on their questionnaire and interview answers. The protocol included the headings I saw, I heard, I thought; and below each heading, I wrote what was occurring in the classroom at that time. While conducting observations, I also observed the content of the classroom and its walls to determine whether there was consistency between teacher interviews and their actual practice. I was a nonparticipant observer in the classes, although I was introduced to the students in two classes. Two of the teachers ignored my presence, but one teacher at one point exclaimed: "Sarah, how's that for a connection!"

## Data Analysis

Following data collection, data were transcribed, coded, and analyzed, and emergent patterns and themes throughout were noted. After each observation, I transcribed my notes. I also verified with participants the content of our interview. Once the data was collected and analyzed, it was synthesized to triangulate the responses from the questionnaire with those from the interviews and observations. For example, 67 percent of questionnaire study participants said that their overseas experience helped them develop sensitivity to cultural differences among their students. Thus, the theme of cultural empathy was mentioned explicitly by three of the four interview participants, and one participant addressed it during my classroom observation. The emergent themes suggested that in some areas an overseas teaching experience influences teaching decisions.

## FINDINGS

The most prevalent theme throughout the study was how an overseas experience expands one's global perspective and how it can be leveraged in internationalizing a classroom. All interview participants agreed that their overseas teaching experience helped develop their global perspectives, both in and out of the classroom. For some, their newfound global perspective informed their classroom curriculum choices. "[I have] a more global view and it informs my workshops," said Martha, who currently develops workshops for public school teachers. Mark went a step further and said that the experience had a direct effect on his views about the United States: "I think the overseas experience kind of opened my eyes to the United States, but specifically the global political sense of the United States and the rest of the world." Similarly, Matthew said, "I think sometimes as Americans we have these awful stereotypes of other nations and I feel like our students need to know that [so I bring in other cultures]." Mary followed the same idea when she commented that as people of the world, we Americans are unable to escape the multiculturalism that surrounds us. She said, "When you see yourself not as American, but as a citizen of the world [that is when you know you have been influenced] by teaching overseas."

While all of the participants commented in general terms about helping students develop a global perspective, Mary was the only one who commented that students should be exposed to an international classroom if they want to succeed in today's economy:

> Not only are we having more cultures moving to our area, but our kids are going to be competing against those different cultures for regular jobs. You know, it used to be just Americans at a company for these jobs. Now you've got the Indian market, you've got the Chinese market. Brazil itself is a huge market that is up and coming. . . . They [students] need to know because their customers are going to be from abroad, their bosses are going to be from abroad, their competition is definitely going to be from abroad. And because of the way politics and business are . . . it's not just a country thing anymore, it's a global thing. I think it's really important that we try to understand that.

The survey's findings supported the data from interviews in showing that an overseas teaching experience does influence the development of a teacher's global perspective, specifically in teachers' commitment to cross-cultural education because of their willingness to bring other views into their teaching. Specifically, more than 50 percent of respondents answered "a great deal (5)" when asked about the influence the overseas teaching experience had on their acceptance of differences, abilities to use illustrations from other cultures in their teaching, and their willingness to bring other than the dominant U.S. views in the classroom. The results demonstrate that participating in an overseas teaching experience has also informed and framed teachers' global perspective.

Answers to open-ended questions supported the above findings, with three of the twelve respondents referencing global perspective when asked to complete the statement "Before I taught overseas I _____ and now I _____." Additionally when asked "In what ways is your teaching different than your colleagues who have not taught overseas?" seven of the twelve respondents provided answers that referred to global perspective. One participant, in discussing what it is like to return to a U.S. school, said:

I have a unique perspective on students who are new to the school, a different view of the systems that are taken for granted in the school, and a different long-term view of myself. . . . In some ways I am an outsider to the school culture. —Study participant

While global perspective was the major idea to come from the study, another theme was cultural empathy, which can also contribute to internationalizing classrooms. A study participant wrote in the survey answers, "I illustrate lessons with global content and challenge kids to see beyond the ends of their noses. I can relate to exchange students and immigrants who struggle with our language and culture. Everything is washed with a layer of multiculturalism." Additionally, three of the four interview participants readily acknowledged that their experiences overseas heightened their awareness of other cultures and of the feelings students from other cultures experience when moving to a new country. Mary, who taught at a private school in Brazil where the majority of the students came from wealthy families, said she would connect with those students when teaching *Catcher in the Rye* and draw parallels with their lives and the life of the main character. Upon returning to the United States, she said she would use her experiences of living in a Brazilian city and ask her American students to imagine living in a place where the majority of people have bars on their windows. "[My students] tend to get really quiet and wide-eyed when I bring up things like that because it seems so otherworldly." In doing this, she thinks she helps create a more empathetic student and "hopefully, adult." She added, "You realize that even though people's cultural ideas are different that they still have the same basic needs." In the same vein, Matthew commented that going overseas "sensitizes you to every student's potential and differences and I think you become more accepting of students, and I think you have to have that overseas experience to get to that level." Martha reported, "I feel that I understand new Americans more . . . that awareness, that sensitivity is heightened."

The survey findings also suggest that an overseas teaching experience increases cross-cultural understanding, with 65 percent or more of the respondents choosing a great deal (5) as their answer to the following categories: ability to communicate across language barriers, ability to communicate across cultural barriers, interest in future cross-cultural experiences, and the ability to adapt to cultural diversity. Specifically, three of the twelve teachers who filled in the statement "Before I taught overseas I _____ and now I _____" provided answers that referred to cultural empathy. Additionally, of the twelve teachers who responded to the second open-ended question, "In what ways is your teaching different than your colleagues who have not taught overseas?" two respondents referred to cultural empathy in their answers; and one wrote, "When working with non-

English speaking students while teaching overseas, I often used drawings and came up with creative ways to communicate. Now, when teaching math, I use drawing and am able to create examples more relevant to the students more easily than many of my colleagues."

A third theme that appeared in all the conversations was culturally relevant pedagogy and curriculum choices. All four participants said that their time overseas was influential in their desires to teach specific lessons upon their return to the United States, and this effort indirectly internationalized their classrooms. Mary commented that the experience made her a better teacher when it came to teaching various pieces of literature to her students. "To give them colorful stories, to give them anecdotes when reading stories about developing countries, [such as] *Life of Pi*, the experience I had in Brazil helps me explain things more precisely." She added that with literature, she does not

> want to read just the dead White males that the canon says we should, so I teach short stories at the back of our book that are from Zimbabwe and South Africa. . . . It's important to try new perspectives . . . to challenge kids to see things differently because that is the only way we are going to have peace in this world.

Matthew also said he uses his experiences to enrich the lessons for the students. Since he spent time in Poland, he is able to use his experiences to help explain scenes in literature, as well as to include Polish and Russian pieces of literature in his curriculum choices. In this way, he reports, he has expanded the curriculum and opened his students' eyes to other views of the world.

Mark shared that his time overseas "opened up his eyes to the wonders of technology," and as a result he teaches a senior elective that focuses on blogs.

> I came up with this, a blog class, which is really kind of a vehicle for me to get kids to start looking at the news and to talk about the news. They have their own blogs and they need to survey the news each week and choose something that's happening and they have to write an opinion about it; they have to articulate why that event is culturally relevant.

He added that the benefit of teaching the class is that it makes the students aware of the world around them and brings them out of the "bubble" of their high school.

When asked about the influence an overseas teaching experience had in the areas of culturally relevant pedagogy and curriculum choices, study participants reported a strong connection between the overseas teaching experience and areas of developing curriculum, developing cultural sensitivity among students, and developing techniques for teaching non-English speaking students. A high percentage of respondents selected "a great deal (5)" when asked to report the influence an overseas teaching experience had in those areas.

Additionally, teachers responded that the overseas teaching experience influenced the development of curriculum, learning techniques for teaching, working with out-of-class school activities, learning to teach with improvised materials, creativity in teaching, and flexibility in unanticipated situations. It should be noted that many of these areas require teachers to use their creativity and flexibility.

## Limitations

While the results of the study are interesting, especially when discussing internationalizing U.S. school, readers must be aware of the limitations. First, the results cannot be considered generalizable because of the small sample size. Second, many teachers who have worked overseas have done so because of their desire for adventure or interest in another culture. This self-reporting could affect the results because participants who wanted to teach overseas may have described their experience in a positive light and may have already developed a nascent global perspective even before they taught overseas.

## Threats to Validity and Reliability

And, finally, researcher subjectivity is also a threat to the validity of my findings. As a former teacher at The International School of Brussels, my own experiences lead me to believe that overseas teaching experience does positively influence instruction and curriculum choices. Throughout my coding process, I had to keep asking myself: Am I looking for themes that are not there, but I think should be there?

## DISCUSSION

For teacher educators, this study has illustrated that time spent overseas can enable the internationalization of classroom practices, as teachers with overseas teaching experience reported that they use their cultural empathy and cross-cultural competence to develop the tools necessary to help students improve their skills and knowledge about other societies and their own society, regardless of their English proficiency or cultural background. While all teachers should be encouraged to develop curriculum related to the cultures of their students, school departments should actively pursue professional development programs that enable teachers to participate in teacher exchanges overseas. If district and school leaders are interested in improving the cultural empathy and global perspective of their students, they should consider active recruitment of teachers who have worked or studied overseas. Additionally, schools of education should actively encourage preservice and student teachers to spend time in another culture so they can develop better cultural empathy, global perspective, and appropriate curriculum decision-making strategies.

While researchers and practitioners explore how to create culturally inclusive classrooms and prepare students for success in this ever-shrinking world, teachers are the first line of defense in the classroom. Incorporating their overseas experiences into their curriculum design and instruction can have a powerful influence on their students' perceptions of the world around them and possibly could help bring about a more just society.

# REFERENCES

Bryan, Sandra. L., and Marsha M. Sprague. 1997. "The effect of overseas internships on early teaching experiences." *The Clearing House* 70: 199–201.

Cornell, Charles. 2003. "How mentor teacher perceive their roles and relationships in a field-based teacher-training program." *Education* 124: 401–411.

Crossley, Michael, and Keith Watson. 2003. *Comparative and International Research in Education: Globalisation, Context and Difference.* Oxon: RoutledgeFalmer.

Kissock, Craig. 1997. "Student teaching overseas." In *Preparing teachers to teach global perspectives: A handbook for teacher educators.* Edited by Merry Merryfield, Elaine Jarchow, and Sarah Pickert, 123–142. California: Corwin Press, Inc.

Malweski, Erik, Sunti Sharma, and JoAnn Philion. 2012. "How International FieldExperiences-PromoteCross-Cultural Awareness in Preservice Teachers Through Experiential Learning: Findings From a Six-Year Collective Case Study." *Teachers College Record* 114(8): 1–44.

Patton, Michael. 2002. *Qualitative Research and Evaluation Methods* (3rd ed.). Thousand Oaks, CA: Sage.

Pope, Jacqueline, and Joyce Wilder. 2005. "Now That I'm Out in the Field: Student Teaching and Valuing Diversity." *Journal of Instructional Psychology* 32(4): 322–328.

Quezada, Reyes, and Cristina Alfaro. 2007. "Biliteracy teachers' self-reflections of their accounts while student teaching abroad: Speaking from 'the other side.'" *Teacher Education Quarterly* 34(1): 95–113.

Stachowski, Laura, Jayson W. Richardson, and Michelle Henderson. 2003. "Student teachers report on the influence of cultural values on classroom practice and community involvement: Perspectives from the Navajo Reservation and from abroad." *The Teacher Educator* 39(1): 52–63.

Sussman, Nan M. 2002. "Testing the cultural identity model of the cultural transition cycle: sojourners return home." *International Journal of Intercultural Relations* 26(4): 391–408.

Villegas, Ana M., and Tamara Lucas. 2002. "Preparing culturally responsive teachers." *Journal of Teacher Education* 53(1): 20–32.

Wang, Lan. 2005. *Global perspectives: A statement on global education for Australian Schools.* Commonwealth of Australia.

*Chapter Five*

# Implementing and Sustaining Long-Term Partnerships for International Student Teaching Placements

## Eleanor Vernon Wilson

Teachers work within an increasingly globalized and diverse profession. Yet for a variety of reasons, many teachers both novice and veteran, do not feel well prepared to teach the many different student populations entering schools today. A range of factors contribute to this perception: self-assessments, the rapidly changing realities of schools, the lack of personal and professional experience with the populations they serve, personal beliefs, and lack of preparation in teacher education coursework focused on issues of diversity and intercultural development. In a survey conducted by Rochkind and colleagues (2008), over 50 percent of the beginning teachers participating in their study felt that they were not prepared to adequately support the learning of diverse student populations. Preparing future teachers to work with students internationally is another salient and critical aspect of teacher preparation as we seek opportunities for students to work with diverse populations in the twenty-first century (Vande Berg, ed., 2012; Cushner & Brennan, 2007).

This chapter describes the design and implementation of an international student teaching placement for elementary preservice students enrolled in a five-year teacher education program and highlights issues related to envisioning and planning such a program. Critical aspects of the logistics of such programs include creating effective partnerships, gaining institutional support, and creating sustainable structures for such programs. The chapter emphasizes the importance of current research that identifies key issues for such programs, as well as describes hurdles that can impede the progress of internationalizing such placements for preservice students; and finally, delineates the research approach used for purposes of evaluating and determining ways for ensuring students' long-term and enduring cultural awareness.

The chapter details a program designed for elementary education preservice students who participated in student teacher placements in the United States and Cambridge, England, between 2009 and 2014. The program is designed to facilitate and maximize preservice students' understandings of cultural influences while student teaching abroad (Bennett, 2004; Marx, 2008). This chapter then describes the experiences of student participants through analysis of student reflection essays, weekly journal entries, and other related ephemera (Marx & Moss, 2011; Birmingham, 2003; Brindley et al., 2009).

## THE PROGRAM

The program, Curry in Cambridge, described here was designed in response to contemporary concerns about preparing students to teach in an increasingly diverse and global society (Stachowski & Sparks, 2007). In 2007 a faculty member in the elementary education program in the Curry School of Education at the University of Virginia had the opportunity to spend time in the UK and to make contacts with education faculty in Cambridge who were interested in working with a U.S. university to establish an international placement. The elementary education faculty in the United States approved the program as did the International Studies Office which serves the University of Virginia for all study abroad programs. The U.S. faculty worked with the UK faculty to identify primary schools for placement in Cambridge and create the seminar component of the program that accompanied the student teaching. Finding schools in the UK, especially in Cambridge, is always a challenge as schools in Cambridge have many requests for placements, locally and internationally, and the U.S. students were dependent on public transportation to get to their assigned schools.

Students participating in the program are enrolled in a five-year BA/MT program in the University of Virginia's Curry School of Education through which they earned a bachelor's degree in a liberal arts field along with a master of teaching degree. The initial student teaching placement takes place in U.S. schools during the first eight weeks of their final year in the program, August through December. Subsequently, students travel to Cambridge, England, for another eight weeks of full-time student teaching in state schools. These placements are intended to facilitate and maximize preservice students' understandings of cultural influences while student teaching abroad (Bennett, 2004; Marx & Moss, 2011).

This study contributes to the literature by documenting and closely examining the experiences of five cohorts of six elementary preservice students each who were enrolled between 2009 and 2013. The program configuration has altered slightly over the five years, but essentially student teaching placements are evenly divided between the United States and the UK. Faculty in the UK and the United States developed an extensive handbook with details about the anticipated placement in the UK, updating this over time. For the last two years of the program (2012 and 2013), the U.S. faculty created the syllabus for students to use both in the U.S. placements and the UK placements to include research findings related to international placements. With the recognition of the importance of preparing students for these placements and then debriefing students after their study abroad placements, the U.S. faculty meet with students prior to departure and then during the semester following their UK placements.

The theme of the U.S. teacher education program in which students are enrolled is "teacher as a reflective decision maker" and incorporates elements of what O'Doherty and colleagues (2013) refer to as *Powerful Learning Experiences*, which these authors define as an "intentionally designed learning experience that advances understanding of the complex nature of schools and increases participants' abilities to collaboratively address issues of equity situated in authentic problems and relevant school contexts" (p. 6). Nine key attributes comprise the powerful learning experience framework: (1) Explores, critiques, deconstructs from an equity perspective (race, culture, and language); (2) Requires authentic, meaningful, relevant, problem finding that links theory and principal practice; (3) Involves sense making around critical problems of practice; (4) Requires collaboration and interdependence; (5) Develops confidence in one's professional practice; (6) Shifts perspective from the classroom to school, district, or state level; (7) Places both the professor and student in a learning situation; (8) Empowers learners to be responsible for their own learning; and (9) Capitalizes on student reflection. While many of these attributes are incorporated into the U.S. teacher education program, of key importance to this paper is attribute nine: capitalizing on student reflection (O'Doherty et al., 2013).

## THE STUDY

A study was designed concurrently with program implementation in 2009 to identify key aspects of program pedagogy and experiences and their impact on preservice students' understandings of cultural influences while student teaching abroad. This goal was grounded in literature highlighting the importance of preparing future teachers to become culturally competent, reflective teachers is critical in today's world (Bennett, 2004; Cushner & Brennan, 2007; Mahon, 2003; Marx, 2008; Brindley et al., 2009). Research suggests that guiding effective reflection practices and enabling students to maximize their experiences and understandings of international practices is central to this process (Danielson, 2007; Schön, 1987; Cushner, 2005; Pollard, 2008).

Faculty explored a variety of approaches for encouraging student reflection on the cultural aspects of the schools and the communities in which they were teaching (Dewey, 1938/1980; Schön, 1987; Pollard, 2008; Cushner & Brennan, 2007; Vande Berg, 2012). As the program evolved, so too did the reflective components of the program. Over time strategies have become increasingly powerful in enhancing students' reflective processes on both their instructional practices and on their own emerging global awareness or what Wilson (2013), building on the work of Bennett (2004), described as an "ethno-relative understanding of teaching." Faculty involved with leading the program increased time for meetings with students pre- and post-international placements as well as during placements. They developed specific targets for students to identify and describe in both placements, and provided readings for students that reflected current research on international learning experiences, particularly focusing on Bennett's (2004) research relating to developing one's sense of cultural relativity while involved in international placements.

During the first year of the program students worked under the guidance of an affiliated lecturer in the faculty of education at the University of Cambridge. This faculty member led the seminars and directed their work much as if the students were in their "final" placements in the UK. The students worked with a faculty member from the primary U.S. program for two of the eight weeks in the UK and also engaged in weekly group discussion reflection sessions with the U.S. faculty member via Skype. Based on student feedback regarding challenges they faced within their UK classrooms, not the least of which was understanding and the letting go of any prior judgments they might have of their experiences, adjustments were made to increase the level of contact with faculty and the opportunities for reflection for the next four cohorts, first by arranging for the U.S. faculty member to travel with students to the UK and to participate in seminars and observations; and second, by providing more structure and "targets" for students to address in both the United States and UK placements (Marx & Moss, 2011).

The importance of reflection quickly emerged as central to the first cohort's experiences, and remained the most effective aspect of determining students' growth as professionals teaching on both sides of the Atlantic. Self-reflection is an essential aspect of developing future teachers' perceptions of working with diverse populations and is central to developing a lens through which preservice students determine and apply strategies that are appropriate for students from differing backgrounds and cultures (Landson-Billings, 1995; Paris, 2012). Teacher candidates who are self-reflective and are aware of the changes they need to make in their professional practice exhibit a valuable skill for continuous development throughout their teaching career

(Gaudino, 2012). Reflection and ensuing changes in one's professional practice are skills that can be improved with guidance and effort (Costa & Garmston, 2002). University professors, supervisors, and cooperating teachers are in an ideal position to guide candidates in developing these skills (Glickman, 1990) and provide opportunities to work in a variety of contexts with a variety of student populations and to critically reflect on those experiences.

## METHODOLOGY

The theoretical framework grounding this study stems from Bennett's concept of developing "cultural competence" (2004), and the study was conceptualized as a case study (Yin, 2009). As noted, the faculty founding this program believed that careful supervision and analysis of students' participation in the program would lead to creating a stronger framework for long-term sustainability. Central to the viability of such programs is determining ways to evaluate program impact for those students participating in the program.

### Data Sources

Analysis of qualitative and quantitative data gathered from five cohorts of preservice students served to provide the background for this study (Yin, 2009). Initially, several instruments were used by program faculty for assessing teaching efficacy and student understanding of diversity at the beginning and end of the placement: a Multicultural Efficacy Scale (Guyton & Wesche, 2005); analysis and coding of video records using the CLASS, a standardized measure of teacher effectiveness (Pianta, La Paro, & Hamre, 2008; MyCAP, Marx & Moss, 2011). As noted in table 5.1, artifacts and documents related to the students' experiences were also collected throughout the semesters in which the students were engaged in student teaching experiences.

After the first two years of the program, it was determined that quantitative data gathered did not adequately reflect students' underlying understanding of differences encountered in placements; nor did it identify ways in which cultural immersion in the UK placement impacted their views of teaching. Thus, in the past three years, we focused on examining students' weekly reflections in their journals and pre- and post-statements of their goals for working in the United States and the UK placements. Additionally semi-structured focus groups were conducted during and after student completion of the program in the UK.[1]

## Data Analysis

Data were analyzed using the constant comparative method, meaning analysis was ongoing, open ended, and inductive (Lincoln & Guba, 1985; Patton, 2002). After unitizing the data (i.e., identifying units of information in the interview transcript), we identified working categories in which we located specific data units. These categories were subsequently modified as we worked through each of the data sources, seeking what Lincoln and Guba (1985) described as a "saturation of categories" and an "emergence of regularities" (p. 350). Comparative pattern analysis, which involved searching for categories exhibiting "internal homogeneity" and "external heterogeneity," was used to illuminate recurring patterns in the data (Patton, 2002).

Table 5.1.   Study Data: Fall 2009–Spring 2014

| Data Sources | Dates | Cohort |
|---|---|---|
| Multicultural Efficacy Scale | Mid-September | 2009–2010 |
| | Early December | |
| First Focus Groups | Late September | 2009–2013 |
| First "Purpose/Goal" Statements | Early October | 2009–2013 |
| First MyCap | Early October | 2011–2013 |
| Second Focus Groups | Mid-October | 2010–2013 |
| First Video-Recording (CLASS) | Late September | 2009–2010 |
| Second Focus Groups | Mid-October | 2009–2013 |
| Third Focus Groups | Mid-November | 2009–2013 |
| Second Video-Recording (CLASS) | Mid-November | 2009–2010 |
| Fourth/Final Focus Groups | Early December | 2009–2013 |
| Final "Purpose/Goal" Statements | Mid-December | 2009–2013 |
| Final MyCap | Early January | 2011–2013 |
| Reflective Journals | Ongoing: August through January | 2009–2013 |
| Lesson Plans and Feedback | Ongoing | 2009–2013 |

Note: IRB approval granted Project 2009-0086-00, renewed 3/1/2013.

## RESULTS

The findings discussed in this chapter are grouped by cohort. For each cohort, the pre-statements about their goals for the UK teaching were remarkably similar: they noted a desire to learn how to teach in a new curriculum, how to manage classes in a new country, and ways to assess learning in their new placements. One student's goals included her professional intentions:

> in compliance with the personal and professional conduct standards for Great Britain, I plan to observe appropriate boundaries between me and my students while simultaneously building relationships with my students founded on trust, respect, and dignity. As with my other placement in Virginia, I fully intend on respecting others and tolerating other beliefs, ideas, and lifestyles while teaching in the United Kingdom.

The most significant finding emerging from the data analysis, for all cohorts, is that students in the international program report they "reflect, and reflect and reflect more" throughout their time abroad. Given the underlying focus of the American program on enabling teachers in training to become reflective decision makers, students have varied opportunities throughout the U.S. program to reflect on their teaching (Marzano, 2012; Schön, 1983, 1987). "Decision making" implies instructional decision making for (most) students, and without scaffolding to support ways to probe more deeply for reasons instructional practices vary, may not lead to evolving awareness of the subtleties of issues and challenges occurring in classroom practice. The majority of program participants' reflections focused on "what works" and what to change in given situations, often after feedback from observers. Final reflections and summary statements from U.S. placements typically include students' increasing self-confidence in management along with developing their instructional ability to successfully plan and assess effective lessons and units. Yet probing for the rationale underlying most students' reflections often does not go beyond changes in approaches to instruction to a level that illustrates the impact on students' current pedagogical beliefs along with anticipations of how these changes will be incorporated in their future classrooms. Hence, it became apparent that focusing on students' reflections provided a way to deepen students' understanding of living and working in another culture, albeit one that shared the same language, many of the same approaches to instruction, yet also differed in many ways.

Once abroad, the centrality of reflection for these students expanded beyond the expected parameters (Gaudino, 2012). Students reported, they benefited from the more extensive written reflection on lessons required by schools in England, the more detailed lesson plans, goals, and that "in America we did not have this experience. . . . We had so much attention from professors and our cooperating classroom teachers [in the UK]. All the reflection was something I didn't feel was as important here in America, now I feel it was important and overlooked. . . ." All students agreed that they had not anticipated developing reflective skills to be the most significant benefit of the international experience as it had not been a significant part of their clinical experiences in the United States. The constant reference to the importance of reflection and the ways in which it became central to the preservice students' teaching lives has emerged as key to this international experience.

The preservice students consistently identified the wide diversity within their international placements as a significant factor in their growing cultural awareness while overseas: "It's just that the class IS diverse . . . we don't celebrate but just live [diversity] . . . in some ways it puts a lot less pressure as it's an approach to diversity that we're very comfortable with." Admittedly, the nature of the placement and the fact that all five cohorts were "strangers in a foreign land" encouraged the preservice students to reflect and to constantly make sense out of their placements: "Reflecting constantly, discussing everything that was going on in school, would never have happened if I was in the States" (Gaudino, 2012). Along with identifying the diverse populations they worked with and their initial understanding of growing awareness of working within a diverse culture, the content of students' reflective observations of differing approaches to instructional practices in the United States and the UK remains consistent over all five cohorts: students identify approaches to differentiation, classroom management, and assessing instruction as key areas in which they not only observe differences, but also place these differences within expectations of teaching practices in both countries.

The following five subsections illustrate key themes that emerged from data from each of the student cohorts. The findings highlight the important role that reflection played for students in each of the cohorts by helping them to make sense of their experiences in the UK. These then provide a framework that demonstrates change over time, particularly as program leaders focus on encouraging more targeted reflection about instructional practices in the United States and the UK and ways in which schools are influenced by cultural expectations along with political demands and other state/country standardized expectations.

## The first group, 2009: "I'm tired of translating."

When the first cohort of elementary preservice students traveled to the UK, the centrality of reflection for these students expanded, going beyond the expected parameters of effective classroom experiences. As one student indicated, they "reflected again and again and then reflected more." Journals and early interviews indicated the ways these students were encountering, and understanding (or not), the cultural influences on their classrooms, yet it became more obvious that guiding students to integrate their reflections in future teaching environments became more important than anticipated. One of the students in the first cohort observed that she was "tired of translating," an astute observation in many ways, but also an indication of the cultural dissonance she was experiencing, a reflection that did not change during the time she was in the UK.

Additional feedback from this first cohort, regarding students' sense of being a part of an international community, is consistent throughout the ensuing five years of the program: "my school's environment was so internationally diverse that multiculturalism was not even a topic for discussion, it just was." The final reflections from this group indicated their confidence in mastering the UK curricular requirements and their increased self-confidence in becoming teachers. These students agreed that their experiences had given them an added dimension of instructional skills and that they felt confident seeking jobs in teaching.

Yet based on feedback from this cohort, U.S. faculty still questioned whether students effectively addressed ideas of an expanding worldview of cultural competency, an aspect essential to these placements. It is one thing to describe and compare instructional experiences in both countries, but it is another to understand reasons underlying these differences. Simply comparing and contrasting events will not reflect underlying cultural and other influences that determine what is taught in schools. It is at the juncture of reporting details of instructional practices as compared to the United States and the UK where students need to be encouraged to recognize to understand that "new and different teaching and learning norms and practices are grounded in the values and beliefs of the local culture" (Vande Berg, p. 18).

## 2010: "This experience opened my eyes to how different classrooms can be in different cultures and what it is like to be an outsider."

Previous studies have shown the importance of a "cultural translator" to work with students engaging in study abroad placements (Marx and Moss, 2011; Brindley et al., 2009). After the first year of the program it became apparent that having a supporting faculty member on site would enhance and help "decode" the experiences of these students (Gaudino, 2012). The second year (2010), six students went to the UK, and program faculty negotiated time to go to the UK with these students to work with them on a regular basis. This programmatic change contributed significantly to assisting students in creating a foundation for critically approaching their experiences and was maintained through the fall of 2013. Along with weekly seminars held by the UK faculty, the U.S. faculty met with students to analyze their progress and reflect on the ways teaching practices were embedded in a culture of expectations different from the United States, yet with a focus on very similar outcomes. Providing prompts and urging students to "think beyond the box" of the immediacy of their experiences led them to deeper understanding of the cultural and instructional differences between the United States and the UK placements.

Analyzing the experiences of the 2010 and 2011 cohorts, led to further understandings of the importance of working with the preservice students to balance opinions about how they viewed instruction in both countries, and working with their professional colleagues was a critical component of the program. As a result of providing more specific targets for students to observe in the UK (e.g., management, assessment, curriculum development) student feedback indicated a movement toward a more holistic self-awareness of cultural influences of teaching practices in the UK. Striving for a balance as they compared their experiences in the United States and the UK, one student observed: "the greatest bit of wisdom this experience has taught me is that kids are kids and good teaching is good teaching no matter where you are . . . the true heart of the teaching profession I have found to be largely the same cross culturally."

In spring 2011 a student enrolled in the U.S. teacher education program was interested in the outcomes of the UK placements for her colleagues and chose to interview the group about their perceptions of the international experiences for a class assignment (Blunden, 2011). This student was unable to apply to the program herself due to her status in the United States but was a great supporter of experiences such as the Cambridge program offers. One of the students she interviewed for this project from the 2010 cohort reported:

> You can read as much as you like about adapting to students' cultural needs and taking on diverse perspectives, but I found that these ideas only truly sunk in when I had my own experiences with them.

Another student interviewed for this paper cited learning the pros and cons of both the American and British education systems: "There were things that I saw there that made me really question what I've been taught and then things that I saw there that made me glad that I had learned another way . . . I've been able to figure out what my preferences are and how I might set up my own classroom so that it's my own personal hybrid of the two systems." In the final summary paper, this student continued:

> I got to see teaching in two very different styles and contexts. The nature of the British curriculum (more practically based) and the way my school taught (more hands-on, multimodal, real world experience, integrating the arts) gave me a much different picture of school than my American placement. Not that my American school was bad, they were simply different styles- and seeing

both helped me find myself (and my style) as a teacher I learned about the pros and the cons of both the American and British Education curricula. I learned what it feels like to be new and scared in an education setting—it was weird having to go to a totally different place, where they speak a semi-different language, and where I had to be competent enough to teach. . . . I think in America, we're very stuck in this quantitative assessment: SOLs, percentage scores on everything are what tell us about the kids. But in England, they really emphasize the importance of qualitative assessment and observations, and I found that I really highly valued that and hope to do it in my classroom.

## 2011: "The true heart of the teaching profession I have found to be largely the same cross culturally."

There were eight students in the 2011 group, and the larger number provided more challenges in travelling for observations, although the faculty of education lecturer continued to share observations with the American tutor; the seminar continued to be taught by the UK instructor accompanied by the U.S. faculty member. The final presentations for this group addressed their changing views of adapting to UK curricula along with discussions of the ways in which they viewed their role adapting to UK classrooms. This group was part of the 2012 study (Gaudino, 2012) and again, highlighted the importance of reflection in their personal professional growth: "Learning how to self-reflect and reflect on my practice with my supervisor was the best benefit of this experience." "We really became peer advisors to each other. . . . As peer advisors, we were interdependent and I valued opinions of the other students in this group."

Another student added that they all benefited from the "more extensive written reflection on lessons required by schools in England, the more detailed lesson plans, goals, etc.," and that "in America we did not have this experience." Students cited attention from faculty and classroom teachers as critical to their pedagogical growth along with understanding the ways in which cultural influences impacted their teaching. And of reflection, they said: "All the reflection was something I didn't feel was as important here in America, now I feel it was important and overlooked." Another student continued, "Developing a network of coworkers was key to our development in England. The teachers and professor in England opened my eyes to how supportive teachers can be with each other." One student asked, "Why have I not had this the whole time I was in America?" These students also concurred that their weekly seminars with an education professor "'helped us to understand': similarities I noticed between the United States and England, yet also helped to develop my own sense of myself as a reflective and responsive teacher" (Gaudino, 2012).

A student from this cohort (2011) described the challenges of the UK placement:

> Taking on a placement in a different country has certainly been a challenge, but at the end of this experience I am positive that I have grown in ways that I never would have if I had completed a placement solely in the United States. I was challenged to adapt quickly to students needs in the three different class-rooms I taught in, I observed differences in staff interaction between U.S. and English schools. I learned how important communicating with support staff is, I saw how Maths and science curriculum are structured and taught, and I came face to face with how crucial differentiated instruction is. Observing class-rooms as an outsider not only encouraged me to reflect on the differences and similarities I noticed between the U.S. and England, but also helped to develop my own sense of myself as a reflective and responsive teacher.

Another student in this cohort described lessons learned during the UK placement as well as the U.S. placement as follows:

> The greatest bit of wisdom this experience has taught me is that kids are kids, and good teaching is good teaching no matter where you are. Differentiation, behavioral management, engaging lessons, and relationships with the students are so important regardless. The differences between the school systems are definitely there, however, the differences are mostly found in the details. The true heart of the teaching profession I have found to be largely the same cross culturally. I have benefitted from this experience so much, and as cheesy as it sounds, have enjoyed every minute of it! I am so glad that this experience has been a part of my teacher training!

## 2012: "This experience has provided me with a critical lens of my teaching . . . "

Several changes occurred with the fourth cohort, the most significant being that the faculty supervisor in Cambridge felt it was no longer possible to work with the students during their UK placements. This necessitated chang-ing our affiliation to an organization (Educators Abroad) that ensured stu-dents could acquire the necessary visas to enter the UK and complete student teaching in the UK. The U.S. faculty member served as site supervisor and led the weekly seminars. This change led to more focused discussions and analysis of the students' experiences along with introducing students to UK curriculum and related procedural issues in schools. Pollard's (2008) work on the cycle of reflective teaching, with an emphasis on interpreting actions within a specific framework, was incorporated into the program. Students were also assigned readings on intercultural learning along with the text, *Getting the Buggers to Behave* (Cowley, 2010), which provides an approach to classroom management. This framework proved helpful as students ana-lyzed themselves and their experiences in ways they had not previously.

Student perceptions of teaching across international boundaries and their influence on cultural constraints were reflected in the pre- and post-purpose statements for the 2012 cohort. The cultural relativity in which one strives to define oneself in authentic terms and the need to retain one's sense of self mark shifts in students' ability and become part of their repertoire of behavior that they "own" by living in different cultures (Bennet, 2004, p. 71). We used the MyCap (Marx & Moss, 2011) instrument both as a guide for discussions throughout the semester and also as a pre- and post-instrument. The prompts from the individual sections that highlighted global competencies encouraged students to review more thoughtfully their work both in the United States and in the UK.

Additionally, students in the 2012 and 2013 cohorts were asked to respond weekly to specific targets relating particularly to classroom practices in the United States and UK: classroom management, classroom instruction, and the impact of cultural differences in classrooms. Their journals and pre- and post-position papers illustrated a deeper understanding of the ways in which teaching in the United States and the UK were the same, and yet different, in their approaches to instruction, and the reasons for these similarities and differences. In her final reflection paper, one student said, "there is no way to describe everything I learned over this placement . . . I have learned to meet the needs of students in two completely different types of classrooms and learned that no matter what the demographics of the students, there will always be an extremely wide variety of levels and abilities that need to be catered to through differentiated instruction."

> Prior to my student teaching placement in England, my goals for the trip were to continue strengthening my professional skills in classroom management, differentiation, time management, parent-teacher relations, and assessment design. I also wanted to continue practicing flexibility in the classroom since it is a key characteristic for good teachers to possess.
>
> Overall, I learned an exceptional amount of information from my experience in England. I not only met all of my personal and professional goals, but also exceeded them far beyond what I previously anticipated. I feel very confident now in the areas of classroom management, differentiation, time management, parent-teacher relations, designing assessments, and flexibility.

As with prior groups, students all commented on differences in assessment strategies and in differentiation or providing individual responses to student work. In some cases they found UK teachers simply creating "more work" in this process: and in others, they found this to be a meaningful way to assess student work. They also learned to work with whole class instruction in ways that contrasted with U.S. schools where the emphasis is on small group instruction. All acknowledged they were more prepared than prior groups for this placement to teach students about global issues although one student observed that the UK placement was "more of a culture shock than I expected." Yet in the end she delighted in the final feedback from her class-

room supervisor: "Never think you know it all. As a teacher you keep learning new things all the time and keep developing. Be open to suggestions and
ideas; it is all about sharing good practice" (Amber, 2012).

An interesting tangential aspect of cultural experiences encountered by
the fourth group of students arose not from the classroom but from the U.S.
presidential election. Students commented on the "bluntness" of their English colleagues when discussing political issues and were slightly thrown off
guard by the interest shown in their personal political preferences. Students
noted that in the United States their political views were private and, as a
rule, they are not asked to comment on them in a public way. However, they
experienced their British colleagues as "blunt" and felt somewhat defensive
about their political opinions.

One of the students chose to summarize various "lessons learned":

> The education system is currently in flux and consequently lacks state-spon-
> sored objectives. "Fresh air" actually means cold. Students change into their
> PE kits for PE and do so in the classroom. Ofsted is a significant impetus to the
> school community expecting a visit. We don't quite speak the same language.
> Small differences can make a big difference. Children in state schools cannot
> legally be required to wear the school uniform. Until recently special educa-
> tion teachers were not required to have any "special" education themselves.
> Students here are classified as More Able or Gifted. Gifted means truly superb
> and gifted in some specific area of life, even one beyond the school. More
> Able typically refers to high achieving students. No special services are pro-
> vided for More Able or British schools refer to a child's level of schooling as
> his or her year, rather than his or her grade. Grading is referred to as mark-
> ing. . . . Daily assemblies are a significant part of the school culture. Guided
> reading takes the same form as it does in the U.S. British students often
> holiday in Florida. Binders have two rings in the UK. Paper is longer in the
> UK than is it in the U.S. You can see a hedgehog rustling around in the
> schoolyard. . . .

Her paper then continued to reflect on why the UK placement had provided
her with a "new lens" through which she would balance her approach to
teaching in the future.

## 2013: "Being in a new culture forced me to truly reflect on my practices as a teacher, and to find what works the best."

Embarking on the fifth year of the program, faculty had become more attuned to the need for focusing students on careful "unpacking" of reasons
that influence teaching, teachers, and schools by providing students with
specific targets to address each week, first in the United States and then in the
UK. These targets included observations about classroom managemen, in-

struction, assessment, and overall strategies for classroom running procedures.

Prior to departure for the UK, the study-abroad leader assigned readings
on developing cultural competencies, and during the UK placement, used
two texts recommended by classroom teachers in the UK for preservice
students: Cowley (2010), *Getting the Buggers to Behave* and Denby (2010),
*How to be an Outstanding Primary School Teacher*. Once in the UK she
observed students each week and held weekly seminars in the United States
and the UK. Weekly instructional topics were identified to specifically observe in the UK (e.g., WALTS, ongoing assessments, and management strategies). Students kept weekly logs beginning with the U.S. placement in
which they were encouraged to think deeply about the underlying issues
influencing their teaching: from annoying and often long bus rides, to lesson
plans and the overall culture of their schools.

In each cohort, the requirements for final presentations were designed to
address the goals students identified in their initial purpose statements. These
presentations included oral discussions of forty-five minutes each about their
experiences in the UK, contrasting them to the United States; and then written papers in which they elaborated on their overall experiences during the
semester.

In the 2013 cohort, a student summed up the presentations of her fellow
cohort members by noting six different "takeaways" provided by all students,
which she felt showed the depth of understanding this group gained:

> For all of us, it was a solemn day, as we took a breath, full of accomplishment:
> These takeaways included thinking about differentiation, cultural competen-
> cies, developing a teacher presence, being part of a welcoming school commu-
> nity, Reflecting on our lessons, meetings, seminars, journals, and experiences
> here in Cambridge. Actively reflecting within our actual lessons—to change
> an activity before the lesson is even over! Altering and being flexible to
> disturbances or hiccups.

And concluding: "the seminars, teaching in the classroom, and presentations
all gave us a chance to truly develop who we are going to be as future
educators. We all walked away from our schools with so much more knowledge than any of us could have ever first imagined."

The developing awareness of preservice students' abilities to make sense
of an international student teaching experience placement does not happen
overnight, nor does it have a finite ending, or happen with all students. This
is also true of affiliated faculty in such programs as the conditions associated
with these placements are often in flux. But guiding students in the development of their global competencies to a space within Bennett's (2001) "ethnorelative understanding of teaching," which involves students' abilities to let
go of critical comparisons and instead see differences embedded in differing

settings that are influenced by differing conceptions of teaching and learning. Reflective practices that encourage such development in perceptions are key to this process and are equally important for faculty working with these programs.

## LESSONS LEARNED

There are many complexities related to framing the international student teaching placements: academic course requirements, creating course numbers that align with the teacher education program and the study-abroad office, expectations for actual amount of full-time teaching in the UK, and expectations for students' final research presentations. Most important, the sending faculty need to be actively involved in the design of these programs and encouraged to insert ideas for students to incorporate in the UK schools.

First, and probably most importantly, it is important to become familiar with existing research on maximizing international experiences for students, whether study abroad or student teaching placements, as the developing research base is most helpful.

Second, it is critical to have institutional commitment for the program and the support of teacher education faculty. Initially the faculty director of this program consulted with all elementary education faculty members and the head of teacher education while planning for the program. We then developed the proposal and worked with the University's International Studies Office to facilitate the logistics of placing students overseas. The program is now run concurrently with several other international programs by the director of field services in the teacher education program.

Third, there is the issue of obtaining Tier 4 visas for students along with housing and developing a strong cohort of supporting schools. Currently we work with Educators Abroad to facilitate these arrangements.

Fourth is the importance of accurately communicating program goals with our UK colleagues. It is important to clarify the initial preparation of students prior to traveling abroad and the specific expectations for the timing and responsibilities of the placement progression once in the UK. As stated earlier, finding a partner to facilitate the international placement is critical; and identifying an agency or faculty member in a university who is willing to oversee placements and facilitate arrangements is equally important for successful outcomes. There are many and varied expectations for students enrolled in teaching practica internationally, and specifying the conditions for this placement was critically important. The importance of working with talented and supportive classroom teachers and schools in the UK, as in the United States, cannot be overestimated. Classroom teachers in the UK gave generously of their time and input to support the American students' developing teacher presence in a completely new setting from their U.S. placements. Just recently (June 2014) a UK teacher who is responsible for American placements in one of our affiliated schools wrote to say that the feedback from a paper I had sent her that focuses on synthesizing reflections of the United States sending students to the UK was extremely helpful and that she intended to use this focus as the program continues in her school.

Fifth, the role of a "cultural translator" to mediate, debrief, and support students while abroad and on their return cannot be overestimated. Misconceptions and misunderstandings of observed classroom running procedures and requirements in the British schools at first seem overwhelming, and helping students to share experiences and observations in seminar is critical to their developing cultural sensitivity.

Finally, in terms of pre-departure preparation of preservice students it is critical to provide as much detail as possible in handbooks describing placement expectations along with other aspects of life when students are placed overseas. The focus on reflection as students develop their observational "lenses" is central for maintaining long-term programmatic impact and is a practice most frequently described by students on their return.

As the previous discussion has shown, the more focus and structure for preservice students' reflective lens, the deeper becomes the understanding and self-assessment of students' professional growth in both the U.S. and UK. Providing students with specific targets to observe and discuss during the United States and UK placements has over time given a framework for this. With each year, we all become more aware of ways to guarantee an enriching and positive experience for students. A student in the 2013 cohort wrote:

> For me, a reflection is much more than a single thought, idea or opinion. A reflection is an in-depth process that forces you to evaluate yourself and your experiences and make choices on how you will implement your findings in your future. I hope to use this reflection as a guide to create my future classroom and to be the best teacher that my students have taught me to be.

## CONCLUDING THOUGHTS

> I learned the importance of recognizing the difference between planning instruction and providing instruction.

It is an understatement that one has to be prepared for the unexpected on both sides of the Atlantic. As the discussion illustrates, and as faculty learned, it is one thing to establish an international student teaching placement and it is another to guide students in their understanding of cultural influences on teaching practices, whether in the United States or the UK. Second, determining the ways in which data can be collected and used in an ongoing and deliberative way to discuss student growth continues to be central for determining programmatic impact and ways to ensure long-term professional growth for preservice students. Certainly, multicultural efficacy does not equal global competencies.

The shift from an objective standpoint of reflection to a more person-centered standpoint of reflection is a critical aspect of participants' experiences and growth. This dynamic lends itself to long-term application. In students' comments on their placements following these experiences, they consistently discussed the importance of balanced perceptions, the ways they viewed instruction in both countries and their colleagues and their progression toward a more holistic self-awareness of their worldview, personal beliefs, and expectations for future roles as teachers. During the first meeting on our return in January 2014, one of the students indicated that this experience led her to reflect on "why" she was approaching instruction in ways she did not in the United States: "I really had to think about WHY I was doing things (instructional) in the UK." Clinical practices that emphasize the art and application of reflection can provide a foundation for preservice students' use of reflection to become aware of their own growth as future teachers.

Never underestimate the lasting influence of the preservice students' experience abroad! In this vein, we created a closed Facebook account for students enrolled in the program, and each year the new cohorts sign on and share their experiences. Not only has this proved helpful for students to respond to each other about basic issues in the UK such as printing lesson plans, catching buses, and working in schools, it has served as a source of information for students who are looking for jobs. Many students move to areas where other students are currently teaching and have found it helpful to share experiences. As one of the student in the 2012 cohort indicated when wishing the 2013 cohort well: "Now I understand why prior groups were 'stalking' us on Facebook as we arrived, eager to hear of our experiences along with dispensing advice!"

As evidenced by the discussion, these international placements require thoughtful deliberation of practice and beliefs regarding educational practices in both the United States and the UK, and can be a "tricky slope" to navigate. In the end, the student who wrote of her expectations for her future role as a teacher summarized: "Be flexible, adapt, but maintain your own style, feel prepared to take on a wide variety of teaching jobs, and maintain cultural sensitivity and global awareness" (Liz, 2012). In closing, the following entry from a student enrolled in the 2013 cohort shows her perceptions of experiencing the UK teaching placement:

Experiencing the different education systems and standards of the UK and U.S. has helped me illuminate what the true importance of teaching is—*student learning*. Sometimes teachers and student teachers get so caught up in the organizational aspects of a classroom that they forget that the main purpose of their role as a teacher is to help students LEARN! One of the aspects I have been working to develop over my time here is how to better engage student's learning. I first started off by adapting the UK's emphasis on lesson objectives. At the start of every lesson I introduced the WALT (we are learning to) and referred back to it throughout my lessons. This helps students become more self-aware of what they are learning. After becoming more comfortable with the format and requirements of a UK lesson plan, I was able to better engage and converse with the students to further enhance their learning. I wasn't just teaching to the students, but I was also learning with them.

## NOTE

1. IRB approval was granted for years 2009–2015.

## REFERENCES

Bennett, Milton (2001). *Intercultural competence for global leadership.* The Intercultural Development Research Institute. Retrieved at www.idrinstitute.org idri@idrinstitute.org.

Bennett, M. J. (2004). Becoming interculturally competent. In J. Wurzel (ed.), *Toward multiculturalism: A reader in multicultural education.* Newton, MA: Intercultural Resource Corporation, 62–77.

Birmingham, Carrie (2003). Practicing the Virtue of Reflection in an Unfamiliar Cultural Context. *Theory into Practice 42*(3), 188–194.

Blunden, Megan (2011). "The benefits of study abroad for preservice teachers." Unpublished paper. Curry School of Education, University of Virginia.

Bradfield-Krieger, P. (1999). Mediated cultural immersion and antiracism: An opportunity for monocultural preservice teachers to begin the dialogue. *Multicultural Perspectives 1*(2), 29–32.

Brindley, Roger, Suzanne Quinn, & Mary Lou Morton (2009). Consonance and dissonance in a study abroad program as a catalyst for professional development of preservice teachers. *Teaching and Teacher Education 25*, 525–532.

Cowley, Sue (2010). *Getting the Buggers to Behave.* 4th ed. London: Continuum Publishing Company.

Cushner, K., & Brennan, S. (2007). The value of learning to teach in another culture. In K. Cushner & S. Brennan (eds.), *Intercultural student teaching: A bridge to global competence.* Lanham, MD: Rowman & Littlefield Education, 1–12.

Dewey, John (1933). *How we think.* Boston: D.C. Heath.

Dunn, David (2011). *How to be an Outstanding Primary School Teacher.* London: Continuum.

Gaudino, Ann (2012). Key issues in an international clinical experience for graduate students in education: Implications for policy and practice. *Journal of International Education and Leadership (2)*3. Retrieved at http://www.jielusa.org.

Groulx, J. G. (2001). Changing preservice teacher perceptions of minority schools. *Urban Education 36*(1), 60–92.

Guyton, E. M., & Wesche, M. V. (2005). The multicultural efficacy scale: Development, item selection, and reliability. *Multicultural perspectives 7*(4), 21–29.

Hall, E. T. (1998). The power of hidden differences. In M. J. Bennett (ed.), *Basic concepts of intercultural communication: Selected readings.* Yarmouth, ME: Intercultural Press.

Hammer, M. R., & Bennett, M. J. (2001). *The intercultural development inventory manual.* Portland, Oregon: The Intercultural Communication Institute.

Hammer, M. R., Bennett, M. J., & Wiseman, R. (2003). Measuring intercultural sensitivity: The intercultural development inventory. *International Journal of Intercultural Relations 27*(4), 421–443.

Harford, Judith, and MacRuairc, G. (2008). Engaging Student teachers in meaningful reflective practice. *Teaching and Teacher Education 24*(7), 1884–1892.

Kaszniak, A. W. (2014). Contemplative pedagogy: Perspectives from cognitive and affective science. In O. Gunnlaugson, E. Sarath, C. Scott, and H. Bai (Eds.), *Contemplative learning and inquiry across disciplines.* New York: State University of New York Press.

King, P., & Baxter Magolda, B. (2005). A developmental model of intercultural maturity. *Journal of College Student Development 45*(6), 571–592.

Landson-Billings, G. (1995). Toward a theory of culturally relevant pedagogy. *American Educational Research Journal 32*, 465–491

Mahon, J. A. (2003). Intercultural sensitivity development among practicing teachers: Life history perspectives (PhD, Kent State University).

Marshall, Catherine, & Rossman, Gretchen (2006). *Designing Qualitative Research.* 4th ed. Thousand Oaks, CA: Sage Publications.

Marx, H. (2008, October). *Learning about self far from home: Preservice teachers' intercultural development during international experiences.* Conference Proceedings of the Annual Meeting of the Northeastern Educational Research Association.

Marx, H. & Moss, D. M. (2011). Please mind the culture gap: Intercultural development during a teacher education study abroad program. *Journal of Teacher Education 62*(1), 35–47.

Marx, H. & Moss, D. (2012). *MyCAP: A Cultural awareness profile.* Retrieved at http://www.nafsa.org/_/File/_/itlc_moss_handout.pdf. NAFSA, unpublished document.

Marzano, Robert J. (2012). *Becoming a Reflective Teacher.* New York: Marzano Research Library.

McGarr, Oliver, & Moody, Janet (2010) Scaffolding or stifling? The influence of journal requirements on students' engagement in reflective practice. *Reflective Practice: International and Multidisciplinary Perspectives 11*(5), 579–591.

Mezirow, J. (1978). Perspective transformation. *Adult Education 28*, 100–108.

O'Doherty, A., Generett G., & Young, M. D. (2013). *Powerful Learning Experiences.* Charlottesville, VA: UCEA.

Paris, D. (2012). Culturally sustaining pedagogy: A need for change in stance, terminology, and practice. *Educational Researcher 41*, 93–97.

Patton, Michael Quinn (2002). *Qualitative Research and Evaluation Methods.* Thousand Oaks, CA: Sage Publications.

Pianta, R. C., La Paro, K. M., & Hamre, B. K. (2008). *Classroom assessment scoring system (CLASS) manual, K-3.* Baltimore, MD: Paul H. Brookes Publishing Company.

Pollard, Andrew (2008). *Reflective teaching.* 3rd ed. London, UK: Continuum International Publishing Group.

Rochkind, J., Immerwahr, J., Ott, A., & Johnson, J. (2008). *Lessons learned: New teachers talk about their jobs, challenges, and long-range plans. Issue No. 3, Teaching in changing times.* Washington, DC: National Comprehensive Center for Teacher Quality and Public Agenda. http://www.tqsource.org/publications/LessonsLearned3.pdf.

Romano, R., & Cushner, K. (2007). Reflections on the importance and value of the overseas student-teaching experience. In K. Cushner & S. Brennan (eds.), *Intercultural student teaching: A bridge to global competence.* Lanham, MD: Rowman & Littlefield Education, 215–225.

Schön, Donald (1983). *The reflective practitioner.* New York: Basic Books.

Schön, D. (1987). *Educating the reflective practitioner.* San Francisco, CA: Jossey-Bass.

Stachowski, L. L. (1994). Realities constructed by international student teachers (PhD, Indiana University).

Stachowski, L. L., & Mahan, J. M. (1998). Cross-cultural field placements: Student teachers learning from schools and communities. *Theory into Practice 37*(2), 155.

Stachowski, L. L., & Sparks, T. (2007). Thirty years and 2,000 student teachers later: An overseas student teaching project that is popular, successful, and replicable. *Teacher Education Quarterly 34*(1), 115–132.

Trilokekar, Roopa Desai, and Kukar, Polina (2011). Disorienting experiences during study abroad: Reflections of preservice teacher candidates. *Teaching and Teacher Education (27)*.

Tschannen-Moran, M., & Hoy, A. W. (2001). Teacher efficacy: Capturing an elusive construct. *Teaching and Teacher Education 1*(7), 783–805.

Vande Berg, Michael. (2007). Intervening in the learning of U.S. students abroad. *Journal of Studies in International Education 11*(3–4), 392–399.

Vande Berg, Michael (ed.) (2012). *Student Learning Abroad: What Our Students Are Learning, What They're Not, and What We Can Do About It.* Sterling, VA: Stulus Publishing.

Wilson, Eleanor Vernon, Moss, David, & Marx, Helen. (2013) *Exploring Cultural Awareness of Preservice Candidates Participating in International Teaching Placements: A Documentary Account.* American Educational Association, Division K.

Yin, Robert K. (2009). *Case Study Research: Design and Methods.* Thousand Oaks, CA: Sage Inc.

Zeichner, K. M., & Melnick, S. L. (1996). The role of community field experiences in preparing teachers for cultural diversity. In K. M. Zeichner, S. L. Melnick, & M. L. Gomez (eds.), *Currents of reform in preservice teacher education.* New York: Teachers College Press.

*II*

# Technology

*Chapter Six*

# Promoting Global and Comparative Understandings of Education

*My Yearlong Journey*

Alexandra Brown

## INTRODUCTION

Many American colleges of education have strong programs that produce highly qualified teachers. However, one vital component lacking in some of these institutions is the internationalization of their education programs. If the ultimate goal of a teacher education program were to produce thoughtful, broad-minded, knowledgeable, and worldly future educators, then involving student teachers from the United States and from abroad in an international collaborative project would be an advantageous addition to the teacher education program.

During one academic year, a small group of student teachers from a large university in the New York City metropolitan area were involved in an international pedagogical collaboration with a comparably sized group of student teachers from a large university in Spain.

An international pedagogical collaboration requires organization, preparation, creativity, knowledgeable information technology (IT) staff, enthusiastic participants, and patience. The use of various technologies throughout the course of any collaboration makes the communication between two international groups of participants possible. The following chapter details my personal journey of the process of engaging American student teachers in an international pedagogical collaboration. It also explains how the project was conceived, organized, and implemented.

There are multiple reasons why I initiated an international collaboration within my education class. The goals of this project were to help student teachers from both countries:

1. Develop a less insular and a more global understanding of education issues. Through this project students were provided the opportunity to explore current issues in their education system and to learn about the challenges and successes of another country's system.
2. Compare and contrast teaching methodologies with student teachers from another country. It is advantageous for novice teachers to share methods of teaching.
3. Learn new technologies that promote cross-cultural communication. The hope was that the student teachers who participated in this project would then transfer what they had learned about videoconferencing and online discussion boards into the public schools where they find employment.
4. Promote social justice through democratic practices in teaching. It was important for all of the students to share their definitions of and experiences with democratic practices in teaching.

The ultimate goal of this chapter is for teacher educators to use the information in this chapter to help them forge their own international pedagogical collaborations. The appendixes serve as useful templates to guide the collaborative process. The description of the technology utilized during the collaboration can help inform information technology (IT) departments as to the technology that can best support an international pedagogical collaboration.

## RESEARCH QUESTION

This research project was my personal reflective journey as a teacher educator implementing a yearlong international collaborative experience for teacher candidates. It was centered on the following research question: What did I, the professor, and my students learn in this yearlong journey? This question is important since it involves both the description of the project and its implementation as well as a deep reflection on its opportunities and challenges. Teachers who research their own practices can help other teacher educators learn from their personal experiences.

## SETTING AND PARTICIPANTS

In this section I will provide a description of myself, the people with whom I collaborated, and I will elaborate on the unfolding of the collaboration.

I am an adjunct professor at a large university in the New York City metropolitan area, and I teach both in the education and the Spanish departments. I came to the university as an experienced teacher, for I had previously taught all levels of Spanish at public high schools in the metropolitan New York City area. As I had spent my junior year studying in Spain I wanted to share my transformative international experience with my students by opening their eyes to the world. Moreover, I applied and was awarded a Teaching the World Fellowship by the Rutgers Graduate School of Education in conjunction with the Longview Foundation. This project was partially funded by the grant and it included a research presentation about this project at the Rutgers Graduate School of Education's Teaching the World Forum at the conclusion of the collaboration.

The twelve American student teachers were enrolled in a yearlong class that concludes their undergraduate teacher education program. The class included a semester of fieldwork and a semester of student teaching experiences in a variety of urban or suburban settings. Student teachers in the class were studying to be teachers in middle or high school content areas such as English, social studies, and so on, as well as K–12 in fine arts, music, or physical education.

The class curriculum stresses the importance of teaching the whole child, and in the first half of the year it focuses on topics such as the adolescent brain, multiple intelligences theory, backwards design in lesson planning, and social and emotional learning. During the second half of the year, discussions about current issues in education and deep reflection on their teaching were a crucial part of the class. Students were aware since the first class that this class involved an international pedagogical collaboration. Students had the option to switch course sections if this project did not interest them. Luckily, all the students expressed interest and they remained in the class. Teaching the same group of students for a year provided ample time to organize the collaboration during the fall semester and to initiate the international student-to-student interaction during the spring semester.

In Spain, three professors were interested in internationalizing their teacher education program were part of this project. One of them was the chairperson of their English as a Foreign Language program and the others were teachers in that program. All of them visited and had previous international experiences. The two junior professors stayed at the large New York City metropolitan university as part of a Fulbright exchange program. Moreover, the chairperson of the program came with a group of administrators from the Spanish institution to cement an agreement between the universities.

The Spanish undergraduate and graduate student participants were not part of one education class. They were selected by the professors to be part of this international experience. They were all bilingual Spanish-English, studying to be teachers of English in either elementary, middle, or high schools.

The majority of the students were student teaching at the elementary school level. They conducted their student teaching in different contexts (rural, urban, and suburban settings).

The Spanish student participants were eager to work with us to both practice their English and to learn about our education system in order to achieve a high level of English proficiency, particularly since scholarships to study in an English-speaking country have been reduced due to the fiscal crisis in Spain.

## The Description of the Collaboration

In terms of the collaboration, the following section will describe the organization, the conceptualization, and the implementation of the international experience.

The organization of the experience took place during the fall semester. It began with a one-hour Skype meeting among the chairman of the department where I work, the Spanish professors, and me. During this session the technology that would be implemented for the collaboration was discussed.

The decision to create a closed group on Facebook, maintain a discussion board through a Ning website, and conduct two three-hour, whole-group videoconferences was made. The American and Spanish students began signing up to the Facebook and Ning sites during this time. A Ning site is a customizable platform used to build an online community.

The Spanish professors requested a letter from the administration of the college of education of my university stating that the project had been approved. Once letters and a stamp of approval were exchanged, the Spanish professors began amassing undergraduate and graduate student teachers of English interested in collaborating with my class.

Spanish and American students were paired based on some commonality, and student e-mail addresses were exchanged. Also during this organizational phase the American students were introduced to the Spanish education system through various class readings. As a final step during the organizational process, a series of documents were created to guide the collaboration:

1. Topics for discussion and reflection on the Ning discussion board (appendix A)
2. Topics for discussion during videoconference (appendix B)
3. Topics for discussion during the one-on-one Skype session (appendix C)
4. Requirements for the student teaching presentation (appendix D)

The conceptualization of the collaboration entailed a variety of experiences:

1. Independently each group watched an online education documentary about the Spanish education system. The idea was to have all the participants watch the documentary *Educación prohibida* prior to the first whole-group videoconference. The film discusses the incorporation of teaching methods such as Montessori and Waldorf into Spanish and Latin American schools. The schools in the film emphasize the importance of teaching the whole child by relying on the students' natural creativity and curiosity rather than merely teaching to a standardized test.
2. Biweekly asynchronous reflections on shared experiences. Students began using e-mail, Facebook, and commenting biweekly on the Ning discussion board about various pedagogical issues that were designed by the teachers in both settings (appendix A).
3. Two whole-group synchronous meetings (one at the beginning of the experience and one at the end). The first whole-group synchronous meeting was designed to introduce the overall experience to both groups. Moreover, it started the discussion about the comparison between the school systems in both countries. The discussion centered on *Educación prohibida*, and other pedagogical issues such as diversity within public schools, learning world languages, discipline in the schools, classification of students, and immigration issues. A list of guiding questions was created to guide students' discussion (appendix B).

The second whole-group synchronous meeting was designed to provide a forum to share presentations they created in dyads about their student teaching experiences. The presentations compared and contrasted the demographics and settings of the schools where they were student teaching and provided a forum in which the students could share their teaching methodologies and lesson plan ideas. Despite having specific requirements for the presentations, the students were given some degree of academic freedom in the assignment as well. Appendix D lists the specific requirements for this assignment.

4. Developing dyads of students to collaborate on a final presentation. At the end of the first whole-group synchronous meeting, students were encouraged to connect on Skype with their assigned dyads and to decide on the use of synchronous and asynchronous meetings as needed (see appendix C for more information about the questions during this experience). Moreover, they were encouraged to discuss later on the required elements of their final presentation to compare and contrast the student teaching experiences in both countries (see appendix D).

The implementation of the collaboration took place during the spring semester. The utilization of various technological tools made the American and Spanish student-to-student interaction possible. First, the students began interacting via e-mail. Then, messages, posts, and comments were made to the closed Facebook group. Facebook was useful for posting reminders and updates about the collaboration. Occasionally, shared articles or other documents would be posted to this site. As a group folder had been created on a Ning site, the students began commenting biweekly on the Ning discussion board about various pedagogical issues (appendix A). The topics discussed on the Ning discussion board revolved around what the American and Spanish students experienced and learned during their student teaching semester. The students were responsible for responding to the topic posted and commenting on another student's post.

During the implementation of the first videoconference, the American and Spanish groups met to discuss the online documentary, *Educación prohibida*, and other pedagogical issues such as diversity within public schools, learning world languages, discipline in the schools, classification of students, and immigration issues (appendix B). Technologically speaking, the Vidyo technology was used on the American side, and the Spanish group used a standard definition polycom system. Vidyo is an enhanced form of Skype that provides better clarity of sound and picture and allows for multiple users. In addition to the American and Spanish professors, students, and staff, American public school administrators and World Language teachers attended this initial videoconference. Once the whole-group question and answer session part of the videoconference concluded, the Spanish-American student dyads used Skype in the computer labs to ask their international partners questions about their education system (appendix C). This initial videoconference lasted three hours.

During the implementation of the second videoconference with the Spanish group later in the semester, the American and Spanish student pairs shared presentations they created together about their student teaching experiences. The presentations compared and contrasted the demographics and settings of the schools where they were student teaching and provided a forum in which the students could share their teaching methodologies and lesson plan ideas. Despite having specific requirements for the presentations, the students were given some degree of academic freedom in the assignment as well. Appendix D lists the specific requirements of this assignment. The shared presentations were created either online using Google Docs or in PowerPoint. As university servers are not always reliable, all of the students' presentations were converted from a Google Doc format to a PowerPoint format. The presentations were sent to one computer and then saved to a flash drive in order to be shown from one computer the day of the videoconference. Vidyo technology was used during this videoconference, and the

Spanish group dialed into our Vidyo connection. The participants of the conference were the American and Spanish professors and students and an additional professor from my department.

The IT staff that had helped manage the technology for the first videoconference was initially unavailable for the second videoconference. Therefore, I had to get training on the Vidyo system and create my own Vidyo account. A backup team was on call in case of any technical issues, and they were brought in during the initial phase of the second videoconference to fix a sound issue. A trial run of the compatibility of the Spanish and American videoconferencing equipment was conducted two days prior to each videoconference.

Despite a few technological glitches, for the most part the technology of the Facebook page, Ning site, and Vidyo worked well.

## LITERATURE REVIEW

There are multiple benefits to internationalizing a teacher education class within a university's teacher education program. In the highly competitive world in which we live, leading student teachers through an international experience in which they are collaborating with another country rather than competing with it demonstrates to students that positive professional relationships can be forged with another country and that all can benefit through this enriching process. However, initiating and following through with an international collaboration involves the willingness to take risks. Ultimately, though, as the literature suggests, those risks are well worth taking. Interestingly, Dewey and Duff (2009) state that "surprisingly little work has been published that addresses the roles, responsibilities, and problems faced by faculty" when embarking on an international collaboration (p. 491). Scovotti and Spiller (2011) state that "there is a surprising dearth of curricular attention related to developing cross-border student collaboration opportunities using high-tech formats" (p. 57). Overall, Spencer-Oatey (2012) states that in the field of education, "there is a dearth of information on the details of people's experiences" in international collaborations (p. 246). Therefore, it is the hope that this chapter provides advice and encouragement in the process of organizing and implementing a technology-enhanced international pedagogical collaboration within a teacher education program.

There are many rewards in initiating an international collaborative experience. As Cooper and Mitsunaga (2010) state in their article, one of the rewards of engaging in an international project is learning from others (p. 69). Scovotti and Spiller (2011) state that, in "addition to mastery of course content, students on both sides of the Atlantic . . . [experience and conquer] . . . cultural, language and logistical complexities associated with cross-border collaboration" (p. 57). Similar to my collaborative project, the participants in Scovotti's and Spiller's collaboration felt that the "use of videoconferencing promoted stronger relationships among . . . [participants] and increased student satisfaction with the cross-border assignment" (Scovotti & Spiller, p. 57).

Although there are many rewards affiliated with engaging in a collaboration, there are also risks involved.

> Three things happen when today's faculty members enter the challenging arena of international collaborations: 1) Faculty members leave the safety of their traditional classrooms and enter a broader and more complex world of global interactions . . . ; 2) They encounter cross-cultural challenges that are often unanticipated and for which they may be ill-equipped; 3) They encounter collaborative challenges, which can be accompanied by technological challenges. (Cooper & Mitsunaga, 2010, p. 70)

As Scovotti and Spiller (2011) found in their international collaborative project, there are "complexities [associated with] working internationally" as "the mechanics involved in cross-border collaboration can and have presented real problems" (p. 58). A few of the issues encountered in their collaboration stemmed from "cultural differences, time zone variations, and finding communication tools for effective collaboration" (Scovotti & Spiller, p. 58). As was the case in my collaboration, in Scovotti's and Spiller's project, the "biggest problems involved the lack of timely response, periodic disappearances of . . . [participants], and miscommunication due to language differences" (Scovotti & Spiller, p. 58).

The first advice offered to those who wish to involve their students in an international collaboration is to stay flexible (Cooper & Mitsunaga, 2010). Second, the incorporation of videoconferencing and the visual contact this affords the students is a wonderful way "to bring the students [of the international collaboration] together and help them understand the importance of teamwork" (Scovotti & Spiller, 2011, p. 58). As was the experience in my project, the participants in the Scovotti and Spiller collaboration stated that "Videoconferencing provided a visual forum by which students and professors could meet and interact despite" the vast distance in time and space (Scovotti & Spiller, p. 58). "Videoconferencing permitted better cross-cultural collaboration, enabling students to work together remotely, build valuable relationships between . . . [participants], manage content . . . and create a . . . [whole-group] synergy" (Scovotti & Spiller 2011, p. 60). Videoconferencing allowed the student groups "to have face-to-face discussions and presentations in real time, which facilitated the successful achievement of the . . . goals" of the collaboration and helped the participants "build stronger personal relationships" (Scovotti & Spiller, p. 60). The third piece of advice offered to those who wish to engage in an international collaboration is "the importance of comprehensive planning" (Scovotti & Spiller, p. 61).

Ultimately, as Cooper and Mitsunaga (2010) state, "Colleges and universities need to understand what entices faculty to begin cross-cultural collaborations . . . [and that] the barriers to success will need to be clearly anticipated and understood in the hope that faculty and their institutions can avoid the pitfalls of their predecessors" (p. 80). Ultimately, the lessons learned from engaging in a collaboration with a university from abroad are invaluable. As the participants in the collaboration that Scovotti and Spiller organized were graduate students, they ask the question, "Could such projects be successfully implemented at the undergraduate level?" (Scovotti & Spiller, 2011, p. 61). The successful undergraduate international pedagogical collaboration proves that they can.

## DATA COLLECTION AND ANALYSIS

The following data sources were collected during the yearlong project for this reflection paper: 1) anecdotal records; 2) weekly journal entries; and 3) my own written reflections on students' reactions to the collaborative process working with Ning and the videoconferences.

1.  Anecdotal records: The anecdotal notes were taken during all meetings related to this project (the initial Skype meeting with the Spanish professors; the meetings with my mentor to discuss the direction of the collaboration; the viewing and discussion of the education documentary, *Educación prohibida*; during Teaching the World Forum meetings at the Rutgers University Graduate School of Education; during the two videoconferences; during presentations made at the Teaching the World Forum at Rutgers University; and when meeting with various IT professionals to determine which technology to use in the collaboration). Recording anecdotes related to the different aspects of the project was a very helpful source of insights.
2.  The weekly journal: The weekly journal was used to keep record of the online correspondence with the Spanish students and professors and to reflect before and after my professional presentation at the Rutgers University Teaching the World Forum.
3.  Personal written reflections on students' assignments: Reflecting on my students' assignments allowed me to have a deeper understanding of the collaborative process and of the effectiveness of the Ning discussion board and the videoconferences.

I purposefully used a triangulation of data, a very well-established practice among teachers researching their own practice (Guion, Diehl, & McDonald, 2011).

The data were analyzed primarily through emergent theme analysis. My analysis entailed looking for emergent themes that came out of the analysis of the anecdotal records, weekly journal entries, and personal written reflections on students' assignments. As I am an emerging scholar, some of the strategies highlighted in this section were rudimentary and evolving as part of this research project.

## FINDINGS

In this section I will answer the research question: What did I, the professor, and my students learn in this yearlong journey?

I learned that there are many similarities and differences between the Spanish and American education systems. Three themes emerged about the similarities between the education systems: 1) curriculum development; 2) concerns about the teaching profession and its future; and 3) technology as an integral part of education. Three other themes emerged about the differences between the education systems: 1) critical understanding of language, culture, and disability; 2) curricular issues; and 3) organizational issues. In addition to these six themes, other unexpected findings emerged from the data.

### Similarities

*Curriculum development*

In terms of curriculum development, there were many similarities between the American and Spanish groups. In my own education classes I emphasize democratic practices in the classroom by providing students with choice of assignment and by promoting multiple points of view. In reflecting on students' online discussions I wrote: "There is a commonality between both groups in that they emphasize democratic practices in their teaching" (weekly journal). The use of democratic practices in the classroom demonstrates that education has the potential to be a great equalizer in society.

Also in terms of curriculum development I wondered if the Spanish professors taught their education students about project-based learning, multiple intelligences theory, and how to differentiate instruction for all learners, for these are topics covered in education classes in the United States. Reflecting on students' assignments I wrote: "Both groups create innovative lesson plans that have real-world application, promote critical thinking, and differentiate instruction for all learners" (personal written reflections on students' assignments). It was interesting to observe that both groups had similar teaching philosophies and that they were able to openly exchange lesson plan ideas.

## Concerns about the teaching profession and its future

In terms of concerns about the teaching profession, both the American and Spanish students were in agreement on several issues. On issues related to grading, both groups had similar opinions. In education classes we discuss how public school students tend to place more emphasis on the grade they receive than learning for learning's sake, how overly concerned parents are about their child's grades rather than being concerned about what their child has learned, and how the administration in some schools makes it difficult for a teacher to fail a student. In reflecting on student online discussions I wrote: "Both groups are dismayed at the grading policies at their schools and the parents' reactions to the policies" (personal written reflections on students' assignments).

Regarding concerns for which subjects are given more time and importance in schools, the American and Spanish students were in agreement. When discussing the fact that many schools emphasize literacy arts and mathematics classes and leave little time for other subjects, while reflecting on the notes I wrote: "Both groups agree that not enough time is spent in physical education, art, and music classes during the elementary school years" (anecdotal records). I wonder if lack of funding for the arts is a similar issue in Spain as it is in some districts in the United States.

Regarding community involvement in the schools and employment in the field of education both groups were in agreement. Reflecting on students' assignments I wrote: "Lack of parental and community involvement in American and Spanish schools makes the teacher's job more difficult" (weekly journal). While reflecting further on students' assignments I wrote that an additional common challenge that American and Spanish teachers face is "the wide range of ability within a classroom" (personal written reflections on students' assignments). Additionally, the lack of teaching jobs for recent college graduates (Medina, 2013) is a shared concern as is the overall lack of respect for the teaching profession.

## Technology as an integral part of education

Despite the fact that technology is an integral part of modern society, it was interesting to observe the lack of technology in many of the American and Spanish student teachers' schools. Although both groups of students agree that technology is important, reflecting on students' assignments I wrote: "There tends to be a paucity of technology in the schools as a few schools have Smart boards but little else regarding technology" (personal written reflections on students' assignments). I wonder, does the use of technology in a classroom enhance learning or distract students? Can students learn just as well without having the latest technological tools?

Regarding the technology used in the collaboration such as the Ning discussion board and the Vidyo videoconferencing tool, both groups of student teachers agreed on the importance of having access to these tools. In reflecting on students' assignments I wrote: "All the students agree that Ning and Vidyo are important in that they allow for collaborative experiences to take place" (weekly journal).

## Differences

Although there were similarities between the Spanish and American education systems, we learned that there were major differences as well.

### *Critical understanding of language, culture, and diversity*

The first major difference lay in the Spanish and American students' critical understanding of language, culture, and diversity. The Spanish and American groups framed the experience of cultural diversity and immigration in different ways. Reflecting on the students' discussion of the demographics of their student teaching placement I wrote:

> The Americans use data sources and proper terminology in their description while the Spaniards confuse terminology related to nationality and religion while describing their student population. (anecdotal records)

I was wondering if perhaps this was a second language issue as English was the primary language used during the collaboration. Reflecting on further points made during the videoconference I wrote: "The American students occasionally use the incorrect pedagogical term when describing their teaching methods" (personal written reflections on students' assignments).

Reflecting on comments made during the videoconferences, when asked who has students with special needs in their classrooms, I wrote: "All the American students raise their hands whereas only a few of the Spanish students raise theirs" (anecdotal records). This made me wonder, are there fewer students with special needs in Spain than in America or is it just that the students are classified differently? Reflecting on additional comments made during the videoconferences, when asked who has immigrant students in their classes, I wrote: "Once again all the American students raise their hands while only a few of the Spanish students raise theirs" (anecdotal records). As I know Spain has experienced an influx of North Africans, Eastern Europeans, and South Americans over the past decade I was wondering why these immigrant groups were not represented in the schools (DeParle, 2008). As I had lived in Spain and was aware of a large gypsy population in the cities, why was there no mention of the gypsy population within the schools?

Additionally, reflecting on students' assignments I wrote: "The Spaniards use Catholic names for some public schools and hang crosses in the Spanish public school classrooms" (weekly journal). According to a recent article in the *Christian Science Monitor*, education reforms in Spain

> favor the Catholic church. They . . . divert public funds to semi-private Catholic centers and gender-segregated schools, mostly run by the Catholic Church, and reinforce the importance of religion classes in public schools . . . [rolling back] a partial limitation on the academic weight of religion classes enacted in 2006. (Cala, 2013)

## Curriculum

The second major difference between the American and Spanish school systems were issues relating to the curriculum. While standardized testing and the recent pressure to base teacher evaluations on student test scores are major concerns for American teachers, standardized testing is not an issue in Spain. Reflecting on students' discussion I wrote: "Spanish teachers are not evaluated on standardized testing but rather on how well they implement the lessons of the textbook" (weekly journal).

Regarding curriculum guidelines, while reflecting on students' assignments I wrote: "Spanish teachers follow regional curriculum guidelines whereas the American teachers need to teach to the Core Curriculum Content Standards" (anecdotal records). This made me wonder if teachers in Spain have more freedom and time to innovate in their teaching than do the American teachers as adherence to the curriculum guidelines is not as stringent in Spain.

Regarding diagnosis of ADD, reflecting on the students' assignments I wrote: "Americans medicate their children more readily when there is a diagnosis of ADD than they do in Spain" (personal written reflections on students' assignments). This made me wonder, why is it harder for children in Spain to receive prescriptions for this type of issue and why do we, Americans, medicate our children so easily?

## Organization and settings of the schools

The third major difference between the American and Spanish schools lay in the organization and settings of the schools. Through online discussions it was revealed that there are basic differences between the organization of the typical American and Spanish school day. Reflecting on the students' online discussions I wrote:

> Spanish school days tend to be shorter than the American school day, Spanish
> class sizes tend to be a bit larger, Spanish students have to pay for their
> materials and food whereas the American students do not have to pay for their
> books, and in some schools the dress code for the teachers seems more infor-
> mal in the Spanish schools than in the American schools. (weekly journal)

This makes me wonder if there is an educational advantage to having a
longer school day, as we tend to have in America. Overall, if the quality of
instruction is not good, then having a longer school day makes little difference in what is learned. Conversely, if the instruction is good, then perhaps
having a shorter school day does not have a deleterious effect on the students' overall education.

The setting of the American and Spanish schools is different as well.
Reflecting on students' presentations I wrote: "While the skyline of New
York City is visible from one American school the snow-capped peaks of a
Spanish mountain range are visible from one of the Spanish schools" (personal written reflections on students' assignments). This is a visual reminder
that children around the world are a product of their geography and the type
of living conditions that their physical space provides them. That, in and of
itself, is a basic difference between the American and Spanish student experiences. For this makes me wonder, do the students in the American school
described above have a green space in which to play and do the Spanish
students occasionally have difficulty getting to school as a result of weather
patterns caused by the rugged mountain range.

## Unexpected Themes that Emerged from the Data

In addition to the similarities and differences between the Spanish and
American education systems, other unexpected themes emerged from the
data.

### World language proficiency

From the videoconferences it seems more Spanish students graduate being
proficient in multiple languages than do students in the United States. Having
been a high school Spanish teacher in the United States I observed firsthand
the lack of importance placed on the learning of world languages in comparison to other subjects. Reflecting on student discussions I wrote that, although
the Spanish students study various languages, "English is the preferred language to study in Spain, so much so that in the elementary grades some
science classes are taught in Spanish and then the same content is repeated in
English" (personal written reflections on students' assignments).

This makes me think that if English is the preferred language to study in Spain and in other parts of the world, then this may in part account for why Americans are more hesitant to study world languages.

*Incorporation of international experience in students' future practice*

Both the American and Spanish groups exhibited enthusiasm during the videoconferences. Students were observed engaging excitedly in discourse during the whole-group videoconferences and during the one-on-one Skype sessions. Reflecting on student discussion board comments I wrote: "Both the Spanish and American students seem interested in attempting to incorporate videoconferencing into their future classrooms" (anecdotal records). Discussion focused on the future possibilities of using videoconferencing to showcase public school students' work internationally, connect with other public schools and students worldwide, reach out to experts in their field, and/or to share teaching methodologies with teachers in other countries.

*Creating an "international" community of learning*

During the student presentations it was apparent that a sense of community had formed between the American and Spanish students as a result of having worked closely on the final presentations and from having worked together over the course of the semester. American and Spanish students expressed warmth to each other when conversing. Reflecting on the students' assignments I wrote: "A collegial connection has been established between the presenters and students expressing a desire to stay in touch with each other" (anecdotal records). A few students even expressed interest in visiting each other and sharing their first-year teaching experiences. Each year I strive to create a community of learners in the classes, but doing this internationally was an unexpected result of the collaboration.

*Technological tools*

This yearlong journey was also useful in terms of understanding which technology would best support an international collaboration. The use of the Ning to maintain a discussion board and the use of Vidyo for the videoconferences were the correct technological tools. The Ning site was a user-friendly platform, and there were few difficulties with it throughout the maintenance of the discussion board. Although the Vidyo technology required having an account and having an expert on hand in case of a malfunction, once the initial errors in the system were fixed, Vidyo proved to be a reliable system for videoconferencing. The closed group on Facebook was useful for posting reminders, sending quick messages, and for sharing documents. However, in future collaborations it would be better to find a more professional technological tool than Facebook to accomplish these same tasks. For, even when students set their privacy settings on their own Facebook pages we would still be able to see their personal photos, and this diminished the professionalism of the correspondence. Sensitive material that occasionally was shared on the group Facebook page should have been sent in an e-mail instead.

## CHALLENGES AND OPPORTUNITIES

Although I am an emerging scholar who has more to learn regarding collaborative experiences, the international pedagogical collaboration described in this chapter was a success. This project began a dialogue about pedagogy among student teachers from two distinct universities that had, prior to the project, known little about each other. Opening student teachers' eyes to differing systems of education, new points of view regarding pedagogy, different methodologies used in the classroom, and the implementation of various technologies was an invigorating process for all involved in the project. The collaboration allowed student teachers to create international contacts in their field and to learn how videoconferencing can be conducted in a classroom. Exposure to all of these experiences will make the student teachers better educators. However, as is inherent in any new endeavor, there are things to learn from the first time a project like this is attempted. Therefore the following section will describe some of the challenges and opportunities of collaborating internationally and will offer advice to teacher educators interested in creating an international experience for their student teachers.

### Challenges

The first challenge was the response time on the part of all the participants. At times, information was not provided and questions were not answered in a timely fashion. The organization of the collaboration took longer than was needed. The professors dominated the discussion during the first videoconference rather than letting the student teachers fully participate in the experience. In order for student teachers to be held accountable for their work in a collaborative project it is better when all the participants are participating within the confines of a graded class.

Weather interferences, time zone differences, and differing university schedules were other challenges of the collaboration. The harsh American northeast winter forced us to reschedule multiple tests of the technology. Finding a common time and date for students to meet via Skype to work together on their presentations was a continual challenge considering the time zone differences and the students' teaching schedules. As the American and Spanish universities had different semester start dates, finding an exact date in which to begin the student-to-student interaction was challenging.

The overall reliability of technology and the compatibility of technology between the two universities were additional challenges. Although the technology worked well during the trial runs, during the videoconferences there were occasional glitches in which the Spanish group could see us but could not hear us. During the one-on-one student Skype session a few computers did not allow a connection to Skype, and several students had to move to computers that could access Skype. Once the initial glitches were fixed the technology worked seamlessly the duration of the videoconferences. Moreover, the lack of continuity of IT help from one videoconference to the next posed another challenge. Although I created a Vidyo account and had brief training in the use of Vidyo to prepare for the second videoconference, I was not equipped to handle sound issues that presented themselves during the videoconference, and a technician was called to help at the last minute.

A final challenge was that little time was left at the end of the second videoconference to reflect upon and discuss topics mentioned during the student presentations. As the videoconference took place during the last day of semester classes there was no time to debrief with the students to ascertain what they learned from the presentations. It would have been advantageous to conduct the videoconference earlier in the semester to allow time for reflection and discussion. Considering that the American and Spanish students had worked together all semester, the termination of the second videoconference seemed abrupt and was less ceremonious than it should have been. The videoconference took place late in the semester because it was the only day that all the participants were able to attend.

## Opportunities

There were many positive opportunities in this collaboration as well. Collaborating internationally has been an opportunity to learn more about education at home and abroad, the nuances of another culture, new technology, how to cooperate with others, and how to proceed with future collaborations.

First, I observed that the students developed a deeper understanding of their country's education system and became more interested in learning about education in other parts of the world as a result of this project. As students gained more answers to the questions they had about the Spanish education system they began formulating more questions about our education system in comparison to other global education systems. The students' desire to continue questioning and seeking answers is one of the most successful aspects of the collaboration. The students' willingness to provide their future public school students with the opportunity to collaborate with students from another country is another successful aspect of the project.

Second, collaborating internationally allows for a deeper understanding of the nuances of how professors and students from another country conduct themselves and think. In working with the Spanish group I had to assert myself appropriately so that my vision in this collaboration was carried out while at the same time stepping back to allow the Spanish professors to express their goals as well. I began the collaboration in Spanish in order to show respect to the Spanish group, and once I oversaw the organization of the collaboration I made the decision to conduct all correspondence in English.

A third opportunity in collaborating is learning about the latest technological tools that allow for communication between two countries. The technological advances happen so quickly that the best way to keep abreast of all of the changes is to learn with the IT staff while they research the best technology and to be involved in every step of the trial runs conducted between the participating universities. Networking was a useful skill learned through this project, for if one person was not sure of an answer then I was able to get the answers I needed from a different source.

An additional opportunity is being able to work cooperatively with others to achieve a common goal. In order to have all the participants remain enthusiastic about the project, the timing and dates of the collaboration had to be convenient for all the participants. Learning how to manage different schedules was an opportunity to work cooperatively. Appropriate gratitude and respect had to be shown throughout.

A final opportunity of this collaboration is emerging with a clearer understanding of some of the pitfalls and successful aspects of working with a university abroad and understanding what needs to be improved when conducting future collaborations. For instance, although this particular collaboration focused on learning about the challenges and opportunities within the American and Spanish education systems, in the future it would be beneficial to discuss possible solutions to the challenges.

Ultimately, advice offered to those interested in internationalizing a class within a teacher education program is that it is crucial to have the support of the departments of both universities and a helpful and knowledgeable IT staff when embarking on an international pedagogical collaboration. Despite the challenges that exist in organizing a collaborative project, the opportunities for professional growth for all of the participants far outweigh the occasional inconveniences. Overall, it was invigorating to open student teachers' eyes to the educational opportunities that exist in both the collaborating country and their native land.

## CONCLUSION

In conclusion, the process of involving student teachers in an international pedagogical collaboration enriched our understanding of the education systems at home and abroad. It was exciting to observe American and Spanish professors and students learning from one another as a result of this project. Through the Ning discussion board and the two videoconferences we all opened our eyes to a reality that is distinct from our own daily experiences in the field of education. The success of the collaboration was due to the preparation and the enthusiasm of all the participants.

University administrators and faculty should not be intimidated by internationalizing a class within their teacher education program. In this era of advanced technology, it is possible to connect with university classes around the world quite easily if given the correct technology, IT help, and cooperation from the collaborating university. Internationalizing teacher education should be an important component of every college of education as it is an invaluable experience for the student teachers who will become the educators in the public school system. A project such as the one my students experienced broadens students' perspectives and helps future educators look at the education system, at home and abroad, with a more critical eye. The ability to critique and reflect ultimately helps strengthen one's own system of education.

## ACKNOWLEDGMENTS

I would like to thank the Graduate School of Education at Rutgers University for providing partial funding for the completion of this research through the Teaching the World Fellowship I received.

## APPENDIX A

### Topics for Discussion and Reflection on the Ning Discussion Board

1. Describe a typical day for the students in the public school where you are student teaching. What seem to be the priorities of the school? Do you agree with these priorities?
2. What are the most challenging issues teachers in your country are facing?
3. What technology is available to students and teachers in your school and how is it used?

4. Share with us a lesson that you thought went well. What teaching methodology did you employ? Why do you think the lesson went so well?

5. As you have just seen how video conferencing works through our collaboration, how could you effectively incorporate video conferencing into your teaching? What have you learned as a result of this collaboration?

## APPENDIX B

### Topics for Discussion during Videoconference

1. Strictness of the teachers
2. Diversity in the schools
3. Importance of, or lack thereof, learning additional world languages
4. Degree to which public school students receive prescription medicine for apparent "hyperactivity" or ADD
5. Mainstreaming of special education students
6. Number of special education and immigrant students in the schools
7. Degree of parent and community involvement in the schools
8. Degree to which teaching, as a profession, is respected
9. Job possibilities, or lack thereof, upon graduation
10. General satisfaction with the teacher education program

## APPENDIX C

### Topics for Discussion during the One-on-One Skype Session

1. What and where are you teaching?
2. What is the American dream? What is the Spanish dream? How is this dream fulfilled in the schools?
3. What is obligatory in public schools? What is voluntary?
4. What are the most difficult issues facing public school teachers in your country?
5. What is the majority gender of educators in the public schools?
6. How long is the public school day?
7. What is the average age of a student entering the university?
8. How are immigration issues impacting public education?
9. How much control do the local, regional, and national governments have as to what is being taught in the public schools?
10. What is the purpose of public education?
11. Is there a sense of fairness and equity within the educational system?

12. What does "democratic practices" in education mean to you and do you see them employed in your school system?
13. What is your definition of multiculturalism? Is it embraced in schools?
14. To what degree is technology used in the schools?
15. How are students assessed?
16. What educational resources are available to immigrant students?
17. How is testing managed in your country?
18. Is a dual language approach to learning in place?
19. How large are class sizes in your school?
20. Are there after-school sports/extracurricular activities/field trips offered in your school?
21. Is the learning of English obligatory?
22. How does diversity play a part in educational policy?
23. Have you had experience working with refugee students?
24. Do you feel safe in your school?
25. What is your experience with diversity?
26. Do teachers give a lot of homework?
27. Are many students identified as being autistic?
28. Is it common for students to have after-school jobs?
29. Are social services readily available to help students in need?
30. Is it common for the school and/or teachers to reach out to the community to get to know the parents/guardians?

## APPENDIX D

### Requirements for the Student Teaching Presentation

Following are the basic requirements that each PowerPoint or online Google Docs presentation has to include:

1. A description of the demographics and the setting of the school where the students were conducting their student teaching
2. Photos of their classroom and the school (photos that did not include people)
3. A description of how the American and Spanish schools where the student teachers were teaching were similar and how they differed
4. A lesson that had been taught well and why they thought it went well

## REFERENCES

Cala, A. (2013, May 17). Spain's controversial educational reform: Will the Green Tide wash it away? *Christian Science Monitor*, pp. 1–3.

Cooper, J., and Mitsunaga, R. (2010). Faculty perspectives on international education: The nested realities of faculty collaborations. *New Directions for Higher Education 150*, 69–81. DOI: 10.1002/he.391.

DeParle, J. (2008, June 10). Spain, like U.S., grapples with immigration. *New York Times,* pp. 1–5. http://www.nytimes.com/2008/06/10/world/europe/10migrate.html/?pagewanted=all&_r=0.

Dewey, P., and Duff, S. (2009). Reason before passion: Faculty views on internationalization in higher education. *Higher Education 58*, 491–504.

Guion, L. A., Diehl, D. C., and McDonald, D. (2011). Triangulation: Establishing the validity of qualitative studies. *EDIS*, 1–4. http://edis.ifas.ufi.edu/fy394.

Medina, J. (2013, October 24). Spanish students, teachers protest against education cuts, reform. *El Pais*.

Scovotti, C., and Spiller, L. D. (2011). Cross-border student collaborations: Opportunities for videoconferencing. *Marketing Education Review 21*(1), 57–61. DOI: 10.2753/MER1052-8008210108.

Spencer-Oatey, H. (2012). Maximizing the benefits of international education collaborations: Managing interaction processes. *Journal of Studies in International Education 17*(3), 244–261. DOI: 10.1177/1028315312454545. http//jsi.sagepub.com/content/17/3/244.

*Chapter Seven*

# Participating in a Technology-Enhanced Internationalization Project to Promote Students' Foreign Language Motivation

Tina Waldman and Efrat Harel

Collaborating with people from a different culture highly enriched me as a future educator, and helped me gain confidence in speaking English.

Cooperation with the U.S. students added joy to the project, and raised my willingness to talk in English.

—Students' reflections

## INTRODUCTION

The purpose of this chapter is to share a technology-enhanced internationalization project between the largest teacher training college in Tel Aviv, Israel, and a university in the New York City metropolitan area. The experience was designed around a project-based learning task approach (PBLT) in which student teachers from both institutions compared and contrasted the challenges and experiences of minority students in both educational contexts. Finally, they constructed an electronic poster presenting their findings. The objective of the Israeli research team was to provide an authentic language experience in English using telecollaboration with members of the target language culture in the United States. The project was designed mainly to promote the student teachers' motivation to use English as a foreign language with their international partners, as well as to elicit student teachers' reflection on education as a means to social justice in a global context. Although data were collected by both the American and the Israeli teams, this chapter reports research carried out on the Israeli students only.

## LITERATURE REVIEW

### Motivation and Language Learning

Social justice in education is a timely issue and one that is close to the hearts of many student teachers in democratic societies, "empowering democratic and critical education environments" (Hytten & Bettez 2011). Facilitating students to become stewards of social justice through participation in authentic learning tasks is likely to positively affect their motivation. Dornyei (2001) provides an overview of theories of motivation pertaining to language learning tasks. He contends that task motivation is influenced by several factors: for example, when students have favorable dispositions toward a task, they tend to participate more actively in the task than those students whose disposition is unfavorable. Therefore, authentic tasks that encourage students to take an active role in creating a critical education environment, in which they become ambassadors of diversity within their country, are expected to positively influence motivation. Another interesting factor of task motivation is that task participants seem to influence each other's motivation. If participants work in pairs or teams, one member's disposition affects the disposition of the others toward the task. In addition, motivation in foreign language learning has shown that it is socioculturally oriented and is influenced by language attitudes, cultural stereotypes, and political considerations toward the foreign language. When learners have an interest in the target language, motivation is high, and learners make an effort by investing time and energy in learning (Gardner 2001).

Theories of foreign language learning motivation tend to combine psychological and psycholinguistic approaches to better understand the process of learning a foreign language. Self-Determination Theory (Ryan & Deci 2000), though not specifically pertaining to language learning, helps to highlight the relationship of externally and internally generated factors linked to motivation. La Guardia (2009) claims that external factors connected to the quality of the learning experience involve feelings of self-efficacy and relatedness to others. Hence, collaborative tasks structured around communication and feedback foster confidence and enhance motivation because of feelings of satisfaction in getting one's point across. Internal factors, on the other hand, involve behaviors linked to motivation that can be thought of as on a continuum with intrinsic motivation at one end and extrinsic motivation on the other. Intrinsic motivation involves performing an act to experience joy or satisfy one's curiosity, whereas extrinsic motivation stems from performing an act to receive a reward. Between these two extremes are degrees of intrinsic and extrinsic motivation involving recognition of instrumentality of an activity and internalizing the values of an activity. So in this particular study, learners may recognize the value of English to be a citizen of the world and will become actively involved in learning.

## Technology Enhanced Collaborations

Internationalization of education is rapidly expanding worldwide, and tele-collaboration, also called online intercultural exchanges between classes of learners in geographically distant locations, are proliferating (Helm, Guth, & O'Dowd 2012). In many cases, these telecollaborations involve Internet-mediated intercultural engagement with classes of foreign language learners and have proven to be an effective tool in the development of students' foreign language proficiency and intercultural communication skills (Mackinnon 2013).

As Klapper (2006) suggests in the case of language teachers, "perhaps the most exciting application of the web in language learning is its capacity for bringing together students and native speakers" (p. 191). As well as a recurring theme of authenticity in the literature on telecollaboration, research has shown that online exchange projects can contribute to the development of learner autonomy, and intercultural awareness (Ware 2005). Telecollaboration is seen

> not so much to teach the same thing in a different way, but rather to help students enter into a new realm of collaborative enquiry and construction of knowledge, viewing their expanding repertoire of identities and communication strategies as resources in the process. (Kern et al. 2004, p. 191)

Telecollaboration projects are conducted using either asynchronous, synchronous, or both methods of interaction between students. Asynchronous communication is typically facilitated through e-mail or forum discussion threads and supports communication when learners cannot be online simultaneously. Synchronous communication is commonly supported by chat programs or video conferencing and involves real-time communication. Oztok et al. (2013) provide an overview of the research comparing asynchronous and synchronous interaction. The writers claim that some of the benefits of asynchronous interaction involve flexibility of time as learners correspond independently, so there is time for reflection and time for in-depth, thoughtful interaction.

Synchronous communication, like asynchronous communication, can be one to one or group to group. Pointing to the research, Oztok et al. (2013) provide evidence showing that synchronous communication fosters social contact and activity between participants. They also suggest that it creates a sense of urgency in terms of the task or debate at hand. Overall, the comparison of asynchronous and synchronous activity reveals that asynchronous discussions are more productive with regard to student engagement in learning, and that learners are likely to encourage each other during interaction, whereas synchronous discussion has been shown to generate a lot of content. Therefore, in this current study we used both forms of telecollaboration to ensure optimal conditions for the success of the project.

## Research on Motivation and Telecollaboration

Interactivity and social interaction are one of the main themes of telecollaboration research. Researchers have noted that successful interaction can impact significantly on learner motivation and learning outcomes (Conole & Oliver 2007). This type of interaction is learner centered, involves the learners in negotiation of meaning, and offers a reasonable amount of learner autonomy. Thus, both formal and informal learning are encouraged. A recurring theme isolated by Mackinnon (2013) in her survey of online interactive learning is authenticity. Unlike many learning tasks which are artificial reconstructions of authentic situations, telecollaboration involves an online presence of authentic interlocutors.

There are few studies in the literature that employ both synchronous and asynchronous communication, and those that do focus on written communication such as synchronous "chat" and asynchronous forum discussions. These studies are quantitative and investigate the number of posts or notes that students send, or pedagogical outcomes (Oztok et al. 2013). However, research by Freiermuth and Huang (2012) takes a look at a synchronous chat task and its effect on motivation. The project took place between a class at a university in Japan and one in Taiwan. The students were given a prompt to discuss using chat software. Questionnaire data were collected, and results suggested that synchronous activity and task enjoyment fostered students' willingness to communicate with students from another culture. In addition, students felt relaxed and compelled to accomplish the task goals. These factors contributed to learner motivation.

Other research investigating synchronous online communication revealed relationships between motivation and learners' feelings of control over their own learning; motivation and willingness to take risks; and enjoyment over authentic discussions (Freiermuth & Jarrell 2006; Darhower 2002). In the current study, a combined approach to use synchronous telecollaboration through videoconferencing and asynchronous telecollaboration through e-mail and Ning posts to complete an international, collaborative PBLT is employed.

## Research Question

Following are the research questions guiding this project:

1. Does the international PBLT impact student teachers' motivation to increase their English proficiency?
2. Does participation in the international PBLT on social justice and global awareness increase the student teachers' intercultural understanding?

These questions are important because we aim to discover whether telecollaboration with international partners positively affects motivation for learning a foreign language. Second, we aim to discover whether an international PBLT impacts on intercultural learning and global understanding. Our findings are relevant to our own future teaching and for other educators of foreign languages who are interested in fostering international project-based learning task experiences for their students.

## SETTING AND PARTICIPANTS

The study was a joint project between a large state university in the NYC metropolitan area in the United States and the largest teacher training college in the center of Israel. The researchers met at an international conference of education in Jerusalem in the summer of 2013. The American researcher saw parallels between the linguistic landscape of Israel, where people speak a variety of mother tongues, and the linguistic landscape of the NYC metropolitan area where the U.S. university is located. Hence, he was interested to discover how student teachers were being prepared for multiculturalism in the Israeli public school system.

An international PBLT was planned involving intensive communication between a group of American and a group of Israeli student teachers over a period of four weeks during which time they would compare and contrast some aspects of each other's culture and public education system. The PBLT included two synchronous video-conferences between the two entire groups, one at the beginning of the process and one at the end; the latter was designed to allow the students to showcase what they had learned from each other. Between the first and the second synchronous videoconferences, teams of students—one or two Israelis and three Americans—communicated using synchronous discussion—Skype, and asynchronous tools such as e-mail or Ning posts to exchange information about their culture, values, and education systems, as well as to co-construct an electronic poster to be presented in the second synchronous meeting.

The U.S. university is a well-established teacher training institution in the NYC metropolitan area. Over the last few years, the institution has been interested in promoting the internationalization of teacher education programs by creating agreements with universities all over the world. In the current collaboration, thirty student teachers were registered in an undergraduate foundation course—one of the first courses in their teacher training program. Student teachers studied a variety of majors, including content areas for middle school and secondary education as well as sports, music, and arts. The course was taught by an adjunct professor and lasted for the winter semester.

The Israeli college, which is supervised by the Ministry of Education and the Council for Higher Education, serves a population of all sections of Israeli society. It prepares educators and teachers for K–12 education settings, and its curriculum places emphasis on community involvement and social justice. Fifteen students participated in the study, ranging from ages twenty-five to thirty-five. All participants were female except for one. They were majoring in various disciplines including early childhood education, special education, and drama and dance. Some of the participants were first-year undergraduates and some were completing their degree after a hiatus from studying during which time they gained work experience.

All the participants in the Israeli college are required to reach a specific level of English by the end of their BEd program. They had studied English for eight years to high school graduation level, and after completing the national higher education entrance exam (psychometric) they needed to complete this last two-credit English as a foreign language class. Most of them had spent some time abroad as is typical in Israel among young people finishing their army service, and as a result some of them spoke English fluently although their literacy skills lagged behind their speaking skills. The English course was primarily online and lasted for fourteen weeks, involving a total of five face-to-face meetings between the lecturer and the students. The focus of the course was academic literacy, and the students prepared and discussed academic reading materials that were relevant to their studies in education. Dr. Efrat Harel (second author) instructed the course, and Dr. Tina Waldman (first author) supervised the whole process.

Tina was born in England and has been living in Israel for almost thirty years. She completed her PhD in applied linguistics at the University of Haifa. She is bilingual and at home speaks English to her husband and three children, all of whom are bilinguals. She heads the English for Academic Purposes department at the teacher training college, where she also teaches applied linguistics in the English teacher training department. With the intention of fostering communication intercultural competence, Tina has incorporated online foreign language exchanges in some of her courses since the mid-1990s with students from various parts of the globe learning English as a foreign language, including Spain, the Netherlands, and China. Being aware of some of the challenges that such interactions pose, she is interested in investigating the complexity of such exchanges and trying to understand how learners view their learning processes through them.

Efrat Harel is a researcher in the domain of language acquisition and a lecturer in English for Academic Purpose. Efrat was born in Israel and has been learning English as a foreign language since the age of ten. She completed her PhD in psycholinguistics at the University of Bar Ilan. Her research line focuses on language acquisition among bilingual children as well as second language learning. Efrat trains student teachers to deal with issues of multilingualism, multiculturalism, and cultural diversity at preschools and schools in Israel. Being sensitive to cultural diversity in the Israeli education system, as well as to challenges of learning English as a foreign language, she is interested in investigating the impact of both factors on motivation among Israeli student teachers learning English.

## THE MODEL OF THE INTERNATIONAL PBLT

The model of the project included three phases: conceptualization, implementation, and reflection. The conceptualization phase involved negotiations between the lecturers involved regarding the details of the international PBLT including: instructions to the students and grading rubrics; type of background multitextual materials for the task, and the logistics of the telecollaboration. The implementation phase involved the actual synchronous and asynchronous experiences presented to the student teachers in both settings. Finally, the reflection phase involved an analysis of all data collected from the students prior to, during, and after the completion of the PBLT.

### Conceptualization

Arrangements for the collaboration began in the summer of 2013. Using Skype, the lecturers held a number of teleconferences to discuss the details of the PBLT. Unlike most telecollaboration partnerships, the context of the participating student teachers' learning environment in Israel and in the United States was very different. In the United States, the student teachers begin studying at the beginning of September, and in Israel they begin in the middle of October. In the United States, the focus of the course was on education, and in Israel the focus of the course was on English as a foreign language. Nevertheless, the lecturers decided to use the same multitextual preparation materials in each of their courses to provide background to the PBLT. The reading materials included the textbook *Current Issues and Trends in Education* (Aldridge and Goldman, 2007). All student teachers in both settings read the chapter on multiculturalism to facilitate their collaboration. Other materials included two documentaries: one about the Israeli public education system and the other about the American one. The Israeli documentary, *Strangers No More* (2010), tells the story of a school in South Tel Aviv where children from forty-eight different countries and diverse backgrounds come together to learn. The parents of these children are among over 300,000 transnational migrant workers who have arrived in Israel. The American documentary, *Waiting for Superman* (2010), focuses mostly on the failure of inner city schools in the United States. These materials were chosen to broaden the student teachers' knowledge about each of the educational systems and promote comparative thinking.

During the teleconferences between the lecturers, they made arrangements for two online synchronous videoconferences: one at the beginning of the PBLT and the other at the end of it. Together, the lecturers prepared a list of questions, which served as a framework for the first group meeting (see appendix A), as well as the guidelines for the final task presentation of the PBLT in which student teachers were to develop electronic posters that compare and contrast the educational system in both countries. The guidelines and rubrics were distributed to both groups prior to the first synchronous videoconference, so the participants could properly prepare for the discussions. (For the guidelines, see appendix B, part 1.) Finally, rubrics for assessment of the electronic poster task were also constructed by the lecturers (see appendix B, part 2) in order to set up future grading criteria.

## Implementation

Implementation of the international collaborative PBLT included three stages: first, a whole-group synchronous videoconference between the United States and the Israeli student teachers took place; followed by student teams' synchronous and asynchronous meetings scheduled on their own for the construction of the electronic poster; and finally, a second whole-group synchronous videoconference in which the student teams presented their posters.

The first whole-group synchronous videoconference was scheduled at the beginning of the term during a Sunday night in Israel and Sunday morning in the United States (due to the time difference between the two countries). Sunday is a working day in Israel, and in the United States it provided time flexibility for the students who have classes all other days of the week. The videoconference was carried out using Skype and a projector and screen, so each group could see and hear the other. After a brief introduction by the two lecturers, the participants began to exchange information about their life and education experiences. They discussed several topics that ranged from customs and lifestyles of college students in both countries, required versus voluntary military duty, and the "American Dream" versus the "Israeli Dream."

It quickly became apparent that the American student teachers, who were younger and less experienced than the Israelis, took on the role of the inquirers; and that the Israelis, who were less fluent in English than the Americans, took on the role of providers of information.

The meeting was very animated; and after two hours of discussion, the groups were divided into ten teams, comprising one or two Israelis and three American participants. The Skype videoconference was completed, and the student teams then dialed up each other on their individual computers to organize their team work schedule.

They used either Ning, which is a forum discussion platform that also facilitates private note writing, or e-mail for asynchronous messaging. In addition, each team set up several synchronous Skype meetings during that month. The purpose of these interactions was to further reflect on the comparative nature of education and social justice in both countries, and create the electronic poster according to the guidelines of the PBLT. Here the American students took on the role of the language experts by doing most of the writing, and by helping their non-native partners in terms of language usage.

Four weeks after the first whole-group synchronous videoconference, the second one took place. The teams uploaded their virtual posters to the Ning, where they could be viewed and shared. The purpose of the videoconference was to create an authentic forum for students to present their PBLT. These joint presentations took place in English. Each presentation lasted for five to ten minutes, and student teachers from each country took turns talking about their findings regarding the education system in their respective countries. Both lecturers graded the posters and presentation according to preplanned criteria (see appendix B, part 2).

## Reflection

In order to fully investigate the research questions in this study, the students were asked to reflect on the process they had experienced, prior to, during, and after completion of the PBLT. The researchers collected multiple data in order to facilitate their reflection process. Following is a description of the data collection, analysis, and findings that better explain the insights gained from this teacher/research project.

## DATA COLLECTION

In order to answer the research questions, multiple sources of data from the Israeli students were collected. In terms of quantitative data, a motivation survey was distributed both pre- and post-collaboration. It was distributed twice to document change in student attitude over the duration of the course (see appendix C for the full survey). In terms of qualitative data, personal interviews were conducted with all students during the collaboration period. A post-PBLT questionnaire with open-ended questions was distributed at the end of the collaboration (see appendix D). Finally, copious notes were taken during the two synchronous videoconferences annotating the student interaction.

The motivation survey, which was completed anonymously both pre- and post-collaboration, asked the students to assess the degree with which they agreed or disagreed with fifteen statements regarding various aspects of their motivation toward the English language and learning English (twelve questions), as well as toward the collaborative project with the American university (three questions). Students responded using a five-point scale ranging from "Strongly Agree" to "Strongly Disagree" to statements such as "I like English." Using the same scale, they assessed their agreement with the statement "The project with the American University will be very beneficial to me." The personal interviews and the post-PBLT questionnaire asked the students to report on their understanding of global education following the collaborative PBLT, and to reflect on their degree of motivation to use English as a result of such collaboration and the required task.

## DATA ANALYSIS

The data was analyzed both quantitatively and qualitatively, as follows:

1. Quantitative analysis of the motivation survey based on:

    a. Comparison between the means in the pre and post-collaborative PBLT survey.
    b. Comparison between four representative questions in the pre- and post-collaborative PBLT survey.

2. Qualitative analysis based on:

    a. Students' reflection gathered via the personal interviews.
    b. Students' reflection gathered via the post-PBLT questionnaire.

The pre- and post-survey results were organized in a manner which allowed for quantitative group comparisons. The mean of each question in the pre-survey was compared to its counterpart in the post-survey. In addition, group comparisons were carried out, first with the means of the twelve questions about learning English, and second with the means of the three questions about the collaborative project. Finally, detailed analysis was carried out on four representative questions: the first is about intrinsic motivation ("I would like to be proficient in English"); the second is about extrinsic motivation ("knowing English will make me an educated person"); the third addresses a blend of intrinsic and extrinsic factors ("knowing English will enable me to understand books, movies and music in English"); and the fourth is about the project ("the project with the U.S. University is interesting for me"). The students' reports in the personal interviews and post-PBLT questionnaires were analyzed qualitatively. The analysis referred to three major points: the students' attitude toward such projects as a way to improve their English proficiency skills; the students' reflection on the electronic poster presented during the second synchronous meeting as a tool to increase their motivation in the course; and finally, the students' rate of global education awareness via the project.

## FINDINGS

Our first research question asks whether this international PBLT impacts students' motivation to increase their English proficiency. In order to answer the question, fifteen Israeli students completed a pre- and post-survey of fifteen questions. Students responded using a five-point scale ranging from "Strongly Agree" to "Strongly Disagree," when five presented a positive attitude toward the question and one a negative attitude. Table 7.1 presents a group comparison between the means, SDs, and ranges of questions 1–12 (motivation for English use) and questions 13–15 (project with the U.S. institution) in both rounds of the survey.

The table shows similar mean scores for pre-survey and post-survey for the motivation for English use questions. For the questions about the project, the table reveals a decline in the mean scores for the post-survey. An independent-sample t-test was conducted to compare attitudes between both surveys for the two types of questions. The analyses showed that a significant

Table 7.1.   Israelis' attitude toward using English and the project with U.S. university as reflected in the surveys

| | English Use (Q 1–12) | | | Project (Q 13–15) | | |
|---|---|---|---|---|---|---|
| | Mean | SD | Range | Mean | SD | Range |
| Pre-Survey | 4.27 | 0.29 | 1–5 | 3.95 | 0.54 | 1–5 |
| Post-Survey | 4.25 | 0.24 | 1–5 | 3.44 | 0.75 | 1–5 |

difference between pre-survey and post-survey was present (t[28]=2.12, p<0.05, p=0.42) for the project questions, but did not exist for the English use questions. More specifically, while motivation toward using English existed at all phases of the course, the students' motivation toward the project slightly decreased at the end of the course. Question 14 ("I believe that in the long run the project with the U.S. University will contribute to my English skills") was responsible for this borderline difference, as will be discussed later.

Comparing the means of each of the fifteen questions in the pre- and post-survey showed no statistical differences, apart from question 14. As aforementioned, the questions about English use tested levels of intrinsic motivation, extrinsic motivation, as well as both. Detailed analysis for three out of the twelve questions showed high levels of motivation. For example, the question "I would like to be proficient in English" was directed to test intrinsic motivation. Results showed that 80 percent of the students marked "Strongly Agree" (scale five) in the pre-survey, and 100 percent of them marked it in the post-survey. Similarly, the question "knowing English will make me an educated person" was directed to test extrinsic motivation. Results showed that 93 percent of the students marked "Strongly Agree" or "Agree" (scale five or four) in the pre-survey, and 87 percent of them marked these scales in the post-survey. Another question was directed to examine a blend of these motivation types: "knowing English will enable me to understand books, movies and music in English." The analysis showed that 87 percent of the students marked "Strongly Agree" (scale five) in both rounds of the survey. With regard to a question about the project: "the project with the U.S. university is interesting for me," results showed that 87 percent of the students marked "Strongly Agree" or "Agree" (scale five or four) in the pre-survey, and 67 percent of them marked these scales in the post-survey. The following analysis of the interviews and questionnaires will shed some light on the latter decline.

In conclusion, in the quantitative analysis we found that motivation toward learning and using English remained high throughout the course; however, not all students thought that the project contributed to their English skills or created interest.

## Qualitative Analysis of Interviews and the Post-PBLT Questionnaires

The qualitative analysis relates both to our first research question about motivation and to our second research question that asked: Does participation in the PBLT on social justice and global awareness increase the students' intercultural understanding?

Personal interviews with the students were carried out during the month that they were working with their American peers in teams, and a post-PBLT questionnaire was conducted following the second synchronous videoconference. Generally, the students showed a more positive attitude in the questionnaires than in the face-to-face interviews.

Three themes emerged from the qualitative analysis: the PBLT as a catalyst for English proficiency, the electronic poster presentation as a tool to increase motivation, and global education awareness.

## The PBLT as a Catalyst for English Proficiency

The students were asked to reflect on their level of motivation via their collaboration project with English-speaking peers. The students' attitude toward the PBLT as a way to improve their English proficiency skills was mostly positive, both in the interviews as well as in the questionnaire. They expressed their willingness to communicate in English and improve their skills in an authentic way, using technology as a tool for learning. Some of them emphasized the self-confidence they gained through the synchronous meetings through comments like, "I had confidence to speak about the subject," "I gained more confidence," "I regained my confidence in oral and writing." Others said they "loved the interaction," and one said she felt like an ambassador. In addition, expressions such as "refreshing," "break from routine," "varied," "fun," "enjoyable," and "interesting" were repeatedly uttered or written by different participants. Some negative attitude was noted in the questionnaire, as a few of the students claimed that integrating such a project in an online course is limiting because the PBLT was too short to have a lasting influence on the students' English skills. Nevertheless, using English (especially speaking) triggered by this collaboration yielded multiple positive reactions from the Israeli students.

## The Electronic Poster Presentation as a Tool to Increase Motivation

The students were also asked to reflect on the electronic poster task they had to present in the second synchronous meeting, together with their U.S. teams. They had to estimate whether the task affected their motivation in the course. Analysis showed similarities between the interviews and the questionnaires, though with different emphases. In the interviews, about a third of the students claimed that the task increased their motivation in the course, and they were happy to do it: "the collaborative work with the U.S. students was very fun. I was more interested and motivated to work." However, most of the students emphasized that the task increased the need, but not the motivation, to use English. Sentences such as "my need to use English academically was increased," "I'm not sure if the task affected my motivation, as I think I was already motivated," and "the task is overbearing and I will be happy when it is over," were uttered. They explained that the collaborative task was time consuming and difficult, especially due to the time difference between the two countries and technical difficulties in communication and cooperation.

In the questionnaire, the students referred to the second synchronous videoconference, and noted that though the poster presentations were potentially interesting, they were repetitive, long, and mainly technically complex. Examples of questionnaire comments written by students are "the meeting was too long," "unfortunately, technological problems hindered the meeting, which was too long." It is important to note that some of the students were affected by the level of communication with their U.S. peers—both synchronous and asynchronous during the month of task preparation. While some succeeded in interacting well, others had more difficulty in managing effective discussions, accounting for the decrease in motivation shown in the post-survey in questions 14 and 15 ("I believe that in the long run the project with the U.S. University will contribute to my English skills"); ("the project with the U.S. University is interesting for me").

*Global Education Awareness*

During the face-to-face interviews, only a few students reported on meaningful learning with regard to global education. Some of the students explained that discussing such issues raised their awareness about the subject, but they felt that most of the essential information was received via the movies and the chapter they had read rather than the discussion with the American students. The trend reflected in the questionnaire, however, was different. Among students' reports were sentences like "I was exposed to new, intriguing contents," "the discussion about education in Israel and abroad enriched me and presented other aspects in education," and "I think it is important for us, as future educators, to expand our knowledge about global education." More than half of the students emphasized the importance of such discussions about education with students from a different part of the world. Many of them reported on a meaningful feeling of increased awareness of global education through interaction, as well as experiencing enriched learning. In conclusion, in the qualitative analysis we found that:

a. The students' attitude toward the PBLT as a way to improve their English proficiency skills was mostly positive.
b. Some of the students claimed that the electronic poster task increased their motivation in the course, and they were happy to do it, while many of them focused on frustrating drawbacks: technical difficulties in communication and time demanding.
c. The students' attitude toward their intercultural understanding via discussions on social justice and global awareness was different in the

interviews and post-PBLT questionnaires. In the interviews, most students said that the PBLT had little impact on their global awareness, whereas in the questionnaire, many of them reported on a meaningful feeling of increased awareness of global education through interaction. The difference in timing of the interviews and the questionnaire may explain this disparity. The interviews were conducted while students were actively involved in the process of the PBLT. In other words, they were in the midst of a demanding assignment and were not in the position to reflect on their learning processes. However, the questionnaire was collected a few weeks following the completion of the PBLT, allowing the students to reflect on the process and consolidate the knowledge they had gained through the intercultural exchange.

## Opportunities for Teacher Educators

Overall, the Israeli students reported a positive attitude toward the collaborative PBLT as a way to improve their English proficiency skills. In addition, many of them reported on a meaningful feeling of increased awareness to global education through interaction with overseas students. Hence, we can conclude that such a collaboration is worth the effort for students of a foreign language, as authentic communication sustains motivation, and an engaging task increases learning.

The ten virtual posters, which were presented in the second synchronous meeting, strengthen this conclusion. Two excerpts from the students' presentations further exemplify the learning gained by the PBLT. One group compared the agenda and values of higher education in Israel and the United States. In order to discuss the Arab situation in Israel as a minority group (20 percent of the population), the Israeli team members collected theoretical information about the subject, summarized the material in English, and then presented it in English together with their American peers. Another group reported on the atmosphere of the classroom in different socioeconomic sections of society (hours, size, buildings) and the purpose of education (Israel: values; United States: critical thinking). They compared public schools in the two nations, focusing on schools in poor areas and middle-class areas. In order to help with visualization, the groups integrated pictures of schools that were photographed in these areas in Israel and the United States, and they spoke about the similarities and differences, drawing conclusions that in fact they were very similar.

In sum, these two examples, among other presentations, display the effort that was made by the Israeli students to share reliable information about the education system in Israel, and to use the opportunity of this collaboration to present the information in English, and gain more confidence to speak and interact in English.

## Challenges for Developers of Technology-Enhanced Partnerships

As previously stated, negative reports by some of the students emphasized technological problems such as poor sound, and loss of connection during the Skype video-conferences. This was particularly annoying in the second video-conference, and students reported that they did not have enough time to deeply analyze the issues presented in the posters presentations. These findings are parallel to Oztok et al. (2013), who suggest that synchronous interaction does not leave time for reflection.

Other students spoke of inconvenience due to the time difference (United States is seven hours behind Israel), which limited the teams' interaction during the month in which they were constructing their presentation. Also due to the time difference, the meetings in Israel took place at night, constituting an obstacle for some of the students. Here, asynchronous communication—Ning and e-mails—helped to solve some of the challenges. Lastly, some complained that as the English course itself was online and not entirely devoted to social justice in education, there was a feeling of having only skimmed the surface of the subject. These challenges should be considered in setting up future projects.

## CONCLUSIONS

Our study focused on the impact of an international collaborative PBLT on students' motivation to increase their English proficiency and to increase their intercultural understanding. Our findings show the Israeli students reported on an authentic experience gained by the collaboration with the American university students. Being intrinsically motivated to use English and having already internalized the value of English, such collaboration strengthened their enthusiasm and willingness to use and communicate in English. Most students were motivated by the discussion about social justice in education, and even expressed "joy" in communicating about the Israeli culture and the Israeli school system. When the international teams worked well together, they felt a sense of relatedness and recognition of shared challenges that were dealt with through communication in the target language. However, when they did not, they felt the task was a burden and were frustrated by technical problems. Finally, we suggest that such international collaborations are helpful to student teachers as they can help them to develop sensitivity to language and communication strategies for coping with face-to-face encounters with future pupils and their parents in their future classrooms.

APPENDIX A

Questions that may serve as a framework for your discussion:

1. How could you compare your schooling to the one shown in the film?
2. How long is the school day? How old are students when they begin school?
3. What would be the average age of a student entering college?
4. What is the purpose of education?
5. What is the American Dream vs. the Israeli Dream?
6. How does the government play a role in schooling?
7. How large are the class sizes?
8. Is there a sense of fairness and equity with the educational system?
9. Are there extracurricular activities as part of the school day?
10. Are there class field trips?
11. How does diversity play a part in educational policy?
12. Is a dual language approach to learning in place?
13. Do you feel a sense of peace when you are in school?
14. What has been your experience with refugee students?
15. Is it common for the school to reach out to the community to get to know the parents/guardians of the students?
16. Are social services readily available to help students in need?
17. Describe a "normal" school day.

APPENDIX B

**Part 1**

Description of the class presentation:

As part of the international experience of comparing and contrasting the public purposes of education in the United States and Israel, you are encouraged to create an online poster using Prezi, PowerPoint, or any other online software. For more information on Prezi, please visit http://Prezi.com.

The PPT should be constructed as a collaborative final project for the international collaboration between you and the student/s from the other institution. It should have an academic component and a creative one.

Following is a description of the different required sections of the final project:

1. Introduction—this section should include a sentence stating something like: The purpose of this poster is to _____. It should also utilize the resources used in the class to frame the poster. Therefore,

citations from the movies watched and the article/chapter read should be included (at least one citation from each resource).

2. Comparing and Contrasting—in this section the poster should highlight two similarities and two differences between the United States and the Israeli purposes of education in a democratic society.

3. Creative—a drawing/picture/photo/illustration or other semiotic way to represent the insights gained from the experience is required.

4. Conclusion—the poster should include one conclusion on each one of the following issues: the academic, creative, and international experiences.

A five-minute oral or previously audiotaped presentation will be required during the second synchronous meeting.

## Part 2

Following are the criteria developed to evaluate the electronic poster:

Table 7.2.

| Criteria | Strong Impact 4 | Good Impact 3 | Some Impact 2 | Minimal Impact 1 |
|---|---|---|---|---|
| Introduction | -Fully captures the attention of the audience. -Topic has a clear focus. -1 citation from each source. -Citations from each source are relevant to poster information. | -Captures the attention of the audience. -Topic is mostly focused. -1 citation from each source. -Citations from each source are somehow relevant to poster information. | -Few audience members seem interested. -Topic focus is vague. -1 citation from only one source. | -Audience is not captured. -No topic focus. -No citations. |
| Content/ Comparing & Contrasting | -Ideas are interesting and thought-provoking. -Ideas demonstrate depth of knowledge. -Two comparing/ contrasting points made. | -Ideas are interesting. -Some ideas are thought-provoking. -Two comparing/ contrasting points are made. -Comparing/ contrasting | -Ideas do not demonstrate depth of knowledge. -Ideas are not particularly interesting or thought-provoking. -One comparing/ contrasting | -Ideas are unclear or illogical. -There are no comparing/ contrasting points made. |

| | | | |
|---|---|---|---|
| | -Comparing/ contrasting points are well integrated into the poster. | points are not well-integrated into the poster. | point is made. | |
| **Visual Presentation/ Creativity** | -Exceptional attention was given to details. -Outstanding quality. | -Visually pleasing for the most part, but 1-2 details could have been refined for a more attractive product. -Good quality. | -3 to 4 details could have been refined for a more attractive product. -Average quality. | -Appeared careless or messy. -Many details needed for refinement for a strong or attractive product. -Poor quality. |
| **Writing Mechanics; Text Elements; Citations** | -No errors in grammar, usage, mechanics, spelling. -Text elements easy to read (font, size). -Background and color enhance readability of text. -Sources are properly cited so audience can determine credibility. | -Text is written with little or no editing required. -Text elements are somewhat easy to read, but do not distract from the presentation. -Background and color distract from readability. -Most sources are properly cited. | -Grammar, usage, mechanics, and spelling impair readability. -Text elements are too busy or are difficult to read. -Background and color distract and make text difficult to read. -Some sources are not properly cited. | -Grammar, usage, mechanics, and spelling errors distract; major editing needed. -Text elements are extremely difficult to read. -Choice of background color needs improvement. -Most sources are incorrectly cited. |
| **Oral Presentation/ Conclusion** | -Presenters demonstrate thorough understanding of content and speak knowledgably about content. -Presenters make three conclusions: academic conclusion, creative conclusion, and international | -Presenters demonstrate good understanding of content and are able to speak knowledgably about most talking points. -Presenters make three conclusions: academic conclusion, creative | -Presenters demonstrate limited understanding of content and rely upon poster text for most of the presentation. -Presenters make two of the three conclusions: academic conclusion, creative | -Presenters demonstrate little or no understanding of content and read text directly from poster to audience. -Presenters make one or none of the conclusions: academic conclusion, creative |

| | | | |
|---|---|---|---|
| experience conclusion. -Presenters address all three points of the conclusion in an integrated manner in their poster. | conclusion, and international experience conclusion. -The three conclusion points are not well integrated into the poster. | conclusion, and international experience conclusion. | conclusion, and international experience conclusion. |
| **Teamwork** -The project is clearly a group effort. | -Most of the team members contribute to the group effort. | -Few people contribute their fair share of work. | -No collaboration in teamwork. |

This rubric was adapted from the following sources: Food Safety and Sanitation Guidelines. Texas Education Agency, 2012. http://mrsjankowski.weebly.com/uploads/7/3/0/9/7309076/prezi_rubric_22.pdf; http://www.hamden.org/uploaded/HHSlibraryfiles/Prezi_Rubric.pdf.

# APPENDIX C

**Table 7.3.   English for Academic Purposes—A Survey**

| | | Strongly Disagree | Disagree | Tend to Disagree | Agree | Strongly Agree |
|---|---|---|---|---|---|---|
| 1. | I like English | 1 | 2 | 3 | 4 | 5 |
| 2. | I always use English when I have the opportunity | 1 | 2 | 3 | 4 | 5 |
| 3. | An English course must be part of any academic degree | 1 | 2 | 3 | 4 | 5 |
| 4. | I need English in my daily life | 1 | 2 | 3 | 4 | 5 |
| 5. | I need English for my future profession | 1 | 2 | 3 | 4 | 5 |
| 6. | I need English to travel abroad | 1 | 2 | 3 | 4 | 5 |
| 7. | Being proficient in English will make people respect me | 1 | 2 | 3 | 4 | 5 |
| 8. | I would like to be proficient in English | 1 | 2 | 3 | 4 | 5 |
| 9. | I feel confidence when I use English | 1 | 2 | 3 | 4 | 5 |

| | | | | | | |
|---|---|---|---|---|---|---|
| 10. | Knowing English will enable me to understand books, movies, and music in English | 1 | 2 | 3 | 4 | 5 |
| 11. | Knowing English will make me an educated person | 1 | 2 | 3 | 4 | 5 |
| 12. | When I get a task in English, I prefer to copy the answers from a book rather than express myself by heart or by writing | 1 | 2 | 3 | 4 | 5 |
| 13. | The project with the American university will be very beneficial to me | 1 | 2 | 3 | 4 | 5 |
| 14. | I believe that in the long run the project with the American university will contribute to my English proficiency skills | 1 | 2 | 3 | 4 | 5 |
| 15. | The project with the American university is interesting for me | 1 | 2 | 3 | 4 | 5 |

## APPENDIX D

## Interview Questions

1. List three things you liked about the class.
2. List three insights you gained from doing the class.
3. Explain how your understanding of "global education" improved during the class.
4. What were the major factors in the class that helped improve your global perspectives of education?
5. How would you rate your global education awareness at the end of class compared to the beginning?
6. How does the task affect willingness to communicate orally and in writing in English?
7. How does the task affect your need to communicate orally and in writing in English?

8. Does the task affect your motivation in the course overall?

## Post-PBLT Questionnaire

1. Did you work alone or with a peer on the presentation?

   a. In your opinion, do you think working alone/with a peer influenced your motivation while preparing the presentation? How?

2. Did you experience difficulties in your presentation in English? Yes/ No.

   a. Mark the difficulties that you experienced:

   - Lack of collaboration with Montclair students.
   - Difficulty gathering information.
   - Difficulty writing up the information in English.
   - Difficulty presenting orally.

3. Did the collaboration with Montclair students improve your desire to use the English language orally and in writing? Yes/No.

   a. Explain.
   b. Does the topic of the project enrich you? Do you think learning and discussion about education from another part of the world contribute to your knowledge as a future educator?

4. Did the second meeting go well according to your expectations? Explain.

   a. What would you change if you were doing it again?

5. Do you think collaborations between Israeli students and native English students is the right way to motivate Israeli students to improve their English? Yes/No.

   a. Explain.

# REFERENCES

Aldridge, J. & Goldman, R. (2007). *Current issues and trends in education* (2nd ed.). Boston: Pearson.

Conole, G. & Oliver, M. (Eds.) (2007). *Contemporary perspectives in E-learning research.* Oxon: Routledge.

Darhower, M. (2002). Interactional features of synchronous computer mediate communication in the intermediate 2 classroom: A sociocultural case study. *Calico Journal, 19*, 249–277.

Dornyei, Z. (2001). New themes and approaches in second language motivation research. *Annual Review of Applied Linguistics, 21*, 43–59.

Freiermuth, M. & Huang, H. (2012). Bringing Japan and Taiwan closer electronically: A look at an intercultural online synchronous chat task and its effect on motivation. *Language Teaching Research, 16 (1)*, 61–88.

Freiermuth, M. & Jarrell, D. (2006). Willingness to communicate. Can online chat help? *International Journal of Applied Linguistics, 16*, 191–213.

Gardner, J. (2001). Integrative motivation and second-language acquisition. In Z. Dornyei & R. Schmitdt (Eds.), *Motivation and second language acquisition* (pp. 1–20). Honolulu, HI: University of Hawai'i Press.

Helm, F., Guth, S., & O'Dowd, R. (2012). University language classes collaborating online. Available from: http://intent-project.eu/sites/default/files/Telecollaboration_report_Final_Oct2012.pdf.

Hytten, K. & Bettez, S. C. (2011). Understanding education for social justice. *Educational Foundations, 25* (1-2), 7–24.

Kern, R., Ware, P., & Warschauer, M. (2004). Crossing frontiers: New directions in online pedagogy and research. *Annual Review of Applied Linguistics, 24*, 243–260.

Klapper, J. (2006). *Understanding and developing good practice. Language teaching in Higher Education.* London: CILT.

La Guardia, J. G. (2009). Developing who I am: A Self-Determination Theory approach to the establishment of healthy identities. *Educational Psychologist, 44* (2), 90–104.

Mackinnon, T. (2013). Using e-tools to facilitate international collaborations and enhance language teaching. *The higher Education Academy Report.* Downloaded on 17.5.2013 from: http://www.google.co.il/url?sa=t&rct=j&q=&esrc=s&source=web&cd=1&ved=0CBoQFjAA&url=httppercent3Apercent2Fpercent2Fwww.heacademy.ac.ukpercent2Fassetspercent2Fdocumentspercent2Fdisciplinespercent2FLanguagespercent2FUsing_e_tools.pdf&ei=zE-wU8jnMYqHPbnIgfgK&usg=AFQjCNEDEmuO7PHGkHusmuzFc1NW9abMcA&sig2=pQBIp8nwL_aUk66pTOeLPA&bvm=bv.69837884,d.ZGU.

Oztok, M., Zingaro, D., Brett, C., & Hewitt, J. (2013). Exploring asynchronous and synchronous tool use in online courses. *Computers and Education, 60*, 87–94.

Ryan, R. M. & Deci, E. L (2000). Intrinsic and extrinsic motivations: Classic definitions and new directions. *Contemporary Educational Psychology, 25*, 54–67.

Ware, P. (2005). "Missed communication" in online communication: Tensions in fostering successful online interactions. *Language Learning and Technology, 9* (2), 64–89. http://llt.msu.edu/vol9num2/default.html.

*Chapter Eight*

# Using Technology to Facilitate Collaboration between New Jersey and Namibian Teacher Education Students

Hilary Wilder and Perien Joniell Boer

## INTRODUCTION

The purpose of this chapter is to describe a pilot study in which preservice education students in educational technology courses in New Jersey and Namibia were paired up in order to create a virtual cross-cultural collaborative learning experience. The anticipated goals of this experience were threefold: to provide students an opportunity to learn about and work with an international peer, to demonstrate for students a way in which technology could be used to help their own students transcend classroom walls, and to help them to understand the importance of promoting cyber-safety and cyber-ethics to students everywhere. Although this experience was designed to foster growth in both Namibian and New Jersey students, the focus of the results will be on the latter, for reasons discussed later.

It is generally agreed that internationalizing preservice education programs will help prepare teachers for the diversity they will face in their classrooms as well as giving them the skills and understanding that will enable them to help their learners become productive global citizens (Roberts, 2007; Merryfield, 2008; Quezada & Cordeiro, 2009; Quezada, 2012). However, this is a relatively new initiative for most teacher education programs which face a number of hurdles including financial, logistical, regulatory, and lack of buy-in from students as well as many other stakeholders (Schneider, 2003; Eduventures, 2008; Mahon, 2010) and other challenges that may occur when reconceptualizing a teacher education program (Ochoa, 2010). At the same time, the substantial integration of information and communication technologies (ICTs) into teacher education programs, brings with it an opportunity to give preservice teachers virtual "international" experiences that circumvent many of the logistical complications inherent in study abroad and international travel experiences (Kissock & Richardson, 2010; Ochoa, 2010; Longview, 2008; Sprague, 2012).

Because "internationalization" is a much-used and often ambiguous term, the authors have recently been exploring a framework which lets teacher education programs separate out three overarching outcomes which are often part of an internationalization effort: altruism (the commitment to helping others and the planet), interculturalism (the ability to relate to and work with diverse peers), and travel-ism (the inquisitiveness, skills, and accommodativeness to be at ease in unfamiliar locations and situations) (Wilder & Feola, 2014). These outcomes, which are not mutually exclusive, can be thought of as axes in a three-dimensional framework so that developers of internationalization programs can strategically decide which of the outcome(s) they want to improve students on. Strategic planning, which may start with only one outcome, is necessary especially for programs which have very limited resources and/or administrative support, and in the case of the first two outcomes, can often be accomplished through local experiences and/or ICT-based projects, rather than full-on international travel. In this particular project, the primary goal was to move students along on the interculturalism dimension by asking them to work together via technology with an international peer. A secondary goal, along the altruism/making the world a better place dimension, was to promote their understanding of the global nature of cyber-safety and cyber-ethics and the need for all students to adhere to these guidelines as global twenty-first century digital citizens.

## THE NEW JERSEY–NAMIBIA CONNECTION

The authors met in Namibia in 2003 when the first author was presenting workshops at the University of Namibia (UNAM), and in 2004 they collaborated to have one student from each of the four Namibia Colleges of Education enrolled in the first author's online preservice educational technology course at William Paterson University of New Jersey (WPU) (until 2011, the Colleges of Education in Namibia were responsible for the Basic Education Teaching Diploma to prepare primary [grades 1–7] preservice teachers. This diploma program is being phased out and is now offered as a BEd program by the Faculty of Education at UNAM, which merged the Colleges under it). WPU and UNAM are both public universities, with a majority of students who are first in their families to attend tertiary education. For most students at both universities, a study-abroad semester is financially and logistically unrealistic, and the authors were looking at whether technology could help.

The results of the 2004 project showed that having the ability to engage in online discussions with Namibian peers did lead to a greater understanding of Namibia and the Namibian education system by the WPU students and a greater understanding of the U.S. education system by the UNAM students; however, without a required collaborative project, there was very little "deep" interaction beyond the perfunctory social response postings (Wilder & Malone, 2005; Wilder, 2007; Malone & Wilder, 2008). In 2008 and again in 2010, the first author had students in her graduate educational technology course provide virtual mentoring for in-service teachers in Namibia on a technology-integration project. This produced a more noticeable growth in the New Jersey students in terms of their understanding of how contextual factors such as the ethnic and/or racial background of students, teachers, and/ or community; cultural and/or linguistic background; socioeconomic background; historic or political background; and ethical and/or legal standards set locally or nationally affect the adoption and implementation of technology in the classroom (Wilder, Ferris, & An, 2010).

In the second half of 2012 (fall semester for WPU, semester two for UNAM), the authors were each tasked to teach the educational technology course in their respective elementary/primary education preservice teacher programs. Preservice teachers in New Jersey and Namibia are likely to face similar challenges in their teaching placements, including: 1) a high likelihood that they will be teaching in classrooms with English Language Learners students (in Namibia, English is typically the second or third language for most children [after mother-tongue and possibly Afrikaans]); 2) that they will be teaching at schools with considerable financial and resource constraints; and 3) that they will be expected to integrate ICTs into their teaching. In a continuing effort to explore ways in which ICTs can be used to facilitate international education experiences, the authors looked for ways in which their students could work collaboratively with one another. Since both courses had learning outcomes which included an understanding of digital citizenship and knowledge on how to teach digital citizenship to their K–12 learners, a collaborative project addressing this requirement was a logical choice. In addition, the topic of digital citizenship, because it involves ethical/legal behavior (ISTE, 2008, Standard 5), will vary based on the cultural, religious, and political context that it is applied in. The hope was that this project would give students the opportunity to investigate norms within their own culture and country by learning about the norms in their partner's comparative education framework.

## RESEARCH QUESTIONS

The following research questions were investigated in this pilot project. Although we had hoped to study the impact of the experience on both WPU and UNAM students, we were unable to collect data from the UNAM students and had to focus exclusively on the results from the WPU students.

- RQ1: What is the impact of the online collaboration between WPU and UNAM students on the inter-culturalism dimension and cultural awareness of WPU students? Would there be a shift in attitude and self-reflection as measured by the My Cultural Awareness Profile (myCAP) survey (Marx & Moss, 2011)? (The My Cultural Awareness Profile [myCAP] survey was used with permission of the authors and the Association of International Educators [NAFSA]. For more information on myCAP please go to http://www.nafsa.org/.)
- RQ2: What is the impact of the international collaboration on the altruism/ making the world a better place dimension and WPU students' understanding and knowledge of what all K–12 students need for effective digital citizenship? Would their understanding become more global and show a broadening beyond the ethical/legal norms of New Jersey, as observed in the revisions of their project and discussions with their partners as their project develops?

## METHODOLOGY

In September 2012, a total of twenty-three undergraduate students in two sections of the WPU course "Teaching in a Technological World" (both sections taught by the first author) were paired with student peers in the undergraduate "Integrated Media and Technology Education" (IMTE) course at UNAM (taught by the second author), based on the subject/grade they were studying to teach. Interestingly, while English was understandably the second or third language for all of the UNAM students (with Otjiherero being the predominant mother tongue in this particular class), it was also the second language for eight of the WPU students (with Spanish and Arabic being the mother tongue of four students, respectively).

The students were given the assignment to create a Glog that could be used in both Namibian and New Jersey classrooms to provide information and instruction on "CyberSmart" digital citizenship. A Glog (http://edu.glogster.com/) is an online poster that can include graphics, text, audio, video, and interactive links. Each WPU-UNAM pair was given a Glogster student account that they both had login access to, along with the directions (found in appendix B) and links to over a dozen online resources on digital citizenship issues to get them started. This was a required assignment for the WPU, designed to meet the International Society for Technology in Education (ISTE) Standard #4 for Teachers: Promote and model digital citizenship and responsibility (ISTE, 2008).

All students were asked to initially create a "personal" Glog about themselves which was used to introduce themselves to their partners. Students were encouraged to communicate with their partners through a variety of technologies including comments on their Glogs, Skype calls, Facebook group, and e-mail. The resulting CyberSmart Glogs were then evaluated with a rubric (appendix B) at the end of the term.

In addition, WPU students completed the myCAP survey in September (before working with their UNAM partners) and again in December. Due to issues discussed below, UNAM students did not complete the survey.

## RESULTS

### Research Questions Results

When looking at the research questions, the following data were analyzed for the WPU students (again, data was not collected from the UNAM students).

*RQ1: The impact of this project on the cultural awareness of WPU students.*

The following data (shown in appendix A, table 8.1) were collected from pre- and post-myCAP surveys, broken down by the four survey dimensions (Exploring the Global Context, Learning about Different Cultures, Knowing Ourselves as Cultural, and Communicating across Cultural Differences). In this table, SD/D = strongly disagree/disagree; SA/A = strongly agree/agree, and the Wilcoxon Matched-Pairs Signed-Ranks Test was used to determine significant change from pre- to post-survey responses. Pre- and post-exemplar answers to the open-ended questions for each of the four dimension on the myCAP survey were also used to explore changes in attitudes and beliefs of the students. Below is an analysis of the data, based on the four dimensions.

*myCAP Dimension 1: Exploring the global context.* When asked to "reflect on knowledge about the global context," the majority of students believed they are knowledgeable on global/international issues, would be able to teach these issues, and that they stay current on them. These beliefs became stronger at the end of the semester (table 8.1), with a statistically significant increase in three of the items. There was an increase (with a p of 0.5) from 70 percent to 90 percent of students agreeing/strongly agreeing that they had knowledge of global and international issues. There were also increases (both with a p of 1), for students agreeing/strongly agreeing that they are reading international newspapers, TV programs, and/or movies (from 50 percent to 65 percent), and for students agreeing/strongly agreeing that they will be able to teach and assess curricular units that explicitly address global issues (from 70 percent to 85 percent). These are of particular interest as they indicate that after the project, the students were seeing themselves as being more knowledgeable about global affairs. Similarly, students who did not consider themselves global citizens or who had somewhat vague ideas about what global citizenship meant at the beginning of the semester were able to characterize themselves as global citizens, using specific examples, by the end of the semester. For example, one student stated

> *I do not consider myself a global citizen. I am not aware of a lot of things that are happening in other countries. I do take interest however, I just don't think to other[s] I would be considered a global citizen because I do not go out of my way often to spread things & make others aware of what is going on in different places.*

at the beginning of the semester but then stated

> *I feel I am more of a global citizen than I was in the beginning of the semester. Working on a project with another student from a different country opened my eyes to other things I wasn't aware of in the past.*

at the end. At the same time, post-semester scores showed that the majority of students still believed that globalization was something that does not impact their lives and do not see themselves as involved in organizations with global missions. There was also a slight (not statistically significant) decrease in their belief that they think about global implications when making choices (table 8.1). In addition, there was little change in their beliefs about the need to teach global issues to their students, with most (but not all) agreeing that it had a place in the curriculum but only as secondary to more core topics. For example, one student's pre-study response

> *I wouldn't classify it as a central place, I would make it an elective for people who are interested in learning about international and global issues. I think that it should be an option because I see so many people who think (in a political standpoint) that our country should mind it's business and that we have enough problems as it is and we should be more focused on that.*

was fairly similar to the post-study response

> *Along w/ all the other things we learned in school, I think international/global issues can be given a place in our schools curriculum. However, I would not go as far as making it a central place. Only because I don't think it should be*

*mandatory. There are other subjects that I would place a higher importance than global issues.*

In general, students appeared to show growth in their understanding of themselves as living in and being part of a larger/global community but may not yet see themselves as playing an active role in that community or helping their K–12 students play an active role.

*myCAP Dimension 2: Learning about different cultures.* When asked to "reflect on your current understanding of culture and other cultural groups," there were no statistically significant changes in responses, with at least 85 percent continuing to report that cultural characteristics should not be used for stereotyping or get in the way of (nonjudgmentally) seeing similarities and differences with others. Similarly, 65 percent of the students continued to look at culture as being predominantly characterized by outward/appearance factors (rather than inward/nonperceptible factors such as core values), and 75 percent continued to believe that a curriculum should (and presumably could) be culturally neutral (table 8.1). At the same time, in the open-ended responses, ideas about cultural markers expanded at the end of the semester beyond obvious factors such as language, dress, and skin color to include inward factors such as perceptions, norms, values, and beliefs. For example, one student's response changed from

> *Three characteristics/categories commonly used to compare culture groups are skin color, attire, and language.*

to

> *Three different characteristics/categories commonly used to compare culture groups are traditions, values, beliefs.*

At the end of the semester, students also seem to have expanded ideas about what they would teach to include not only outward topics such as language, geographic location, and customs from students' families, but to also cover concepts of "tolerance," "diversity," understanding of differing beliefs, and knowledge of current situations worldwide. For example, one student's response changed from

> *Maybe I would teach about where other countries are on a globe or map and then explain the culture.*

to

> *I will try to bring in newspaper articles or videos of global news to help students see and realize what goes on in other countries.*

One noticeable (although not statistically significant) increase (from 55 percent to 65 percent of students agreeing/strongly agreeing) was in students' belief that international travel (e.g., leaving the familiar) would be beneficial in understanding other cultural groups. While the collaboration did not seem to have much of an impact on students' openness to learning about other cultures (which was relatively high to begin with), the disconnects that resulted from trying to work with someone from another culture via a mediated technology may have led to a stronger belief that you need to be physically near that person in order to really understand him/her.

*myCAP Dimension 3: Knowing ourselves as cultural.* Students were then asked to "reflect on your own cultural identity" and to consider themselves as a cultural "other." Again, there were no statistically significant changes in responses (table 8.1). While the large majority (95 percent) continued to report on the importance of helping their K–12 students respect each other's cultural identity, at least 65 percent continued to believe that their own cultural identity does not influence how they behaved or that it will impact their teaching. They did not seem to acknowledge their own cultural "otherness," or that their non-outward characteristics (e.g., beliefs) might not be the same as the norm (or that there might not even be a "norm") but instead maintained a belief that we all have similar ideas about right and wrong (with a slight decrease in this from 95 percent to 90 percent). The upside was that only a minority of students reported an avoidance to talking about beliefs, values, and traditions, although this increased slightly (nonsignificantly, from 15 percent to 25 percent) by the end of the semester. When looking at the open-ended responses, there was again an expansion of their understanding of "culture" to include inward factors such as political beliefs, with one student's response changing from

> *I am American, Christian, white, a native English speaker, a westerner, have Irish and Italian ancestry.*

to

> *White, American, Middle-class, western, College student, tolerant, male, Rural, young, liberal.*

An awareness that the teacher brings his/her cultural identity into the classroom did not seem to change, and for most students, there appeared to be little reflection on how a teacher's own cultural identity might impact their interactions with students and approach to the material taught even at the end of the semester. For example, one student's response changed only slightly from

> *I don't think that your cultural identity influences the way you teach. I think your educators influence the way you teach.*

to

> *I think that a teacher may show her students some of what her culture is but not influence.*

However, there were a few students who had noted possible influences in both their pre- and post-responses; for example,

> *Some ways that a teachers cultural identity could influence the way they teach could be that they talk about it to the students and incorporate things into the lesson plan about it.*

was revised to

> *A teachers cultural identity could influence the way they teach because of their beliefs. If they strongly agree with something they will teach the students that.*

Again, the collaboration did not seem to have much of an impact on changing students' understanding of how their own culture might influence their behavior or their teaching, and the number of students who started out seeing their culture as being a differentiator stayed pretty much the same by the end of the semester.

*myCAP Dimension 4: Communicating across cultural differences.* When asked to "reflect on your own intercultural skills," the majority of the students (at least 95 percent) continued to believe that they could effectively communicate with others from different cultures, that they would be able to avoid misunderstandings, and that they would be able to increase their teaching effectiveness by learning about their students' cultural background (table 8.1). At the same time, the number of students who disagreed/strongly disagreed that teachers had to only consider cultural implications in certain courses showed only a nonsignificant decrease (from 55 percent to 47 percent) by the end of the semester. However, there was a noticeable (with a p of 1) decrease (from 80 percent to 74 percent) in students who agreed/strongly agreed that they had to adjust their communication styles depending on who they are talking to, and a nonsignificant decrease (from 95 percent to 84 percent) in students who agreed/strongly agreed that their own cultural background does not impact their ability to communicate with others, possibly indicating a budding awareness that communication across cultures may take work. One interesting aspect was that a relatively large minority (35 percent) of the students believed that they had been misunderstood due to cultural differences, perhaps reflective of the Hispanic and Muslim students in the course who had encountered such experiences. Similarly, when looking at the pre- to post-semester open-ended responses, there seemed to be a shift toward acknowledging the possibility of miscommunication, with the inclusion of more specific examples of miscommunication; for example, one student's stated

> *I guess it wouldn't be too different because I would talk to them w/ the same respect I would talk to someone of my own culture.*

at the beginning of the semester but then stated

> *This happens all the time, people still ask me why Im not allowed to sleep away from home or have a regular "American" relationship.*

at the end. There were also more specific ideas for strategies that might be used to prevent miscommunication in their classrooms. For example, one student's speculation changed from

> *I'm not sure yet, maybe try to involve them and ask about their backgrounds. Maybe have a culture project.*

to a more concrete strategy to

> *I will put notes on the board to show what I'm saying so if a student misses something they can re-read my instructions/lecture.*

Again, there was an indication that students were beginning to understand that effective communication needs to be actively thought about rather than just assumed, and this may have been influenced somewhat by them struggling to understand the UNAM partners during the Skype sessions or even to understand what their partners had posted on their personal Glogs.

In summary, although there were only a few statistically significant differences between pre- and post-answers on the survey, there were signs of growth on many of the items when looking at the open-ended responses.

*RQ2: The impact of this project on WPU students' understanding and knowledge of what all K–12 students need for effective digital citizenship.*

Data collected for this question included WPU students' scores on their CyberSmart Glog project, which were evaluated based on a three-point rubric with four items (appendix B). The CyberSmart Glog, as described above, required students to provide explanation and links to support resources for six digital citizenship topics including respectful online/mobile behavior and lawful online/mobile behavior as well as awareness of digital equity and e-waste. We hoped students would think about how technology could be used for both good and bad, as well as foster their caring about technology implications on a local, national, and global level. We were also hoping that by working with their UNAM partner, WPU students would see the universality of this knowledge as being needed by K–12 students in both New Jersey and Namibia.

Unfortunately, due to the challenges noted below, the UNAM students were not able to collaborate on or provide feedback to the WPU on the CyberSmart Glogs, so we were unable to adequately address this research question; however, there were indications that even though WPU students created their CyberSmart Glogs on their own, they did seem to take into account some awareness of how digital literacy skills are needed by all— even those, like their UNAM peers, who might be on the other side of the digital divide and have only limited access. In all but a few cases, WPU students were able to meet or exceed expectations on the project (appendix A, table 8.2). For example, under the category of Cyber-equity, one student included special needs (e.g., use of assistive technology) in addition to promoting access across linguistic, racial, gender, socioeconomic, or political boundaries. Another student included a recommendation for "*being respectful of cultural differences you may find in a blog or website*," recognizing that diverse populations will not only be accessing/consuming online material but will also be producing it. In addition, at least four students created CyberSmart Glogs in both English and their mother tongue (Spanish or Arabic), and a number of students included resource links from non-U.S. websites.

## Project Challenges

The best laid plans, however, often hit snags, and this project was no exception, with scheduling/logistics, technology, and student participation being primary challenges.

## Scheduling/Logistic Issues

Due to the fact that the UNAM students were just winding down their semester, while the WPU students were just starting their semester, there was a narrow window of about two months (mid-September to early November) that this project could run. Although we tried to have as much as possible set up ahead of time, the final pairing up of students took longer than expected, with students at WPU in the midst of add/drop and students at UNAM not forthcoming with their contact information. We were able to hold an initial group Skype session between one of the WPU course sections and the UNAM students who agreed to come into the computer lab at night (there is a five-hour time difference in early fall); however, the UNAM students did not come in for a Skype session with the second WPU section.

Scheduling was also impacted by the fact that the WPU course was designated to be run as a "hybrid," which meant that unlike the UNAM course, which met daily, the WPU sections met only once every few weeks, with all other sessions being carried out asynchronously via Blackboard®. Lastly, and most importantly for the WPU students, the biggest scheduling challenge came when Superstorm Sandy hit New Jersey, resulting in school closure and no electricity or Internet for weeks after for the majority of students in both sections (most of whom did not live on campus). By the time WPU had recovered, the UNAM students had finished their academic year and were gone.

## Technology Issues

Before starting the project, we debated which technology to use that would let our students collaborate and give feedback to their partner while at the same time let us monitor the interactions. We were also cognizant of the fact that UNAM students would be accessing the technology via relatively slow bandwidths, even when they were doing so from the UNAM computer lab. At UNAM, an IT plan to upgrade the campus and bandwidth was behind schedule; however, we went ahead with the promise that the IT infrastructure would be in place when we started, which was not the case. The limited Internet access meant that UNAM students could not always access their Glogster accounts even when working in the computer lab. At UNAM nearly every part of the pilot required addition and special arrangements when it came to IT. The bandwidth was so low that Skype sessions had to happen at times when most Internet traffic on campus was down (on Friday afternoons) so that the IT technicians could dedicate the bandwidth to Skype activities. Even then, visuals were poor; and after the initial introductions, we had to resort to voice and text only.

We were hoping that students would make use of the "Comment" feature in Glogster that would allow them to give feedback and respond to both the personal Glogs that each made and the collaborative CyberSmart Glogs that they were to work on with each other. Although all the students were unfamiliar with Glogster, they were able to quickly come up to speed with it and create their personal Glogs, giving them a way to "introduce" themselves to their partner (each WPU-UNAM pair shared a single Glog account and could see anything the other had done). All twenty-three WPU students were able to create a personal Glog. Of the twenty-three UNAM students, sixteen were able to create a personal Glog—mostly due to the fact that they were given special access to work in the computer lab after hours—again, important since most of the students did not have personal computers or Internet service at home. In terms of WPU-UNAM communication, despite technological and scheduling difficulties, a number of students were able to find workarounds (e.g., instant messaging, Facebook via their mobile phones); and two WPU students were able to speak directly via a Skype phone call to their UNAM partner's mobile phone.

## Student Participation Issues

As noted above, for the UNAM students, enthusiasm in the collaboration fizzled out earlier than anticipated. The project came toward the end of the semester and the particular students who participated in the collaboration were in their final year of a teaching certification that was to be phased out. The students interpreted the phasing out of the certification program as "they simply cannot fail"; hence, motivation was low, and the collaboration was not on their top priority list. Additionally, the IMTE subject was nonexaminable and students' grades were based on their various course-required technology-based projects, which did not include the collaboration project. Many of the students simply focused on achieving the minimum effort for each required project. The technical support issues and logistical aspects surrounding the pilot led to further lowering of morale for the students. Time in the laboratory was limited as the computer lab was scheduled for various other classes using computers. Special arrangements were made for more lab time; however, lack of Internet at UNAM hampered the students' progress, which further demotivated them. As the semester wound down, students focused more on their examinable subjects, and class numbers started dwindling. Furthermore, the lack of motivation resulted in the second author struggling to collect myCAP surveys from students. As with the collaboration project, perhaps the surveys would have been taken seriously if they were part of a tangible motivation incentive.

For the WPU students, this project was a required assignment which counted toward their grade in a course required for their preservice teaching program. Since none of them faced technology challenges (until Superstorm Sandy), they were willing to work on the project, and many were eager to collaborate with peers in Namibia. Over time, however, as their UNAM partners became less and less active, many WPU students became anxious about their grade, and since they could not be held responsible for this, the collaboration requirement for the grade on this project had to be dropped. In the end, the WPU students worked on the CyberSmart Glogs by themselves without input from their UNAM partners.

## Summary of Findings

Although we were unable to collect much of the data that we had been hoping for, and faced a number of the scheduling/logistics, technology, and student participation challenges, we still believe that the experience was worthwhile for both our WPU and UNAM students (the latter reporting in private conversation that they enjoyed making personal Glogs with the WPU partners). Indications of growth in WPU students' understanding and knowledge of culture/intercultural issues were shown on a number of the myCAP survey responses. Similarly, although the CyberSmart Glogs were not produced with the help of their UNAM partners, the large majority of WPU students were able to demonstrate that they recognized the concepts and issues involved in the use of technology at local and global levels and the importance of helping their students understand digital citizenship.

## OPPORTUNITIES AND CHALLENGES: SUGGESTIONS FOR COLLEAGUES

As with our previous collaboration efforts, we continued to face scheduling, technology, and participation challenges on both sides of the Atlantic (although we'd like to believe Superstorm Sandy was a fluke, it certainly served as a wakeup call for New Jersey). We do, however, believe that a virtual collaboration can be useful for teacher educators looking to provide an internationalization experience for their students, and offer the following suggestions.

## Scheduling/Logistic Suggestions

For better or worse, partnering with international institutions will often mean working in opposing time zones, academic calendars, and even seasons, and planning a collaboration with institutions that do not have corresponding schedules or calendars can be challenging. For this reason, most of the communication between the students will need to be asynchronous, and projects confined to the narrow windows where semesters and course syllabi can overlap. Planning needs to be done carefully and allow ample time for delays and technical glitches, with time lost being added to time zone differences. At the same time, the temporal disconnect can help remind students that their "here and now" is not the only "here and now." Currently, formal education typically occurs within the small confines of a "here and now" classroom; however, the future may require a very different paradigm of an "anytime, anyplace" system, and the teachers we are preparing today may be at the forefront of that shift.

## Technology Suggestions

Perhaps, as real-time collaboration technologies such as Skype/FaceTime and document/whiteboard sharing apps become truly ubiquitous, accessible, and affordable by students in both New Jersey and Namibia, then students can be expected to work outside of the classroom and class hours. At the present time, however, it cannot be assumed that all students in developed nations have the financial wherewithal to afford the devices and services for this, in addition to being completely unaffordable for most students in developing nations. While we did try to account for this by offering additional computer lab hours, students often did not take advantage of this. For WPU students, many of whom were commuting from home, this would have been an extra trip in. For UNAM students, many of whom were living in the dormitories, this would have meant walking back to their room via unlit (and not particularly safe) paths.

When we first planned the project, UNAM was in the process of rolling out a student laptop program and campus-wide Wi-Fi; however, as the semester progressed, it became clear that this rollout would be delayed and that committed buy-in from key UNAM administrators was lacking. Even getting the administrative permission to keep the labs open in the evenings was a struggle for the second author. It is therefore strongly suggested that projects rely on technology that is accessible and available to all students, and also that there is a commitment from administration and IT staff to ensure that it is available throughout the duration of the time needed. Before engaging in any technology projects, confirm that the infrastructure is in place with the minimal criteria met. Buy-in from administration is key and not just with the relevant faculty. Support at an administrative level allows for solutions to be quick and less painful when challenges arise. For example, students who were in possession of laptops could have easily collaborated on their own time, but bandwidth solutions were not offered. After the pilot period, the university offered 3G devices to students with 100 GB Internet connectivity monthly as part of their yearly technology fee to alleviate the demands on bandwidth.

Another factor to consider is whether or not the teacher educators want to monitor or be part of the communications that take place. If they do, then they will have to use a platform that provides this functionality in a secure and protected environment that is also accessible by all the students. For example, Blackboard provides a secure and protected platform for threaded discussions and group file-sharing; however, it is very bandwidth intensive and was not usable in Namibia (not to mention unaffordable). Google Groups, which we had also tried in a previous collaborative project, was usable in Namibia but not reliable (as we discovered when Google did away with shared pages halfway through the project). Despite the merits of Glogster and its collaborative features, the software was slow and cumbersome in the computer lab at UNAM due to the low bandwidth. Future recommendation would be to look at software that does not require high bandwidth and that is commonly used by both institutions. To date UNAM has not purchased Glogster and does not have the financial strength to purchase proprietary software that would be useful for student teachers who could use it in their teaching profession. Thus, a further recommendation would be to opt for using open-source software that can be easily used at the teachers' future schools. Additionally, as students may be reluctant to log into yet another platform, it might be better to use a technology that they are already using (e.g., Facebook) but in a way that does not intrude on their personal use. As noted earlier, the more successful collaborations were between those students who connected via Facebook. This appeared to be a "common denominator" for both student groups, where connectivity was not an issue to Namibian students as they could easily access Facebook via their mobile phones even with a non-data phone plan.

## Student Participation Suggestions

Although WPU and UNAM students were all initially excited about "meeting" and working with a partner in another country, the enthusiasm quickly dissolved, and there were very few who were able or willing to work past the scheduling and technology issues that arose and keep the collaboration going. Some of the students did find workarounds (e.g., friended each other on Facebook). Most however did not, and the UNAM students in particular stopped logging into Glogster once they had created their personal Glogs. Again, this was in large part due to the scheduling (as it approached their end-of-semester and final exam time) and lack of accessible technology, but there was also reluctance due to the fact that this was not a graded assignment for them and that the course itself was not an examinable subject. Both authors realized the immense opportunity for collaboration of this nature and hoped for a relatively workable engagement from student to student. We recognized the motivation factor in applying a grade to the Glogster project for the WPU students, whereas the UNAM students did not have the same incentive. Future projects should consider proffering the same or similar motivation to students on both ends of the collaboration.

## CONCLUSION

In conclusion, we strongly recommend that teacher educators look into ways of using technology to help their students gain "internationalization" outcomes which do not require physical travel, as this can be difficult for many students and education programs. Virtual collaborations across country borders, or even across communities with different cultural backgrounds, can give students a way to gain the skills necessary to understand and work with diverse peers. Similarly, assignments based on a goal of making the world a better place that are done in collaboration with others from different backgrounds will give students a way to gain an understanding of how to effectively work toward ubiquitous human rights and universal living standards. As the technology becomes more and more affordable and accessible, this should become easier and easier.

## ACKNOWLEDGMENTS

This project was funded in part by a Teaching the World Fellowship given to the first author in 2012 by the Graduate School of Education at Rutgers University.

## APPENDIX A

## Data from the myCAP Survey and Glog Project Grades

Table 8.1.   Likert-scale data for of myCAP survey (N = 23)

| | Pre | | Post | | Wilcoxon results |
|---|---|---|---|---|---|
| | SD/D | SA/A | SD/D | SA/A | |
| Dimension 1 | | | | | |
| Q1 | 30% | 70% | 10% | 90% | W+ = 0, W- = 28, N = 7** |
| Q2 | 60% | 40% | 70% | 30% | W+ = 22, W- = 6, N = 7 |
| Q3 | 50% | 50% | 35% | 65% | W+ = 3, W- = 25, N = 7* |
| Q4 | 65% | 35% | 65% | 35% | W+ = 7.50, W- = 7.50, N = 5 |
| Q5 | 84% | 16% | 63% | 37% | W+ = 2.50, W- = 12.50, N = 5 |
| Q6 | 30% | 70% | 15% | 85% | W+ = 0, W- = 15, N = 5* |
| Q7 | 35% | 65% | 45% | 55% | W+ = 9, W- = 6, N = 5 |
| Q8 | 75% | 25% | 70% | 30% | W+ = 2.50, W- = 12.50, N = 5 |
| Dimension 2 | | | | | |
| Q11 | 5% | 95% | 10% | 90% | W+ = 10.50, W- = 10.50, N = 6, |
| Q12 | 35% | 65% | 35% | 65% | W+ = 13.50, W- = 7.50, N = 6 |
| Q13 | 45% | 55% | 35% | 65% | W+ = 8, W- = 20, N = 7 |
| Q14 | 85% | 15% | 90% | 10% | W+ = 4, W- = 2, N = 3 |
| Q15 | 65% | 35% | 60% | 40% | W+ = 3, W- = 3, N = 3 |
| Q16 | 0% | 100% | 5% | 95% | W+ = 3, W- = 0, N = 2 |
| Q17 | 80% | 20% | 75% | 25% | W+ = 4, W- = 6, N = 4 |

| Q18 | 25% | 75% | 25% | 75% | W+ = 14.50, W- = 6.50, N = 6 |
|---|---|---|---|---|---|
| **Dimension 3** | | | | | |
| Q21 | 5% | 95% | 5% | 95% | W+ = 1, W- = 0, N = 1 |
| Q22 | 40% | 60% | 35% | 65% | W+ = 6, W- = 9, N = 5 |
| Q23 | 40% | 60% | 45% | 55% | W+ = 6, W- = 0, N = 3 |
| Q24 | 55% | 45% | 60% | 40% | W+ = 6, W- = 4, N = 4 |
| Q25 | 75% | 25% | 75% | 25% | W+ = 4, W- = 2, N = 3 |
| Q26 | 85% | 15% | 75% | 25% | W+ = 2.50, W- = 7.50, N = 4 |
| Q27 | 5% | 95% | 10% | 90% | W+ = 6, W- = 9, N = 5 |
| Q28 | 5% | 95% | 5% | 95% | W+ = 3.50, W- = 17.50, N = 6 |
| **Dimension 4** | | | | | |
| Q31 | 0% | 100% | 0% | 100% | W+ = 2, W- = 4, N = 3 |
| Q32 | 5% | 95% | 0% | 100% | W+ = 3, W- = 12, N = 5 |
| Q33 | 0% | 100% | 0% | 100% | W+ = 4, W- = 2, N = 3 |
| Q34 | 65% | 35% | 68% | 32% | W+ = 7.50, W- = 7.50, N = 5 |
| Q35 | 5% | 95% | 16% | 84% | W+ = 6, W- = 0, N = 3 |
| Q36 | 10% | 90% | 5% | 95% | W+ = 2.50, W- = 7.50, N = 4 |
| Q37 | 20% | 80% | 26% | 74% | W+ = 10, W- = 0, N = 4* |
| Q38 | 55% | 45% | 47% | 53% | W+ = 5, W- = 5, N = 4 |

*p <=0 at .1 **p <=0 at .05

**Table 8.2.  Rubric scores from the CyberSmart Glog project (N = 23)**

| Rubric items for evaluating CyberSmart Glog | Exceeds | Meets | Below |
|---|---|---|---|
| 1. All six issues are addressed with useful and factual information given | 7 | 13 | 3 |
| 2. Project is understandable, meaningful, and appealing to the age level and any special learning needs of the target group | 20 | 3 | 0 |
| 3. Project is sensitive to and supports the social class, gender, race, ethnicity, language, and sexual orientation differences within the target group | 22 | 1 | 0 |

| 4. Project is creative, artistic, and well-formatted without any spelling or grammatical errors | 8 | 15 | 0 |
|---|---|---|---|

## APPENDIX B

### Directions and Rubric for CyberSmart Glog Project

Assignment instructions: You will be working with a partner on the other side of the Atlantic and in the other hemisphere from where you live (find New Jersey and Namibia on a map). You and your partner will be designing an online Glogster poster which can be used to educate your learners about their rights and responsibilities as a Digital Citizen. Create something that will be understandable and meaningful to the age group that you anticipate teaching. It should include useful information for the children about the following six issues:

1. Cyber-safety (protecting yourself online: keeping your information private, etc.)
2. Cyber-respect (conducting yourself with respect to others: no cyber-bullying, proper netiquette, etc.)
3. Cyber-lawfulness (understanding copyright, fair use, plagiarism, protection from computer viruses, legal ramifications of breaking these laws, etc.)
4. Cyber-health (physical [e.g., carpal tunnel] & psychological [e.g., Internet or video-game addiction], etc.)
5. Cyber-equity (your rights, access [e.g., girls as well as boys, all people-groups, all languages], etc.)
6. Cyber-conservation (minimizing your impact on the environment, power usage, natural resources required, e-waste, etc.)

You can include short video clips (you can use your cellphone), photos, drawings, text passages, audio clips, and so on, to give learners a quick overview of what they should/should not be doing and what their rights are. If you think you will be teaching children whose mother tongue is not English, please provide English and mother-tongue translations of anything you include.

**Table 8.3.    Rubric for Glogster poster**

|  | Exceeds Expectation | Meets Expectation | Below Expectation |
|---|---|---|---|
| Covers all six Digital Citizenship issues | All six issues are addressed with useful and factual information given | All six issues are addressed with a minimal amount of information | One or more of the issues not addressed |
| Age-appropriate-ness and special needs | Project is understandable, meaningful, and appealing to the age level and any special learning needs of the target group | Project is understandable by the target group | Project is not understandable by the target group |
| Formatting, spelling, grammar, creativity | Project is creative, artistic, and well-formatted without any spelling or grammatical errors | Project is well-formatted without any spelling or grammatical errors | Project is not well-formatted and has spelling and/or grammatical errors |
| Respectful of learners' diverse backgrounds | Project is sensitive to and supports the social class, gender, race, ethnicity, language, and sexual orientation differences within the target group | Project is not discriminatory to any member of the target group | Project contains evidence of prejudice against any member of the target group, based on social class, gender, race, ethnicity, language, and sexual orientation differences |

# REFERENCES

Eduventures, Inc. (2008). Strategies to internationalize schools of education [Report No. 06SOECRR0208]. Boston, MA: Author.

International Society for Technology in Education (2008). *ISTE standards for teachers*. Retrieved from http://www.iste.org/docs/pdfs/20-14_ISTE_Standards-T_PDF.pdf.

Kissock, C. & Richardson, P. (2010). Calling for action within the teaching profession: It is time to internationalize teacher education. *Teaching Education, 21* (1), 89–102.

Longview Foundation (2008). *Teacher preparation for the global age: The imperative for change*. Retrieved from http://www.longviewfdn.org/122/teacher-preparation-for-the-global-age.html.

Mahon, J. (2010). Fact or fiction? Analyzing institutional barriers and individual responsibility to advance the internationalization of teacher education. *Teaching Education, 21* (1), 7–18.

Malone, T. & Wilder, H. (2008). Chasing Ubuntu: Using ICTs to promote reflective practice. *Multicultural Education and Technology Journal, 2* (2), 118–125.

Marx, H. & Moss, D. M. (2011). *MyCAP: My cultural awareness profile tool* (1st Ed.). Washington, DC: NAFSA: Association of International Educators.

Merryfield, M. (2008). The challenge of globalization: Preparing teachers for a global age. *Teacher Education and Practice, 21* (4), 434–437.

Ochoa, A. (2010). International education in higher education: A developing process of engagement in teacher education programs. *Teaching Education, 21* (1), 103–112.

Quezada, R. (Ed.) (2012). Internationalization of teacher education: Creating globally competent teachers and teacher educators for the 21st century. New York: Routledge. (Also available as a special issue of *Teaching Education, 21* (1), 2010.)

Quezada, R. & Cordeiro, A. (Eds.) (2009). Internationalizing schools and colleges of education: Educating teachers for global awareness [Special Issue]. *Teacher Education Quarterly, 34* (1). Retrieved from http://www.teqjournal.org/TEQpercent20Website/Backpercent20Issues/Volumepercent2034/Volumepercent2034percent20Numberpercent201.html.

Roberts, A. (2007). Global dimensions of schooling: Implications for internationalizing teacher education. *Teacher Education Quarterly, 34* (1), 9–26.

Schneider, A. I. (2003). Internationalizing teacher education: What can be done? A research report on the undergraduate training of secondary school teachers. [ERIC Document Reproduction Service No. ED 480869] Washington, DC: Department of Education.

Sprague, D. (2012). Expanding Horizons through Technology for Teachers and Students, in B. D. Shaklee & S. Baily (Eds.), *Internationalizing Teacher Education in the United States.* Lanham, MD: Rowman & Littlefield.

Wilder, H. (2007). Using e-learning to globalize a teacher education program, in R. C. Sharma & S. Mishra (Eds.), *Cases on Global e-Learning Practices: Successes and Pitfalls* (pp. 73–81). Hershey, PA: IDEA Group, Inc.

Wilder, H. & Feola, D. (2014, April 24). *Why internationalize education? Outcomes on 3 dimensions*, invited presentation given at the annual Teaching the World Forum, Graduate School of Education, Rutgers University, New Brunswick, NJ.

Wilder, H., Ferris, S., & An, H. (2010). Exploring international multicultural field experiences in educational technology. *Multicultural Education and Technology Journal, 4* (1), 30–42.

Wilder, H. & Malone, T. (2005). Intercultural technology education for preservice teachers in Namibia and New Jersey. *Contemporary Issues in Technology & Teacher Education, 4* (4), 456–464. Retrieved from http://www.citejournal.org/vol4/iss4/currentpractice/article1.cfm.

*Chapter Nine*

# Our Twelve-Year Journey Internationalizing In-service Science Education

Jacalyn Giacalone Willis, Katrina Macht,
and Marya Burke

## INTRODUCTION

This chapter recounts the twelve-year Rainforest Connection (RFC) journey and what was learned from the experiences of in-service teachers and their students who came together with other cultures and scientists as a result of the digital connections. The process of writing this chapter helped the authors crystallize both the "model" of the RFC for internationalizing in-service teacher education, as well as its contribution to promote social justice, through open access to high-quality science education. This story is told through narrative in order to convey the thick descriptions of the rich cultural context and educational content of the journey of a colorful and ambitious project that took on a life of its own. We chose to use narrative because it is through stories we are able to make meaning of our world. As Lather (2006) and St. Pierre (2004) explain, "narrative thinking humanizes the field of educational research in ways conventional methods cannot." As a way to understand experience, it places the individual's story front and center, and establishes a milieu within which to frame the discourse.

As this chapter unfolds in the telling and interpretation of the journey, we will use the results of our project evaluation research to unpack the outcomes and lessons learned by our leadership group. These lessons helped us to develop the model we will share with our readers, one that can be applied in low-cost and highly effective ways, to enhance both the science education of

K–12 students, and the content knowledge and internationalization of participating teachers. The chapter starts by describing the setting and participants,
including the philosophical foundations of the project, moves onward to
show what the project looks like in action, and ends by illuminating the path
forward through the lessons we learned.

## SETTING AND PARTICIPANTS
## OF THE RAINFOREST CONNECTION

### The Setting

The home setting for the journey is PRISM, housed in a university-based
science education center, now serving the in-service needs of K–12 teachers
in more than sixty school districts in New Jersey, and funded by government,
corporate, and private foundation sources. In alignment with the National
Science Education Standards (1996), the New Jersey Core Curriculum Content Standards (2009), and, recently, the Next Generation Science Standards
(2013), the program applies a constructivist and inquiry-based framework to
teach science content and pedagogy to in-service teachers.

PRISM is the home program base that gave rise to the RFC, which has
used one of several technology-based platforms that spawned programs
around the world with videoconferencing as one program component. Two
projects in particular—The Flat Classroom Project and Global Nomads
Group—share a number of commonalities with the RFC, but each project is
unique in its own right. Both projects use digital tools for international collaboration, and emphasize global learning to break down cultural barriers and
stereotypes (Ferriter, 2010; Global Nomads Group, 2014).

The Flat Classroom Project is a humanities-based program targeting
upper middle and high school students. It uses such tools of technology as
online discussion boards, videoconferences, e-mail, and e-chats to link students for global collaborations. Once students from two or more different
classes are connected, they work together to study one of the global movements featured in Friedman's *The World Is Flat* (Ferriter, 2010; Friedman,
2005). Participating students collaborate, using a group wiki to research a
particular topic and then create meaningful artifacts. In addition, students
create personal videos not only to share with each other, but also to submit
for judging at the conclusion of the project (Lindsay & Davis, 2012).

The Global Nomad Group (2014) also uses digital tools to connect classrooms from two or more different countries. Again targeting middle and high
school students the group's mission is to "foster dialogue and understanding
among the world's youth" (Global Nomads Group, 2014, *About GNG*, p. 1).
Using interactive videoconferencing, webcasting, social networking, gaming,
and film making, the organization offers virtual exchange programs that run

for either a single semester or all of the school year between students in North America and youth in Africa, Asia, and the Middle East, as well as within North America. Choosing either the STEM-based or civic engagement curriculum, educators are required to receive either virtual or in-person professional development on the program's pedagogy and content before beginning a project.

Although similar in some ways, the RFC is distinctly unique from these and other technology-based programs in a number of ways. First and foremost, professional development of in-service teachers is a more central feature of RFC than it is for either of the two previously described projects. While professional development is included in the Flat Classroom and Global Nomads Group programs, it is targeted at guiding teachers to effectively implement the respective projects. Professional development associated with the RFC, on the other hand, is geared toward fostering greater scientific literacy and supporting K–12 in-service teachers in their pursuit to become more effective science educators. It emphasizes the skills and strategies necessary to creating globally minded science classrooms that are constructivist and inquiry-based. Most participating RFC teachers have received extensive professional development before bringing RFC into their classrooms. Once they begin participating, face-to-face conversations via videoconference are RFC's cornerstone. These videoconference conversations provide opportunities for rich collaborations between practicing scientists in the field and youth of all ages in classrooms across the globe.

## Participants

This section is designed to introduce the researchers of this chapter as well as the profile of the participating in-service teachers.

## The Researchers

The RFC project would not have happened if certain circumstances had not brought together a mix of personalities that created a synergy of creativity, expertise, and technology. Because the lives and expertise of the three authors shaped the philosophical framework and the evolution of the in-service program model described in this chapter, we introduce ourselves here:

*Jacalyn Giacalone Willis* is both a scientist and a professional development designer. She is an ecologist with a doctorate in biology and forty years' experience in tropical forests, specializing in mammal population dynamics. She has twenty-five years' experience as a professional developer in K–12 science education. Willis is the founding director of Professional Resources in Science & Mathematics (PRISM), a professional development center for STEM education at Montclair State University, with a staff of scientists, mathematicians, former K–12 teachers, and administrative person-nel. She created the RFC project, using the Internet to connect K–12 class-rooms globally with researchers at the Smithsonian Tropical Research Insti-tute in Panama, the main location for her research. As a biologist, she carries out field research in a tropical forest at this field station, which had online access early in the inception of the Internet. As early e-mail users in 1998, it seemed natural to include PRISM's in-service teacher-participants and their classes in discussions of the research—how it is accomplished and what the results show—first through in-person workshops in New Jersey, followed by e-mail journal entries sent to participating teachers and addressed to their classes. Students were invited to respond to these correspondences via the project we called the Rainforest Connection. An exchange of journal entries, questions, and responses was carried on by e-mail long before blogging was ever invented. With the improvement of Internet bandwidth that permitted two-way video, the RFC became a videoconference project.

*Katrina Macht* is a sixth grade science and English teacher in a New Jersey public school district. She is a curriculum specialist with expertise in environmental education. For the past several years she has worked with the RFC project of PRISM to link scientists in the field to classrooms throughout the United States by way of interactive video webcasts. She is currently a doctoral candidate for the EdD in pedagogy program at Montclair State Uni-versity.

*Marya Burke* is an educational researcher, evaluator, and editor specializing in educational programming. She received her doctorate from the University of Illinois at Urbana-Champaign in education policy studies. Her primary interests include equity studies, teacher education, parental involvement, and approaches to assessment.

## Participating In-service Teachers

The teacher participants in the RFC play critical roles in outreach to minority students. Within the twenty-three participating schools across fourteen dif-ferent districts in 2014, approximately 45 percent of the students were African American or Hispanic/Latino, with another two percent Native American. Although a statistically low number, this Native American in-volvement is nonetheless meaningful, because this particular U.S. population is traditionally underserved, underrepresented, and often difficult to reach at all levels in science. Ten of the participating schools had 75 percent or more of students receiving free or reduced lunch. Two schools in Panama partici-pated as well as the U.S. schools.

## DATA COLLECTION AND ANALYSIS

In order to write this chapter, the data collected were triangulated. We used all previous reports developed during the past twelve years since the inception of the project, looking at archival materials as well as anecdotal records we collected during our past experiences in the program. The data included surveys, interviews, focus groups, and feedback sent by e-mail immediately after connections.

We used an emergent theme analysis (Denzin & Lincoln, 2011; Lincoln & Guba, 1985) in order to answer our research questions. The analysis revealed a very clear model for the implementation of the program. Moreover, they provided a thick description of the RFC as a basis for other researchers to follow. One of the aims of qualitative research is to describe in detail educational experiences created for teachers as an important part of this research tradition.

## RESEARCH QUESTIONS

This chapter is centered on the following three research questions:

1. What is the underlying model of the RFC to internationalize in-service science teacher education for social justice?
2. What does the RFC program look like in action?
3. How does the RFC align with social justice goals?

## FINDINGS

This section of the chapter will restate each one of the research questions followed by its appropriate answer.

*What is the underlying model of the RFC to internationalize in-service science teacher education for social justice?*

The various evaluation results have been important in shaping the RFC model for professional development and for implementation of classroom teaching. The model evolved into a four-part RFC experience that transforms how teachers think about science, teaching, and the world through summer institutes, follow-up academic-year workshops, and mentoring in classrooms. The philosophical framework of the in-service model was developed by the PRISM staff for a variety of in-service experiences, but was then tailored and expanded to address the needs for internationalizing the in-service program and connecting teachers with scientists. The RFC philosophical model can be characterized as:

1. Engage teachers in constructivist, hands-on, reflective, interactive, international learning experiences in workshops, both indoors and outdoors, that model how science investigations are practiced.
2. Implement similar hands-on, reflective student experiences in classrooms so that students are doing science, using experiential methodologies while interacting with other students, all modeled in the classroom by their now-experienced teachers.
3. Create curriculum materials developed by experienced teachers to implement and spread the experiential approaches.
4. Cultivate teacher-leaders who can spread the teaching and learning approaches of the model to other teachers in their own schools and beyond.

The RFC in-service model is usually co-facilitated by teams of experienced teachers and practicing research scientists. This partnership has stimulated social interactions among scientists, teachers, and their students that have had long-term consequences and resulted in expansion of the in-service model in innovative ways.

What we call the RFC philosophy of teaching—teachers using concrete, hands-on, minds-on experiences—is heavily influenced by the science education methodologies of Lawrence Lowery (1998, 2002). The model evolved to include lively interactive conversations with scientists about their work as well as international learning components about teaching, researching, and living in other cultures.

Further analysis of the data collected highlights some of the effective components of the program:

- *Students characterize the RFC model as a "different way to learn."* Differences included: the opportunity to talk with real scientists; the experience of the real rainforest; the absence of typical learning structures—learning that did not involve books, lecturing, or their teacher; qualities of the experience or participation; the use of videoconference technology; and seeing video clips of animals shot by the teachers and scientists at the remote site. Broadly speaking, reality is important to students. As one student put it,

  These are real scientists in a real rainforest, taking movies like home videos and not a staged National Geographic film made for TV . . . and we can talk with them about their real experiences!

- *Teachers value the engagement of their students.* Teachers expressed that the most beneficial aspects of the video sessions were students' motivation and inspiration from interacting with the scientists and students' science learning as aligned with educational goals. Teachers variously commented that getting students' attention was never an issue during the video chats.

- *Teachers traveling to the field site and, as a result, becoming leaders.* Teachers who participate by traveling to the field site are clearly moved by the experience, and it is unquestionably a valuable motivator for continued learning and growth for them. They spoke of feeling a level of enrichment and engagement that would stay with them for years. This was seen as both a personal benefit and a professional one. As one participant said, "rich experiences make rich teachers." Teachers who went to the Panama site spoke most enthusiastically about how they would build on the experience in future activities with their students.

- *Interactive design as a crucial aspect of the experience.* Teachers found that this "video-chat" format, allowing for direct contact between students and scientists, offers a critical feature of best practice in instruction. Many of the teachers prepared the students ahead of the conferences, helping them develop a base of prior knowledge that they could draw on to engage more effectively when faced with the "expert" in the field. This is also part of teaching with best practice. Students were clearly engaged by this method. They responded enthusiastically to the videos and frequently asked unprompted and unprepared questions that showed they were thinking outside any preset plan. In a touching example, one kindergarten student, upon learning about a species of fig tree that withholds nectar from the offspring of fig wasps as "a punitive" action against mother wasps who do not "pay back" the tree in return for food supplied, asked, "Why do the babies have to pay for what the mamma fig wasps do bad?"

- *The RFC experience enables students to develop more realistic and meaningful understandings* of science as it is practiced and the rainforest as a real place. In this manner, they could then transfer and apply the ecological concepts from the rainforest to their own observations of local environments. Teachers noted that their students gained insights into what scientists actually do as a profession. They were excited to understand that "science could mean traveling to the rainforest and watching a variety of animals." Students also learned that scientists come in all shapes, sizes, and colors, so to speak. Teachers noted that the design was especially powerful for children who are not served well by the standard approaches of the classroom, who are able to connect with the RFC information, see the real-world careers they could pursue, and see that they can do this too.

- *Use of technology as an educational tool.* Teachers noted that students may have little experience with technology; in many school settings, there are limited resources for equipment, and the students lack these resources at home, as well. For others, their use of technology is fairly limited, often consisting of gaming and social networking that does not necessarily contribute to their understandings of the world around them or of the possibilities technology can offer. The use of the computer and the Web in the RFC provides a meaningful way to breach these limitations.

## What Does RFC Look Like in Action?

Brain research studies show that the best way to learn and help learners retain knowledge is to provide them with firsthand experiences (Lowery, 1998; Shapiro, 1994). This is especially true when learning science. However, first-hand experiences are not always possible, particularly experiences in remote locations around the globe. What can teachers do to connect students to topics not directly accessible to them? How can we provide firsthand experiences that reach beyond the walls of our classrooms? Videoconferencing technology is one such medium. It provides the framework for individuals and groups to meet in "real time" through video, to converse and learn together.

The methods for accomplishing the videoconferences themselves are simple. Teachers need to have a computer connected to the Internet, a projector or large TV so that the entire class can view the Web-streamed video, a webcam, a microphone, and speakers. Teachers are required to test their equipment and connection prior to the actual videoconference by calling in to an RFC staff member who can assist with troubleshooting. The conference call is made through software that is licensed to Montclair State University. A link is provided to the teacher, and the software downloads quickly once linked. The software permits participants to show images and videos for sharing with other participants in a separate window. More than one class can join at a time, and participants at different sites can see and hear each other, as well as show various media.

The heart of the RFC story is told in vignettes that were written by the second author, Katrina Macht, a classroom teacher who made valuable contributions to the development of the project since its inception. Four vignettes were selected to represent important aspects of the project that directly impact the internationalization of teaching and learning for in-service teachers, and improve social justice. The vignettes mirror the RFC model of professional development:

1. Teachers' hands-on experiences with the RFC team at a rainforest research station;
2. Experiences of a student not in the rainforest, but at home in the classroom;
3. Curriculum and narrative resources developed as products of the RFC; and
4. Teacher leadership that spreads the teaching practices.

## Vignette #1: In the Rainforest — A Teacher's Experiences

*A typical morning in Panama starts before dawn with a chorus of howler monkeys just outside my window. I am up early to prepare for this day's video connections with classes, collecting artifacts I want to share with the students and organizing photos and videos. I prepare by combing through books, talking with scientists about their research, and, very important, walking the forest trails, documenting the island's diverse flora and fauna. Finally, I am in front of the webcam, waving to my students in New Jersey.*

*"Good morning! Today, class, we have a special treat: I have a guest here who is a scientist studying mammals on this island. Please say hello to Dr. Willis."*

*The discussion opens up to a free-wheeling description of the forest and a research project, illustrated with photos and video clips. The students are asked to compare with the less diverse ecosystem in their community. When a student asks how we know how many monkeys are on the island, the discussion turns to the methods used to study the animal life. When another student asks what the monkeys eat and what eats the monkeys, the talk turns to food webs, and how we know who eats whom, and so on for the next forty-five minutes. Every student asks a question or shares a piece of information, and every student gets a response from the scientist. Every student is engaged, and everyone has a chance to shine: all voices are heard, and the lessons I hoped to teach were "covered" without resort to textbook or lecture in the usual sense. This is what I came for.*

Experiencing firsthand the work of a scientist in an international setting and then sharing that work with other classroom teachers is often a transformational event for the educators. Such firsthand experiences usually lead to teaching without or beyond the textbook, with teachers rediscovering the power of learning as it occurs naturally, and to retention that is long-term and connected to multiple meanings in complex understandings of science concepts.

Thus, the second vignette tells a story of how the project experiences play out in an actual classroom. One of the hallmarks of the project is that it offers an engaging and interactive science learning environment for students who are otherwise disenfranchised, disenchanted, or disabled in the usual learning environments. The RFC director's anecdotal experiences in classroom visits to develop student discourse about research methods had already convinced her that the "special education" student population is a vast untapped and wasted human resource that can be activated by a nontraditional classroom environment and approach. As Calabrese Barton (2003) stresses, "We believe strongly that unless and until an approach to science and science education in our urban classrooms focuses on what it might mean to create a more just world, then we will fall short of our goal of truly building a science education for all" (p. 18). Such a just world must be inclusive of a variety of learning styles, thinking patterns, and personal interests, like those of the student in the next vignette.

## Vignette #2: In the Classroom—Student Experiences

*Because of frigid weather, students were rarely allowed out for recess that winter, and Jeremiah was growing increasingly unmanageable. A special-needs poor, black male adolescent, in a mostly white, affluent suburb, Jeremiah was the poster child of systemic failure. Academically unsuccessful as well as unruly, he spent more of those dreary days in the principal's office than anywhere else. When I assigned research projects, Jeremiah did not respond well. After a rocky start he began to take an interest in research projects the other students were developing. At first he was more of an observer than participant, until one day I accidentally discovered his favorite topic: SNAKES! From that point forward there was no stopping Jeremiah. He was the expert in the room and came alive preparing for the upcoming video chats with a rainforest scientist. He conducted research, wrote articles, created illustrations, and organized an impressive poster presentation to teach his classmates and the school community about snakes and their importance in forest ecosystems. At last the day of the long-awaited RFC lesson arrived, and that same troubled adolescent of just a month ago was the first to arrive to my classroom, so that he could get "the best seat in the house." He wanted to be front and center, and took an enthusiastic lead when engaged in conversations with the scientists nearly 3,000 miles away. He eagerly shared his personal passion with the scientists, asking relevant questions, interjecting his own insights and newfound knowledge about snakes and their roles in food webs. Certain the live snake had been caught especially for him, Jeremiah's face lit up when a vine snake made an up-close appearance on the broadcast that day.*

*Jeremiah's learning interests were validated, and he was motivated to further pursue new research questions. The experience was not a magic bullet; he was still frequently found in the principal's office in subsequent months; however, in the scheme of his overall learning experiences, Jeremiah had tasted classroom success and been encouraged to see the value of academic learning.*

Transformation of how students think of themselves and empowerment to learn are two of the goals the RFC team is able to attain. These are critical components of teaching for social justice, which will be discussed below (Calabrese Barton & Upadhyay, 2010). Jeremiah was resistant to traditional classroom learning experiences and did not practice acceptable classroom behavior, but he did respond to an atypical science experience. Jeremiah's passion was for snakes—a passion fed by the videoconference on "Adaptations of Snakes." His teacher used the moment to create a unit of study based on what had meaning for Jeremiah. Surrounding the video experience was an entire learning landscape, not just one video connection, that empowered Jeremiah to be successful and confident in this learning environment.

According to Calabrese Barton (2003), social justice in education is based on power, control, and identity:

> Student resistance is an active process that students use to make claim to their own space in schools and by which students and teachers negotiate control in schools—control over identity, over what schooling is about, and over relationships and respect. (p. 69)

Success in the form of social justice also requires program sustainability, which in turn requires reaching teachers within their curriculum. The third vignette takes us to some of the curriculum models that spread these approaches to other teachers, so that the components of the program are adopted and have a good "fit" in their teaching plans.

## Vignette #3: In the Curriculum

*I had a significant number of struggling students, who were reading and writing below grade level, and seemed to have already given up on themselves as scholars. They were, however, interested in "doing science," and came to life whenever there was a hands-on investigation. My dilemma was how do I marry that love of hands-on science with the critical need to become better readers and writers, not to mention better thinkers? One major science unit of study was ecosystems. The Rainforest Connection website provided resources to supplement existing curriculum and help me better integrate science with reading and writing. Science became the content, reading and writing the tools needed to learn that content. My students thought we were "doing science" all day, when in fact language arts was the main thrust of our day.*

The overarching goals and objectives of the RFC address the New Jersey Core Curriculum Content Standards and the 21st-Century Life and Careers Standards (2009). Teachers can use the RFC curriculum models to improve scientific practices through hands-on, inquiry-based investigations and interactions with working scientists. While some teachers choose to use the videoconference as a stand-alone cameo appearance to create some classroom excitement, many teachers choose to build a multifaceted curriculum experience that embraces the connection to the scientists in personal ways and extends the learning in rich and relevant ways. In such plans, students work collaboratively to understand the lives of scientists and how they carry out their research. Students may pose, refine, and evaluate questions; design investigations; and use scientific instrumentation to collect, analyze, and evaluate evidence. Students may also gather, evaluate, and represent evidence using scientific tools, technologies, and computational strategies. In many introductory or culminating curricular experiences, students may engage in productive scientific discussion about practices with scientists and peers, both face-to-face and virtually, to learn about scientific concepts and principles.

Students may use mathematical, physical, and computational tools to build conceptual-based models and to pose interpretations of natural phenomena. Some of the most satisfying and productive projects have integrated reading, writing, science, technology, mathematics, and the arts. One mathematics teacher planned with an RFC scientist to deliver an engaging lesson on how to use sampling and understanding of ratios and proportions to estimate population size, using observed mammal numbers with marking techniques from census data from Panama. Another teacher in language arts classes helped her students design "postcards from the rainforest" that were developed, written, and illustrated through conversations with a scientist about ecological principles, and illustrated specific examples of those principles.

The RFC fosters meaningful learning experiences such as those described in the Common Core State Standards (2010): interaction with complex, nonfiction text; conducting independent research; writing technically; and using technology strategically. As the Standards state, "Students must be able to read complex informational texts in these fields with independence and confidence because the vast majority of reading in college and workforce training programs will be sophisticated nonfiction" (p. 60).

Our final vignette is about becoming a teacher-leader. Katrina Macht, author of all these vignettes, is a skilled professional development designer as well as an instructional leader in her district, and often provides workshops for PRISM. Here she describes her personal growth as an educator.

## Vignette #4—Teachers as Leaders: Sharing the Knowledge and Practices

*I was invited to travel to Barro Colorado Island as a member of the videoconference team. My role was to help facilitate videoconferences between scientists at the field station on the island and students throughout the United States, including my own. It has been a transformative experience. To witness firsthand the interconnected themes of tropical ecology and biodiversity within a verdant Panamanian forest has afforded me the opportunity to link classroom learning to real-world scientific research in rich and meaningful ways. The knowledge I have gained by being able to walk the forest's trails, and study the plants and animals I see there, has deepened my understanding of ecological principles and in turn made me a better classroom teacher. I*

*may not be able to take my science classes on "field trips" to remote loca-
tions like tropical rainforests, but with the use of videoconferencing technology I have been able to open new doors to these remarkable worlds. By
providing students with opportunities to talk directly with working scientists
conducting field research, scientific research has come to life for them.*

The PRISM team has developed through various projects several cohorts
of experienced teacher-leaders who can facilitate effective professional development experiences for in-service teachers. Of all the projects, the development of RFC teacher-leaders has been the most effective for a variety of
reasons. The additional international component of the RFC leadership development gives the RFC teachers an added layer of experience that cannot
be attained by staying on the home campus. These teachers have travel experience, they have met and studied with scientists, they have had hands-on
work in tropical ecosystems, they are aware of environmental and social
issues in a global context, and they have befriended teachers in other nations.
Their well-rounded education not only gives them a cachet of experience, but
it also makes them particularly sensitive to the needs and shortcomings of
teachers at home and to the ways in which facilitation helps teachers become
more effective in the classroom.

*How Does the RFC Align with Social Justice Goals?*

Based on all the data gathered and analyzed as part of this research project,
the researchers found that the RFC aligns with social justice in the following
ways:

- It provides access to science education to all through inexpensive Internet
  technology;
- It provides access to high-quality science education through scientists,
  teacher-leaders, internationalized content, and effective teaching approaches;
- It provides learning experiences that are student-centered, that address the
  personal needs and interests of students;
- It provides experiences that break down biases to gender, ethnicity, race,
  and economic status.

Access to high-quality educational experiences is a foundational tenet of
social justice goals. As the UN states:

> Unlike any other medium, the Internet enables individuals to seek, receive and
> impart information and ideas of all kinds instantaneously and inexpensively
> across national borders. By vastly expanding the capacity of individuals to
> enjoy their right to freedom of opinion and expression, which is an "enabler"
> of other human rights, the Internet boosts economic, social and political devel-

opment, and contributes to the progress of humankind as a whole. (UN Special Rapporteur report, May 2011)

In keeping with this goal of access, the RFC was designed to bring scientists located in various global locations directly to classrooms for meaningful discussions of science and science practices with K–12 students and their teachers in a variety of economic, ethnic, racial, and geographic communities. As Dimick (2012) writes,

> Science educators recognize that issues of equity within their field include creating more equitable access and opportunity for students, particularly among students from communities that have been marginalized from participating in science education and pursuing science careers. (p. 992)

The annual RFC programs have become important windows for diverse students to see into the worlds of science. In support of the live telecasts, archived podcast programs that extend access to the RFC have been available free to the public on YouTube and the university website: http://montclair.edu/csam/prism.

However, social justice in science education involves more than simple access. It means addressing ways to provide opportunities for students that are similar to those educational experiences found in the best schools; to offer access to effective educational experiences provided by teachers who are well-versed in science content and pedagogy; and to take care to validate the knowledge and experiences of all students. Thus, one purpose of this chapter is to show how some important issues in social justice can be addressed through simple, cost-effective methods that stimulate learning and help in-service teachers provide sound science content through help from volunteer science experts in international settings.

When Carter (2010) remarks that modern science is part of the "ecology of knowledges," he means that Western science is only one way of interpreting the world. Carter (2010) points out,

> Western science has also been coproductive of hegemonic interests resulting in many unintended consequences not least of which is the global environmental crisis with which we are all faced. (p. 437)

The RFC bridges these knowledges through developing awareness in teachers that helps them view the world through several lenses, not just their own personal lens.

Many of the RFC teachers are teachers of impoverished urban students in underserved schools, children of subsistence farmers, non-English speakers, children of immigrants, children with severe physical disabilities, incarcerated children in U.S. justice system facilities, or children classified as "special needs" or requiring "special education." These children pose challenges to the RFC staff and collaborating scientists and teachers, but the attitude has been that we must find ways to engage all students in meaningful discussions about science, and help them understand how to access science and make it part of their lives.

The RFC staff aspires to focus on how to grab onto those powerful learning moments that intersect with children's lives and use those moments to draw students into learning science. The RFC has been a tool many teachers have used to gain admittance to the negotiating table and help students stake that claim to space and empowerment in ways that are acceptable in classrooms while not destroying student identities. The personal needs, issues, and life experiences of students can be such that their world is on the other side of a chasm between children and the practices of science, such that the role of teacher might be to build bridges between children and science. Calabrese Barton (2003) describes the nature of that chasm through stories of children in poverty learning science in meaningful ways. She compiled and summarized the data from several sources that illustrate the issues of inequities in science education that impact children in poverty, noting that they "have decreased access to rigorous courses, books, scientific equipment, compensatory programs, or qualified teachers; and drop out of school at higher rates than those of their more affluent and suburban counterparts" (p. 7).

The RFC points out one of the major ironies in access to science education. The program has its origins and twelve-year history closely tied to one field research station in Panama, one of the oldest field stations in the world, nearly one hundred years old, and one of the most studied pieces of natural real estate anywhere on the planet. It is run by a unit of the Smithsonian Institution in Washington, DC, and is a U.S. federal facility that houses scientists from countries all around the world who collectively study the flora, fauna, and geology of the area. The island is reached only by Smithsonian boat and only after permits are obtained. It is about one hour by car and another half-hour by boat from bustling, overcrowded Panama City. The island is covered in forest that has been protected from cutting and poaching for many years, and provides a home to animals that are difficult to observe in other parts of Panama because of hunting pressure from humans. Tours and school groups visit it, but for most children in Panama, the forest is a totally new and somewhat frightening experience. Densely populated Panama City has a large metropolitan park that is protected and is home to many of the native species, but most schools do not provide field trips; and the rainforest is as alien to these urban Panamanians as it is to children in New Jersey . . . maybe more so. Most Panamanians who live in this country with amazing biodiversity do not have personal experience with their wildlife, have never met a Panamanian scientist, and have little access to information about or opportunity to visit these protected natural areas that still conserve much of that diversity.

Dimick (2012, p. 1009) notes, "Science acts as a gate-keeping subject, and access to science skills can lead to higher status knowledge and socioeconomic success." Providing access to nontraditional role models, practitioners of science who are capable of meaningful discourse with youngsters, and to teachers with enhanced science content knowledge are important goals of the RFC that move forward the ideals of social justice in science education and may have the power to transform lives. As Calabrese Barton and Upadhyay (2010, p. 2) elaborate in their discussion about the difference between "socially just teaching" and "teaching science for social justice" using ideas from Moje (2007):

> On the one hand, socially just science teaching is about access and opportunity: All children deserve the right to good teachers, to adequate materials, and to a chance to succeed on society's terms whether that be a grade or a test score. Teaching science for social justice, on the other hand, not only provides access to mainstream knowledge and practices but also provides opportunities to question, challenge, and reconstruct knowledge. Social justice pedagogy should, in other words, offer possibilities for transformation, not only of the learner but also of the social and political contexts in which learning and other social action take place. (p. 2)

## MOVING FORWARD

The last part of this chapter deals with insights gained from this project useful for other teacher educators interested in internationalizing in-service teacher education programs within a social justice framework. The following section will be divided into two sections: facing challenges and taking advantage of opportunities.

## FACING CHALLENGES

Over a twelve-year history of an ambitious project it is inevitable that challenges will be multitudinous, but that opportunities also arise from unexpected sources. These challenges include:

1. Overcoming gender bias in students' and teachers' concepts of scientists;
2. Confronting the rigidity of government standards and testing;
3. Addressing the lack of preparedness of scientists to teach K–12 students; and

4. Reaching out to developing nations and school districts in the United States that have limited resources.

*Overcoming gender bias in students' and teachers' concepts of scientists*

The PRISM staff have for many years used "Draw-A-Scientist" pre- and post-assessments for teachers and students, often with discouraging results that depict scientists as white males in lab-coats working in a chemistry-style lab, creating explosions, or scientists who resemble TV or movie villains and heroes. However, in recent trials with educators in Honduras and students in Panama, we were gratified to see a majority of scientists depicted in a variety of ethnic and racial groups, often as women, in various research styles, often outdoors, and dressed in fashion trends that showed realistic views of such people at work. Students of teachers who participated in The Rainforest Connection Live! often send the staff their drawings of scientists and have been submitting realistic drawings of what scientists do and their surroundings, how they do their work, or show themselves as they envision life as a scientist.

*Confronting the rigidity of government standards and testing*

Curriculum, standards, and statewide testing have often made it difficult to bring the RFC into some schools because school administrators and teachers often take these documents literally and rigidly, and fail to see the ways in which the RFC helps students address those performance standards. This is especially troubling in secondary schools, where the endless refrain is, "I have too much to cover in the textbook!" When high school science is finally released from the confines of lecturing and textbook-based curriculum, we will all be able to help more students stay engaged in science, understand the real world of science and engineering practices, and think critically. This "sea change" in attitude is already in process in New Jersey with the 2014 adoption of the Next Generation Science Standards. Alignment to these standards takes the RFC style of teaching front and center in curriculum development when partnered with in-service programs that will deepen the global perspective, content knowledge, and classroom practices of teachers.

*Addressing the lack of preparedness of scientists to teach K–12 students*

Not just any scientist can talk productively with students. This should not be surprising because scientists rarely have any training in pedagogy, and very few are gifted naturally as teachers. The RFC programs have included a Swedish woman, for example, who studies fig wasps that pollinate the ecologically significant wild fig trees of tropical forests. She studies the behaviors of the wasps and how the trees can cultivate the relationship so that more fig flowers are pollinated, resulting in more seeds and better reproduction by both the trees and their pollinator wasps. She was able, with help from RFC staff and well-planned media illustrations, to convey the concepts of pollination and symbiosis to a kindergarten class in Connecticut. The children were engaged and asked questions spontaneously that showed that they understood the lessons. On the other hand, some scientists talking with somewhat older children have had difficulty maintaining engagement with the students even though the topic was not so esoteric as fig wasps and seemed exciting when planned, but was flat in delivery. The main issue was clearly the very serious and monotonous style of delivery that used too many unfamiliar scientific terms. It is clear that choosing appropriate scientists and providing coaching in style and vocabulary is an important key to success. One way to make this work better is to pair a scientist with a teacher who has had some experience in the program and can act as "translator" and host, eliciting deeper explanations as needed by the audience and filling in with explanations or questions when necessary.

*Reaching out to developing nations and school districts in the United States that have limited resources*

Reaching schools in New Jersey had for many years posed great challenges in overcoming teacher reluctance to use the technology so readily available at universities and businesses. Even school "tech specialists" had issues with opening firewalls for a specific two-way connection time and link. Now, with so many New Jersey schools using smartboards and Internet digital textbooks, the difficulties at home have been mostly resolved, and the RFC staff have been putting more resources toward helping developing nations use the RFC. Outreach has included some donations of webcams to teachers in other nations who could not otherwise be connected. The RFC team has also worked with IT companies in other countries to open their doors to schools to visit for RFC events at their corporate offices.

## TAKING ADVANTAGE OF OPPORTUNITIES

Some special opportunities arise each year as the RFC director collaborates with scientists in other countries that have resulted in:

1. The creation of a network of international science researchers interested in K–12 education.
2. Expanding RFC experiences to nontraditional students.
3. The use of RFC for preservice international programs.

*The creation of a network of international science researchers interested in K–12 education*

The creation of a network of international researchers has made it possible for researchers to report on findings and observations in video sessions directly from eco-lodges in the high-altitude cloud forests of western Panama, montane rainforest and coastal mangroves in Thailand, and rainforest in eastern Australia. An important asset of the program has been the opportunities for cultural exchanges. These have included connecting participants with the cultures of research scientists who live a life centered on research in the natural world; working scientists from international cultures, whose research takes them to many remote locations; women scientists who work in nonlaboratory settings and study natural ecosystems; classrooms from different nations that may connect in real time with partnered classrooms; and American urban and suburban or rural communities that demonstrate the diversity of communities in our own state and nation.

*Expanding RFC experiences to nontraditional students*

The RFC is opening windows for students who are unable to attend a traditional school, such as students with severe disabilities. In New York City, students who have physical disabilities such that they must attend class on gurneys or with motorized wheelchairs and support equipment may attend special schools that develop programming tailored for them. The RFC has reached such students, taking them to places and meeting people they would not ordinarily meet in their limited environments.

*The use of RFC for preservice international programs*

Being able to teach a class of preservice teachers in Madagascar was a wonderful opportunity and a landmark in the international expansion of the program. We anticipate that several of those student teachers will soon be using RFC methods and resources even if they have to take their classes to Internet cafés to find a broadband connection.

## CONCLUSIONS

Writing this chapter helped us crystallize a concept of the model that works, so that what we developed intuitively has become more palpable to us. By describing this model we hope that we can help others transpose the model to other content, disciplines, cultures, or locations to create new and effective international programs that address the needs of in-service teachers and their students.

Maybe the most important conclusion from this journey is the uniqueness of our work by establishing a viable model for internationalizing in-service teacher education programs. The RFC project has had ongoing internal evaluation as well as two external evaluations. This evaluation process made it possible to take stock of the current state of the project as a way both to broaden international outlooks through science education and to define the successful components of the model. However, the ongoing evaluation process also helped us define and refine the RFC model. The model that developed for the RFC parallels the PRISM model of professional development through a four-step process of

1. Engaging teachers in hands-on, constructivist, reflective, international learning experiences;
2. Engaging students in similar experiences that involve interaction with scientists;
3. Creating effective, standards-based curriculum materials; and
4. Cultivating teacher-leaders who can help spread the teaching approaches of the model.

What is different from the foundational PRISM model is that the RFC model incorporates internationalized lessons, and interaction with scientists to model how to be international or global in outlook, as part of a scientific culture and within international settings.

Based on our own experiences, developing your own model for the implementation of your personal internationalization experiences is crucial to the success of any such effort.

PRISM in general and RFC in particular effectively reach large numbers of underserved students with valuable learning experiences that simultaneously teach teachers alongside their students. Similar projects can be developed at low cost and using scientist volunteers guided by science educators for assistance in pedagogical styles for K–12 participants. Many university scientists are interested in reaching out to K–12 teachers and students, especially since the National Science Foundation has recently encouraged more K–12 dissemination through requirements for grant-funded research projects.

The RFC implementation model in a nutshell is a constructivist, experiential teaching program that uses the advantages of technology to make science studies international, very immediate, relevant, and engaging, while also bringing this opportunity to teachers and students who would not otherwise have such experiences. Based on our journey, we recommend that providers of professional development and in-class lessons in a variety of content domains identify ways in which components of such outreach can be brought into new "classrooms without walls" for greater impact and broader audiences.

# REFERENCES

Calabrese Barton, A. C. (2003). *Teaching science for social justice.* New York: Teachers College Press.

Calabrese Barton, A. C. & Upadhyay, B. (2010). Teaching and learning science for social justice: An Introduction to the special issue. *Equity & Excellence in Education, 43* (1): 1–5.

Carter, Lyn. (2010). The armchair at the borders: The "messy" ideas of borders and border epistemologies within multicultural science education scholarship. *Science Education, 94* (3): 428–447.

Denzin, Norman K. & Lincoln, Y. (2011). *The SAGE Handbook of Qualitative Research.* Thousand Oaks, CA: Sage.

Dimick, Alexandra S. (2012). Student empowerment in an environmental science classroom. *Science Education, 96* (6): 990–1012.

Ferriter, W. M. (2010). How flat is your classroom? *Educational Leadership, 67* (7): 86–87.

Friedman, T. L. (2005). *The world is flat.* New York: Farrar, Straus & Giroux.

Global Nomads Group. (2014). *About GNG.* Retrieved from http://gng.org/about/about-gng-what-is-global-nomads-group/.

International Group of Experts on Science and Mathematics Education Policies. (2010). *Current Challenges in Basic Science Education* (UNESCO document 191425). Paris, France: UNESCO Education Sector.

Lather, P. (2006). Foucauldian scientificity: Rethinking the nexus of qualitative research and educational policy analysis. *International Journal of Qualitative Studies in Education, 19* (6): 783–791.

Lindsay, J. & Davis, V. A. (2012). *Flattening classrooms, engaging minds: Move to global collaboration one step at a time.* Upper Saddle River, NJ: Pearson Education.

Lincoln, Y. & Guba, E. G. (1985). *Naturalistic observation.* Thousand Oaks, CA: Sage.

Lowery, L. (1998). How science curriculums reflect brain research. *Educational Leadership, 56* (3): 26–30.

Lowery, L. (2002). The nature of inquiry. *NSRC ScienceLink, 13* (1): 3–4. National Science Research Council, Washington, DC.

Moje, E. B. (2007). Developing socially just subject-matter instruction: A review of the literature on disciplinary literacy teaching. *Review of Research in Education, 31* (1): 1–44.

National Governors Association Center for Best Practices, & Council of Chief State School Officers. (2010). *Common Core State Standards.* Retrieved from http://www.corestandards.org/.

NGSS Lead States. (2013). *Next Generation Science Standards.* Retrieved from http://www.nextgenscience.org/.

Shapiro, B. (1994). *What children bring to light: A constructivist perspective on children's learning in science.* New York: Teachers College Press.

St. Pierre, E. A. (2004). Refusing alternatives: A science of contestation. *Qualitative Inquiry, 10* (130): 130–139.

State of New Jersey Department of Education. (2009). *Core Curriculum Content Standards for Science.* Retrieved from http://www.nj.gov/education/cccs/standards/5/.

UN Special Rapporteur report on the promotion and protection of the right to freedom of opinion and expression. (2011). *UN Human Rights Council Reports.* May 2011.

Warren, K., Roberts, N., Breunig, M., & Alvarez, M. A. (2014). Social justice in outdoor experiential education: A state of knowledge review. *Journal of Experiential Education, 37* (1): 89–103.

*III*

# Glocal

## Chapter Ten

# Comparative Reflections

*Glocal Experiences in European Teacher Education*

Francesca Caena

This chapter shares reflections and findings on experiences of *glocality* and *internationalization* in teacher education across European countries—describing a hermeneutic journey of understandings and interpretations along two parallel, intertwining routes. On one hand, it highlights *glocal* developments of teacher education, explored within a PhD comparative study in four European countries coming to terms with the consequences of Bologna process reforms in their own contexts. On the other, it explores processes and issues of *internationalization* in teacher education, experienced within an Erasmus project for a European joint master in initial teacher education, involving eight universities. The project was then followed up by a pilot program offering a selection of the master's curriculum courses to student teachers of the project consortium. The writer has embarked on the journey taking on different roles—researcher, teacher educator, European project coordinator—deploying the opportunities of discussing main issues of teacher education with different stakeholders (teacher educators, student teachers, researchers, teacher education program directors and coordinators, policy makers, vantage point experts) across ten European countries. This has helped an understanding of *glocal* tensions (between *global* influences on European teacher education and *local* cultures), reflected in teacher education curriculum makeup, delivery, and, above all, outcomes—the profile of a European teacher with the knowledge, skills, and values to meet twenty-first-century education challenges (inclusion, diversity, multilingualism, and intercultural issues in the classroom) to guarantee social justice.

# INTRODUCTION

This is a story of intertwining journeys against the background of European and global dynamics of reform in the teacher education field in a very interesting period—the second half of the latest decade—when the ties between economic aspects, educational effectiveness, and social equity had become increasingly close. It deals with the developments in teacher education policies and practices across European countries as a consequence of internationalization processes mostly at odds with existing local cultures and regulations, generating tensions, and unpredictable consequences—*glocal* solutions—that can be of interest.

A sheaf of perspectives was collected along a three-year-long PhD study exploring consequences of global trends (Bologna process reforms[1] internationalizing European higher education) in the tricky field of initial teacher education. The comparative study considered case examples—teacher education institutions in four European countries—and revolved around one key question: can a European dimension of teacher education offer a generative framework of innovation in contexts with rooted local cultures and practices? The perceptions of student teachers about their preparation, against the competence requirements of a European teacher, were integrated with those of other stakeholders, about issues and priorities of a teacher education curriculum accommodating global pressures and national traits in specific contexts.

Along the same time span—between 2007 and 2010—further insights were provided by experiences within a European Erasmus project[2] involving universities in eight countries, which tackled the challenges of developing a joint European teacher education curriculum—walking the tightrope between needs of comparability and peculiar education traditions. The key questions facing the international working group concerned key learning outcomes linked with key curriculum areas and courses as common foundations for an education of European teachers that could be compatible with diverse regulations cross-nationally.

What has been learned along the journey suggests the catalyzing role of European drives to change in teacher education: they can heighten existing issues but at the same time promote local improvements that are not likely to happen otherwise. The main debated culture change concerns the shift of focus from knowledge of content to the competences required of teachers—with implications for assessment and curriculum makeup, to be aligned with needs and learning outcomes of pupils. This can also contribute to tackling equity and personalization issues in education, by ensuring that pupils are taught by teachers who can provide diversified support and strategies to make pupil potential thrive. And this can represent a powerful means to promote social justice in education.

# THE GLOCAL DIMENSION:
## ADDED VALUE IN (TEACHER) EDUCATION

The starting point to understand dynamics of change and reform in European teacher education, under pressures toward convergence of objectives and outcomes in the European higher education area, can be found in insights from diverse perspectives in globalization studies with the ecological-sociological paradigm (Caena 2014a; Crossley and Watson 2003; Bronfenbrenner 1979).

Teacher education can be described as underpinned by shared ideologies—values and beliefs in social and professional communities—about roles of teachers and aims of schooling (Cochran-Smith 2006). Such context-based cultures are interwoven with controlling influences on the macro-level of national governing bodies—which deal with teacher recruitment, selection, and the quality of the education system (Tatto 2007).

Pressures toward harmonization (or standardization) of education policies and systems in Europe can be considered as global phenomena, which interact with local context conditions and produce contradictory developments—*glocal* reactions of adaptation or resistance (Arnove and Torres 1999; Giddens 1999). This is even more so in the case of teacher education, which is particularly vulnerable to global forces because of its institutional character and liability to state control over funding and regulations (Cummings 2003; Tatto 2007).

In a systemic, ecological perspective of European teacher education—characterized by complexity and defined by its multiple contexts—cultural and organizational influences can be viewed within a dynamic system of concentric, interdependent levels constantly interacting and changing (the macro-, meso-, and micro-levels of government, teacher education institution, and teacher education program) (Caena 2014a).

The dialectics between global and local dimensions in education, recently flagged as a focus of interest for comparative research, can generate original, hybrid "translations" which reflect institutional and educational cultures, with the mediating role of national governments (Crossley and Watson 2003; Tatto 2007). Each national context seems to develop peculiar solutions, related to varying degrees of state control over education policies, and diversity of links between university provision and the job market (Bonal and Rambla 2003). According to this perspective, reform variations across national education and training systems are related to a series of factors—history, learning theories, conceptualizations of teachers and citizenship, education technologies, administration cultures, costs, resources and quality control (Cummings 2003). Policy choices can appear complex and contradictory, mirroring varying views on the teacher's role (as a professional or a bureaucrat) and teaching effectiveness (critical and reflective professionalism, or technical teaching skills) (Edwards and Usher 2008).

Within global, fast changes in ideologies, politics, and economics, new conceptualizations of education might result in unprecedented educational reforms and developments—mediating between different answers to key questions: who should be prepared to teach, on what, and how they learn; how to organize training, what kind of institution is suitable, and what opportunities it offers for teacher learning (Tatto 2006).

In this global scenario, education policies and practices in local contexts can be interpreted and understood as *glocal*—set in spaces of (dis)location entailing the meeting and involvement of different cultural identities, beyond binary oppositions that are unable to describe complex, contradictory phenomena. An example of localization expressing cultural identity can be the concept of curriculum, which outlines national interests as distinct from others. As a consequence, the paradoxical concept of *glocality* and *dislocation* can become a dynamic space of meeting and interchange, mediation and building of meanings. *Glocal* translations and interpretations in European teacher education, therefore, can represent interesting developments that tackle the global challenges of shifting concepts of teaching, learning, and learning environments—in a global society of mobile, blurring boundaries between cultures and subjects (Edwards and Usher 2008).

## TEACHER EDUCATION ACROSS EUROPE:
## AN OVERVIEW OF POLICY AND PRACTICE TRENDS

The conceptualization of teacher education as an open system—characterized by multiple settings, diversity, and distinctive cultural traits, inter- and intra-nationally—has underpinned the PhD study that explored tensions in teacher education programs (with case studies across four nations—England, France, Italy, and Spain) from a systemic perspective, on different levels: of policy regulations, institutional implementation, and provision in specific settings (Snoek and Žogla 2009). This conceptualization was also the background for discussing and designing the European joint master curriculum in the Erasmus EMETT project, which started with a comparative analysis of existing teacher education practices in the eight countries concerned (Austria, Cyprus, Denmark, France, Hungary, Italy, Lithuania, and Poland) to outline common ground and local peculiarities.

The balance between trust and control in roles and responsibilities of national or regional authorities (the education ministry, regional bodies, or local education authorities)—that is to say, the governance culture—turned out to be particularly relevant, accounting for most differences in teacher education features across national contexts. In fact, at the macro-level state control mostly determined the routes and length of teacher education, providing guidelines of varying detail and prescriptivity about outcomes, professional profiles and qualifications, while providers could have more or less freedom, cross-nationally, about selection and assessment—with links to teacher status, career, and teacher supply/demand ratios. At the meso- and micro-levels, teacher education providers in different countries could be granted diverse degrees of autonomy in shaping the curriculum and determining its contents and delivery (Caena 2014a).

The PhD study field data (and the Erasmus project background surveys) covered a very interesting period for the impact of "Europanizing" key reforms following up the Bologna process—which was particularly tricky for teacher education, owing to its controversial position in the European higher education area. This was partly due to its "curse of complexity"—involving multiple relationships, actors, and views about learning processes, contexts and roles—and a lack of international consensus on the best options for evidence-based, research-underpinned policies and practices (Cochran-Smith and Fries 2005; Schwille and Dembélé 2007).

Across countries in Europe, Bologna process reforms brought about changes in roles, responsibilities, and organizational structures of teacher education, with sharply different choices and speeds of implementation, due to local governance cultures balancing state control and institutional autonomy, defining quality filters, and professional models. Such peculiar balances did not work in a vacuum; they interacted with markedly peculiar national traditions, which shaped both teachers' professional profiles and the features of teacher education (and schooling).

Hence the anomalies of reform implementation cross-nationally; teacher education programs and requirements in many countries traditionally used to deal with specific qualifications that held no equivalence to bachelor or master level degrees—the two-tiered structure of European higher education based on ECTS credits[3]—and were linked with peculiar recruitment mechanisms and professional careers. This was underlined by the European TUN-ING project—a concrete implementation approach to the Bologna process—which had been developing a methodology for planning, delivering, and evaluating comparable, compatible European study programs as competence- and outcomes-based (González and Wagenaar 2005).

Cross-country diversity in teacher education policy and practice, on which European influences were grafted to promote convergence for professional mobility and transparency, could be mostly found in the following aspects:

- governance and quality assurance,
- the university level of qualifications for teachers,
- the features of teacher education according to school level,
- the use of teacher competence frameworks and professional standards, and
- the length and features of teaching practice in schools.

In the main, decentralization trends in education have been prevailing across Europe, with the role of central ministries often consisting in "steering by goals and objectives," and the increasing devolution of operational control to other system levels—with more institutional or local autonomy of choices, diversification, and flexibility (Caena 2014b). This can be viewed as a way to meet the complexities of modern education and training systems by decision making that can be closer to local needs, and arguably more effective. Decentralization trends have been taking on variable features across European countries, however—with partial devolution to education institutions but state control over budget and teacher recruitment (France, Italy), devolution of some responsibilities to geographical regions (Austria, Spain) and local authorities (Nordic countries), or devolution of administrative and budgetary powers to education institutions (the UK) (Green 2002).

The devolution trend is linked with accountability and quality control mechanisms (often intertwined with "Europeanizing" processes toward transparency and convergence of outcomes), which have been displaying a similar heterogeneity. Evaluation of teacher education widely differs for frequency, procedures, and aims; the autonomy of teacher education providers can be high (as in Austria, France, Spain) or be submitted to tighter control (as in Cyprus, Hungary, Lithuania, Poland, and the UK) (Eurydice 2006, 2013).

Teacher qualifications across Europe, as a consequence of the "universitization" of teacher education, have been showing the tendency to step up to master level for upper-secondary teaching, but can vary widely according to school level and national regulations. They are also intertwined with selection and recruitment issues—tied, in turn, with the professional attractiveness, status, and demand of teachers in specific contexts. Teacher status is becoming predominantly position-based in Europe, with open recruitment entrusted to school institutions or local authorities; only a minority of countries still keep career-based teacher status (among these, France, Italy), usually entailing competitive examinations that select among a surplus of applicants. On the other hand, there are countries with a recruitment and retention issue (e.g., Denmark, the UK), and teaching seems to be considered as an attractive career in only a few national contexts (e.g., Cyprus, Spain) (Eurydice 2013).

Teacher competence frameworks—as references for teacher education learning outcomes, curricula, and qualifications, or the selection and recruitment of teachers—can be shaped and used in a wide variety of ways. Their degree of detail can range from broad, general statements or areas (such as in Denmark, France, Italy, and Lithuania) to structured lists of competences broken down into knowledge, skills, and attitudes (e.g., the Professional Standards for Teachers in England, in the period of the PhD study). Competence frameworks can be mostly used as guidelines for initial teacher education (such as in Austria and Denmark); if issued as professional standards, they can be linked to a teacher evaluation framework (European Commission 2013).

School practice can be said to represent the aspect of greatest variety in Europe, cross-nationally; its importance, however, is crucial—its features, length, and integration with other curriculum areas are indicated as key for effective teacher education and teacher learning (Biesta 2012; Darling-Hammond 2006; Hagger and McIntyre 2006). While school practice can total as many as 1,065 hours in England, its length can be left to the autonomy of providers, as well as vary across school levels of teaching—generally, the higher school level, the shorter practice—dwindling to fewer than one hundred hours in some countries (e.g., Cyprus) (Eurydice 2013).

As far as the professional profile of the teacher is concerned, the Bologna-induced global policy shift toward competences as learning outcomes in teacher education has been working parallel to an increasing focus on the knowledge, skills, and attitudes required of teachers, and how best to prepare them, in European policy documents and recommendations ever since the Lisbon Agenda[4] in 2000 (e.g., European Commission DG EAC 2005; Commission of the European Communities 2007). Further recent developments at the European level, beyond the time span of the experiences presented in this article, have concerned the endeavor of outlining a shared, evidence-based breakdown of the competences required of teachers, which could be deployed as a reference and common ground for national policy choices—as suggested in the European Commission Communication *Rethinking Education* and its related Staff Working Documents (European Commission 2012a, 2012b).

## MOVING TOWARD A EUROPEAN TEACHER EDUCATION: STUDY FINDINGS

Along the first journey on the European teacher education terrain, the comparative, mixed-method PhD empirical study gauged the perspectives of multiple actors of teacher education (student teachers, teacher educators, program directors and coordinators, vantage point experts) in four country contexts (England, France, Italy, and Spain), selecting case-study providers of secondary school teacher education (subject area of foreign languages) as paradigmatic examples of excellence, innovation, and internationalization:

- *Schools of Education, Bristol and Oxford Universities* (Postgraduate Certificate in Education—PGCE),[5] for England
- *IUFM*[6] *Lorraine*, for France

- *Scuola di Specializzazione per l'Insegnamento Secondario*[7] *del Veneto*, for Italy
- *Universitat Pompeu Fabra* (*Facultat d'Humanitats*) and *Universitat de Barcelona* (*Facultat de Formació del Professorat*), for Spain

The period of the study—close to the 2010 deadline of the Lisbon Agenda—witnessed the impact of substantial teacher education reforms, at different stages of implementation in the four countries concerned. On the meso-level of teacher education programs in provider institutions, this impacted on curricular codes—that is, the weight and balance of curriculum components and areas.

Curricular codes can be defined as classic (transmitting and preserving knowledge and cultural tradition), rational (developing meta-competences and skills, with research and inquiry methods), moral (promoting democratic values and active participation) or realistic (developing competences and skills for social and professional life). However, teacher education programs usually show peculiar blends of curricular codes, intra- and inter-nationally; they can be underpinned by varying interpretations of teacher professionalism—whether the key focus is on the teacher as a subject specialist, a researcher and reflective practitioner, or a member of a professional community (Snoek and Žogla 2009).

Considering the four countries in the period of the study, state control over teacher education curricula, teaching practice, and professional qualifications was at its highest in England—where a well-developed quality assurance framework and professional standards were integrated by an extended view of teacher professionalism, open recruitment (entrusted to schools), and prevailingly realistic teacher education curricula. In France, like in England, teaching practice played a relevant role in the curriculum at the time; a centralized education governance placed a highly selective filter (a state competitive examination) for access to teacher education and recruitment. The impact of European influences could be found in the introduction of a reference framework of ten broad teacher competences in 2007; moreover, the French teacher education curricula, traditionally classic and heavily relying on knowledge content, seemed to be shifting toward realistic and rational aspects. Spain and Italy showed similar institutional and professional cultures—with partial autonomy granted to providers, and thus a wide variety of features and codes in teacher education curricula, intra- and inter-nationally (Caena 2014a).

Against these contextual background features, the study focused on two interconnected questions concerned with systemic issues:

- the generative potential of the European dimension of teacher education as a reference framework for improvement in local contexts, cultures and practices

- *glocal* developments that might stimulate innovative change, arising from tensions, contrasting influences, and mediations between global, European, and local priorities in teacher education practices

One key focus of interest concerned the professional profile of the European teacher as mirrored by the teacher education curriculum, across different cultural interpretations, in a crucial period of transition and change in policies on different levels.

On one hand, the qualitative dimension of the study probed the perspectives of twenty main actors involved in teacher education policy, practice, or provision by means of semi-structured interviews across the four case study contexts, focusing on key issues of teacher education on European, national, and local levels in times of sweeping reforms. A phenomenological approach (Grounded Theory) guided the qualitative analysis of interviews, looking for interpretation principles in data themselves, with the help of Atlas.TI software (Charmaz 2006; Glaser and Strauss 1967). Links and relationships between themes were thus visualized in networks, which showed common ground and distinctive traits across national contexts.

In a complementary way, the quantitative dimension of the study was addressed to 231 student teachers across the four national case study contexts and explored their perceptions about the European dimension of teacher education as compared with the features of their own training—considering competence requirements of European teaching professionals as linked with teacher education curricular features. The study questionnaire was designed to focus on student teachers of a subject area (foreign languages) whose involvement in intercultural and multilinguistic policies is key for the European dimension of education. It built on the results of a study on the European profile of language teacher education, which broke down the areas to be covered by the teacher education curriculum, as linked to the knowledge, skills and strategies, and values required of European language teachers (Kelly and Grenfell 2004). Such a professional profile resonates with recurrent views in the literature and presents features of the teacher as a clinician professional, a reflective practitioner and researcher, a social actor, and an adaptive expert (among others, Darling-Hammond and Bransford 2005; Paquay and Wagner 2001; Williamson McDiarmid and Clevenger Bright 2008).

The questionnaire contained items requiring closed answers, by means of paired five-point Likert scales[8] (A and B), about the relevance (answers A) and effectiveness (answers B) of teacher education curriculum components, linked to the European teacher profile and training experiences.

The analysis of quantitative data entailed descriptive statistics, confirmatory factor analysis (Structural Equation Modelling)[9] and MANOVA (multivariate analysis of variance) and was effected by means of SPSS 16.0 and

MPLUS softwares. The analysis of variance results can be interesting to consider the influence of the independent variable of nationality on the two sets of answers (A and B)—about the relevance of the European profile dimensions in the training within each case study context and the perceived effectiveness of the same dimensions for the respondents' professional profiles.

Initially, descriptive statistics results about the whole set of answers underscored the items (elements of a European teacher education curriculum) with the highest gaps between answer A (perceptions of relevance in one's own training) and answer B (effectiveness for one's own professional profile). These gaps are likely to indicate student teachers' perceived needs, which appear to be less addressed in their training. Among these items, two belong to the area of strategies and skills, and regard metacognitive aspects (strategies for self-directed learning), while the other three concern the area of European values—in particular, the attention to linguistic and cultural diversity, as well as to sociocultural values.

The analysis of variance showed that the independent variable of nationality was significant, with differences in the means of answers for items grouped in the three dimensions of the European professional profile (knowledge, skills, and values), and for both sets of answers: A ($F_{9.645}=7.709$; $p<0.05$) and B ($F_{9.642}=4.813$; $p<0.05$). The dimension where there were the widest differences, cross-nationally, was the one of values.

A comparative view of answers according to nationality could also be useful to explore distinctive cultural traits in student teachers' perceptions and the influence of European features in local teacher education programs— contributing to enquiring into *glocal* features of teacher education across national contexts. The analysis of respondents' perceptions in national subgroups was done comparing the answer means, according to the five-point Likert scale for answers A (relevance in own training) and B (effectiveness for own professional profile). Answers were considered as grouped in the three dimensions of the professional profile of the European teacher (knowledge, skills and strategies, values) used to structure the questionnaire sections, and taken from the above mentioned Kelly and Grenfell study (2004). First of all, the analysis of variance highlighted the sharp diversity of French respondents' perceptions from the other three national subgroups, across all profile areas, and for both answer sets; this subgroup also yielded the lowest scores in answers A (relevance in own training). This seems to indicate lower degrees of "Europeanization" in the training in that national case study context.

As shown by figure 10.1, in the area of skills and strategies (SF in the graph) the comparative analysis of answers highlighted the common relevance of the reflective dimension in the training (item 12A in the graph), in accordance with European recommendations and evidence from research (among others, Korthagen et al. 2006). Another aspect that seemed to receive a lot of attention, across national training contexts, was the individualization of teaching (closely linked with the promotion of equity and social justice in the classroom). On the other hand, the development of meta-cognitive skills (learning to learn) did not seem to represent a priority in the training, in the main (as shown by means scores for items 13A and 14A in the graph).

As indicated by figure 10.2, the area of values outlined a wider diversity of perceptions, in particular about promoting values linked to European citizenship (item 25A in the graph) and collaborative work (item 26A)—with Italy and Spain that seemed to display a higher attention to these aspects in the training.

Another interesting finding can be seen in figures 10.3 and 10.4, and concerns the areas and items displaying the highest divergence between the two answer sets (A and B)—to suggest perceived needs of student teachers in relation to the European profile proposed in the questionnaire. To this end, a new variable D (the score resulting from the difference between answer B means and answer A means) was created. Also here, the French subgroup

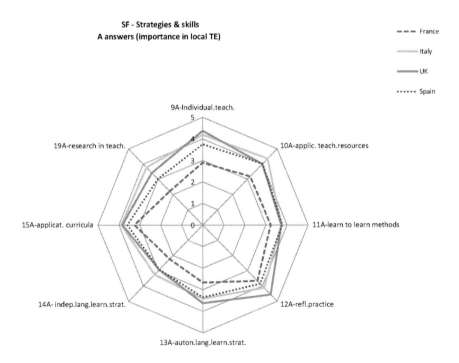

**Figure 10.1.    Graph with answer means for each national subgroup—items SF dimension (strategies and skills)—A answers: importance in one's own training (Likert values: from 1 [not relevant] to 5 [extremely relevant])**

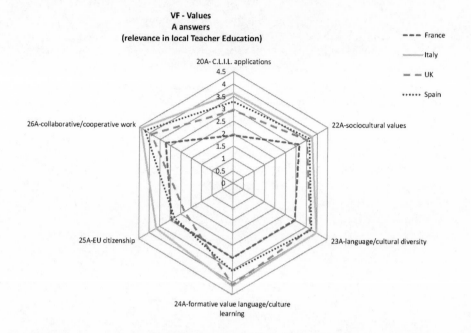

**VF - Values**
**A answers**
**(relevance in local Teacher Education)**

**Figure 10.2.   Graph with answer means for each national subgroup—items VF dimension (Values)—A answers: importance in own training (Likert values: from 1 [not relevant] to 5 [extremely relevant])**

stood out, with higher means differences, especially in the strategies and skills (SF) and values (VF) areas (figures 10.3 and 10.4 respectively). In particular, in figure 10.3 the highest means difference for French respondents regarded the individualization of teaching (item 9D) and learning to learn skills (item 11D), as linked to self-directed learning strategies (item 14D).

In the values area (figure 10.4), training needs of the French subgroup seemed to focus on linguistic and cultural diversity (item 23D) and socio-cultural values (item 22D).

All in all, satisfaction with the training received, against the European profile proposed, seemed to be higher in Italian and English case study contexts of the study (where it could be inferred that European features in teacher education were more marked), and lower in the Spanish and French contexts. A common need (which is linked to subject specialism, but can be considered as transversal to all subject areas of teacher education) concerned the development of strategies for ongoing language competence develop-ment—which can be considered as key for teachers who ought to be able to promote similar strategies in pupils, in a lifelong learning perspective.

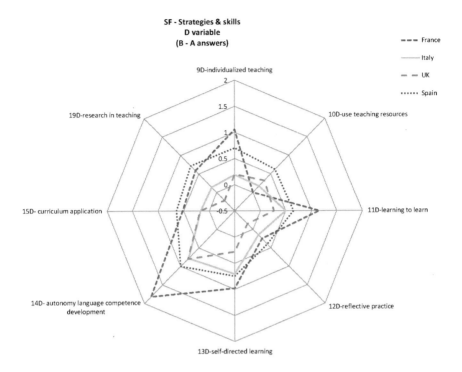

**Figure 10.3.** Graph with D variable = difference between means of answers B (effectiveness for professional profile) and A (relevance in own training) for each national subgroup—SF dimension (skills and strategies)

## DESIGNING A EUROPEAN TEACHER EDUCATION CURRICULUM: PROJECT EXPERIENCES

The second, parallel journey in the arena of European teacher education was offered by the EMETT project (European Master for European Teacher Training), funded by the Erasmus Lifelong Learning Programme of the European Commission, which endeavored to find a few solutions to issues of the "global" scenario of teacher education previously described. Over three years—from 2007 to 2009—the project involved a network of eight higher education institutions in different areas of Europe—"historical" EU countries (Austria, France, and Italy), a Nordic country (Denmark), eastern European countries (Poland, Lithuania, and Hungary), and a southern European one (Cyprus).

The project's aim consisted in the curriculum design and implementation of a European teacher education program, which tackled opportunities and constraints of a joint degree at the master's level. The international working

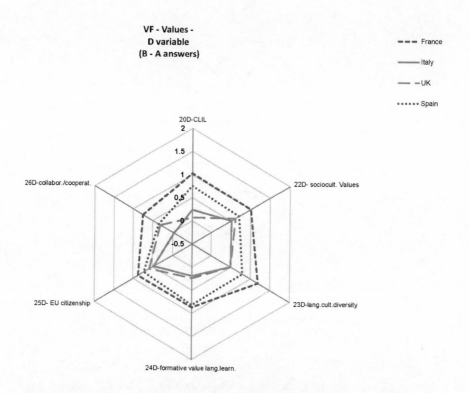

**Figure 10.4.   Graph with D variable = difference between means of answers B (effectiveness for professional profile) and A (relevance in own training) for each national subgroup—VF dimension (Values)**

group took stock of European policy recommendations in the field, discussing and developing feasible applications. It relied on a bottom-up approach, starting from a reciprocal knowledge and understanding of teacher education systems and practices in the eight countries; it deployed project surveys and field data to build a shared awareness of similarities and possible adjustments across different cultures and contexts of education, teaching, and training.

The project main outcome—a comprehensive secondary teacher education curriculum totaling 120 ECTS credits, which could fit into national systems and regulations—was meant to draw criteria for a comparable international academic qualification in teacher education, with a key shift from an input- to an output-based perspective.

By deploying a systemic logic of innovation, a modular, flexible approach was considered the best option, while attempting to avoid the dangers of fragmentation. Therefore, the curriculum framework consisted of six core areas, each containing a varying number of compulsory and elective modules (within an allowed range of credits for each of the six core curriculum areas), defined in terms of expected learning outcomes. Integration of contents and pedagogies was considered as the key organizing principle; theory, research, and practice were thus designed as interconnected by reflective, transversal axes, by means of reflective workshops of analysis of teaching practice.

The practice of teachers as learners and reflective practitioners, who analyze their own professional actions among peers, was thus set at the core of curriculum design. It was underpinned by a conceptualization of teacher competence as "knowing how to act" in a problematic professional situation, to be developed in professional actions, discussions, and contexts.

What soon turned out to be the greatest challenge was the development of a whole, consistent teacher education program—in one of the most regulated areas within higher education. As a consequence, the main concerns of each partner institution about needs and constraints (on a macro- and meso-level within each national context) had to be taken on board, against the background of a period of uncertainty and transition, characterized by reforms and institutional changes. It was soon crucial to set up, facilitate, and monitor a mechanism for ongoing intensive, collaborative work by partnership staff—by means of presence and distance meetings that provided precious opportunities for the negotiation of knowledge and meanings, to underpin shared, effective curriculum development decisions to meet ongoing transformations.

Two major issues in the European teacher education debate—mobility and an updated professional profile for the European teacher—were discussed within the project international team that acknowledged the crucial importance of intercultural and multilinguistic competences as cross-cutting for both issues.

Teacher mobility in Europe, pinpointed as a key challenge in European Council Conclusions, for the attainment of the Lisbon Agenda strategic objective (making lifelong learning and mobility a reality), was—and still is—quite low indeed if compared with other professions (Council of the European Union 2009).

The international project working group agreed that an updated professional profile of the teacher needed to include not only multilingual competences, but also the ability to develop intercultural competences in teachers and pupils—promoting tolerance, reflective attitudes, personal development, active participation, cooperation, and social integration.

The European *White Paper on Intercultural Dialogue* (Council of Europe Committee of Ministers of Foreign Affairs 2008) underscored the key role of language learning for overcoming barriers and stereotypes, and recommended the development of effective teaching strategies for intercultural education—with multidisciplinary approaches across school curricula, valuing expressions of creativity in different cultures. In this perspective, teacher education curricula were required to prepare teachers who could manage

situations of diversity, conflict, and discrimination by promoting self-criti-
cism, self-awareness, and a plurality of perspectives for democratic, active
citizenship.

In order to meet these priorities, two areas of the teacher education curriculum in the EMETT project were dedicated to the development of multilingual
and intercultural competences—hard-wired to compulsory mobility experiences
with teaching practice in school institutions, and reflective seminars abroad,
supported by expert practitioners and tutors (see figure 1.5). This way, the
mobility semester experience was meant to be boosted by being embedded in a
coherent curriculum framework—unlike standard Erasmus mobility for higher
education students. As for the multilinguistic dimension of the curriculum, not
only did it entail the delivery of curriculum modules in the major European
foreign languages (apart from English as a *lingua franca*, French and German
were covered as first languages of two partner institutions), but also the opportunity of learning a minor foreign language (with six options available within the
partnership) in the chosen host country during the semester abroad (Caena and
Margiotta 2010).

In designing the curriculum, the international project team was engaged
in lively discussions about the balance between curricular elements—thus
reflecting different conceptualizations of teaching, teacher education, the educational goals of the school, and the roles of teachers. Even though European discourse promoted an extended view of teachers' roles from a lifelong
learning perspective, beyond classroom and subject boundaries, in practice
teacher education curricula, at the meso-level of higher education providers,
tended to display a heavy subject-knowledge perspective, with secondary
school teacher education falling mainly under the responsibility of subject
studies departments in universities, such as in Poland. Within the international project team, however, it was finally agreed to merge subject studies and
subject didactics as a curriculum area, taking stock of theoretical insights on
the key relevance of pedagogical content knowledge (joining the "how" and
the "what" of teaching) to promote individualization of teaching and effective pupil learning (Shulman 1986, 1987).

The features and amount of required teaching practice represented another key issue. Given a minimum common denominator of at least ten
ECTS credits in all partnership countries, marked differences were found in
teacher education curricula and pedagogies, for the links with relevance and
characteristics of reflective practices. The French perspective was based on a
reflective, ongoing loop between theory and practice, alternating university
and school contexts—with collective, tutored discussions of teaching experiences in student teachers' learning communities. The other partner institutions in the project, however, did not display the same strong focus on the
reflective practitioner model in their curricular traditions.

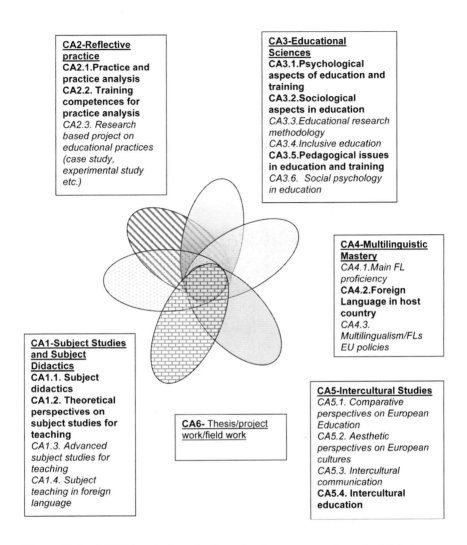

**CA2-Reflective practice**
CA2.1.Practice and practice analysis
**CA2.2. Training competences for practice analysis**
*CA2.3. Research based project on educational practices (case study, experimental study etc.)*

**CA3-Educational Sciences**
**CA3.1.Psychological aspects of education and training**
**CA3.2.Sociological aspects in education**
*CA3.3.Educational research methodology*
*CA3.4.Inclusive education*
**CA3.5.Pedagogical issues in education and training**
*CA3.6. Social psychology in education*

**CA4-Multilinguistic Mastery**
*CA4.1.Main FL proficiency*
**CA4.2.Foreign Language in host country**
*CA4.3. Multilingualism/FLs EU policies*

**CA1-Subject Studies and Subject Didactics**
**CA1.1. Subject didactics**
**CA1.2. Theoretical perspectives on subject studies for teaching**
*CA1.3. Advanced subject studies for teaching*
*CA1.4. Subject teaching in foreign language*

**CA6-** Thesis/project work/field work

**CA5-Intercultural Studies**
*CA5.1. Comparative perspectives on European Education*
*CA5.2. Aesthetic perspectives on European cultures*
*CA5.3. Intercultural communication*
**CA5.4. Intercultural education**

**Figure 10.5. EMETT project curriculum structure: core areas and modules (modules in bold = compulsory; modules in italics = optional)**

As for pedagogies, the delivery opportunities offered by distance learning, supported by information and communication technologies (ICT), represented a distinctive element of the Italian case study context, where the provision of teacher education modules in a blended mode over almost a decade had proved to offer effective opportunities for the development of cooperative, research, and reflective skills within communities of learning and practice (Wenger 1998).

The international project working group could thus count on a wide variety of perspectives and expertise (of higher education professionals of different subject areas and cultures, working in universities with distinctive traits and specializations) which were deployed as key elements in contributing, each with their own strengths, to the provision of the joint master curriculum program delivery.

This was put to the test of practice, after the project end, by piloting curriculum modules by an intensive program (MEITT—Modernizing European Initial Teacher Training), hosted by the partner university of Vilnius in the summer of 2010. It was offered to student teachers of different subject specializations within the university consortium, which engaged academics in planning and delivering courses over a two-week period. The key words of the program were creativity, innovation and modernity, encompassing three topic areas—teacher training and education sciences, subject specific training, sociology and intercultural studies. The program delivery and format were meant to rely prevailingly on seminars and workshops entailing the collaboration, discussions, and presentations of student teachers, who could join "special interest groups" to work on specific topics (e.g., European citizenship, cross-cultural understanding), develop specific competences (such as in foreign languages—e.g., with a crash course in Lithuanian), and collaborate in comparative analyses of European education systems, cultures, policies and practices. The main output of the intensive program was the development of a collective, collaborative report by participating student teachers, drawing the picture of an innovative European teacher from different angles and perspectives on the basis of discussions and input along the program.

Participating student teachers highlighted one key aspect in their feedback: the difference that was often felt between the modernization "discourse" about the program, and the actual practice of delivery and format of the courses. The importance of modeling active, involving, collaborative teaching and learning strategies and delivery modes in teacher education, for student teachers to experience firsthand and later deploy with pupils, stood out—in order to promote deep, meaningful learning, which appears increasingly disjointed from lecturing.

Finally, the main challenge for the implementation of the joint master degree within the consortium, after the project end, was found in the sharp dissonance between European recommendations and the contradictory, uncertain, sluggish pace of reforms and regulations on the level of national policies and politics—which entailed, for instance, the suspension of all teacher education provision in Italy for three years (between 2010 and 2013) while waiting for the lengthy processing of teacher education reforms.

## LESSONS LEARNED ALONG THE JOURNEY(S)

Some lessons learned along these reflective journeys, by intertwining complementary experiences and perspectives, can offer insights into the generative potential of *glocal* developments in teacher education in a turbulent period of change. The impact of the global, European dimension on teacher education policy and practice can thus be explored, indicating possible routes of shared discourse and action across different cultural contexts (Caena 2014a, 11).

A primary, transversal focus of interest across the ten national contexts regards the reflective dimension as linked with practice-based research—which appears to be present in all the teacher education programs concerned, in national and international policy documents, as well as recurrent in the discourse and perceptions of study respondents and project participants.

In study findings and project working documents, reflective practices were linked to formative assessment, practitioner research, as well as the development of intercultural, adaptive, and inclusive teacher competences. However, the concept of reflection turned out to be translated into diverse curricular pedagogies and practices across national contexts. The reflective paradigm could therefore be singled out as a *boundary object*: a shared concept used and understood in variable modes by different communities of interest and practice—working as a mediation element for dialogue and knowledge exchange—and thus *glocal* evolutions (Star and Griesemer 1989).

Furthermore, the responses of teacher education systems to global influences, across the ten national contexts—the mediations with institutional, organizational, and formative needs, opportunities, and constraints on the local level—highlight some common tensions across contexts, which can be viewed as catalysts of change and innovative *glocal* developments (Caena 2014a, 12–13; Engeström 1999; Edwards and Usher 2008). Such tensions can be made sense of with the help of cultural-historical perspectives[10] and teased out as follows (see figure 10.6).

- The tension between academic and professional requirements of teacher education programs—which impacts on selectivity—is linked to the expectations of governments, employers, teachers, and social groups (above all, where tighter government control is coupled with major reforms, as in England and France).
- The tension between polarities in the professional profile, especially for secondary schooling—teachers as all-round professionals, or subject specialists—can be found in most national contexts (except England, where shorter, practice-based teacher education mainly focused on teaching skills and pedagogic subject content knowledge).

- The tension between laying emphasis on either professional knowledge, skills or values can be detected in selection, curriculum content, and assessment across most contexts (in France, the difficult transition from a knowledge to a competence focus with the introduction of a teacher competence framework has paved the way for interesting developments).
- The tension between program delivery in university and school—timing, aims, content and assessment, linked to organization, regulation, and quality control—can hamper the alignment of activities, outcomes, and teacher educators' discourse (the English context offered an example of good practice: joint curriculum planning, monitoring, and delivery by school and university).
- The tension between cultures of collaboration and autonomy can affect teacher education quality and the innovative potential of *glocal* developments (e.g., in French, Italian and Spanish contexts, where education professionals' attitudes to cooperation appeared to need further development).
- The tension between functional and social roles of teacher educators— either developing and assessing teaching competences, or building professional identity—could be felt more strongly in contexts of intensive, demanding training (as in England, where the need to develop the second role was mentioned by study respondents).
- The tension between a formative or summative focus in assessment can imply concentrating on reflective competences by practical theorizing, self-evaluation, and research (e.g., with portfolios and reflective writings), or on products testifying professional knowledge, linked with recruitment and qualifications (reports, essays, and examinations).

## CONCLUSIONS

The journeys traveled along parallel routes on the uneven terrain of European teacher education can be described as journeys of interpretations. This is particularly so when trying to address the difficulty of comparing meanings across language and culture boundaries (Hudson 2007). If interpretation is present in any encounter with others, then the hermeneutic circle—the movement of going beyond and coming back changed—could be defined as a fundamental element of learning—providing projections of *glocal* possibilities that can become one's own (Conle et al. 2006, cited in Caena and Margiotta 2010, 327).

The hurdles and potential of *glocal* teacher education highlight the importance of a reflection, feedback, and collaboration culture involving all teacher education stakeholders on different levels—to agree on common ground and priorities spanning global and local needs, opportunities, and constraints.

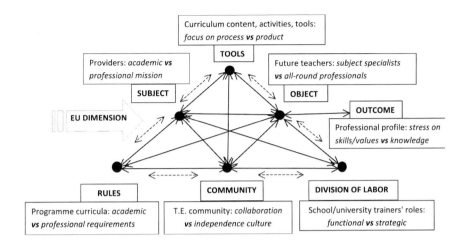

**Figure 10.6.   A cultural-historical perspective: common tensions across national teacher education contexts (Engeström 1999)**

Teacher education is fraught with uncertainties and a multiplicity of relationships between policy making, teaching, training, schooling, learning processes, actors, and contexts. Such complexity is increased—it could be perceived as being "squared"—when it aims to qualify itself with an international dimension. One strategy for coping with this "squared" complexity was suggested by the EMETT experience: strengthening and extending academic networks for reciprocity of research and practice exchanges, in order to exercise bottom-up influences over policy making as responsive to evidence, rather than to politics or short-term, firefighter policy drives.

The self-confidence and agency which come from shared, evidence-based research and practice can thus further a strong, active participation of teacher education actors and stakeholders in policy development and change—for effective improvement in the quality of teachers and teacher education (Caena and Margiotta 2010, 328). This resonates with messages sent within a recent international dissemination conference for a European Doctorate of Teacher Education (EDITE)[11] hosted in Budapest University in July 2014: the importance of academic and professional networks was underscored in playing a relevant role for enhancing effective debate, cooperation, and agency aimed at developing teacher education policies and practices with solid, evidence-based foundations, which can promote equitable education and therefore social justice.

# NOTES

1. The Bologna process is an international reform process, aimed at realizing a common European higher education area by 2010. It started in 1999 with the signing of the Bologna declaration by twenty-nine European education ministers; it aimed to harmonize (the term used in actual European documents) study qualifications within a two-level degree system (bachelor and master), consolidate the European Credit Transfer System (ECTS), promote student mobility, and establish a common quality assurance system for better cooperation.

2. Erasmus Multilateral projects were funded within the 2007–2013 LifeLong Learning Programme of the European Commission, providing support for cooperation of higher education institutions to improve the quality and relevance of higher education, and strengthen quality through mobility and cross-border cooperation.

3. The ECTS (European Credit Transfer System) represents the unit (introduced in 1989 by the Erasmus mobility program) used within the European higher education area to quantify the length of courses and modules, and more recently to recognize study program credits. One ECTS conventionally amounts to approximately twenty-five to thirty hours of work, and sixty ECTS credits represent the equivalent of one full year of higher education studies.

4. The Lisbon Agenda and Declaration, signed in 2000, underlined thirteen common objectives to be reached by European countries over a decade for the modernization and improvement of education and training systems, revolving around three strategic aims (quality, access, opening to the world). They set a series of recommendations (promoting the development of key competences and the transparency of professional and academic qualifications), and marked a turning point for the "unionization" of European education policies.

5. The Post-Graduate Certificate of Education is a one-year teacher education route which is provided by higher education institutions in England.

6. IUFMs (*Instituts Universitaires de Formation des Maîtres*) were regional institutions dedicated to the training of teachers, organized as consortia linked to a group of universities. Their independent status was modified in 2005, placing them under the institutional control of single university institutions.

7. The Scuole di Specializzazione per l' Insegnamento Secondario (SSIS) were regional institutions providing postgraduate, biennial teacher education for secondary schooling, organized as independent consortia linked to a group of universities. They were set up by law in 1999 and closed down in 2010, to be replaced by teacher education provision managed by single universities.

8. The five levels of the Likert scale went from 1 (the lowest level score) to 5 (the highest level score).

9. Structural Equation Modelling is a procedure for estimating relationships between latent and observed variables, often deployed for confirmatory factor analysis in statistics (in order to get an empirical confirmation of model validity—in this case, of the professional model of the European teacher presented in the questionnaire).

10. Cultural Historical Activity Theory (CHAT) offers a reference framework to describe sociocultural activities in complex contexts, with the concept of activity system that can be applied to teacher education practices. An activity system consists of six components: the common object and outcome, the subject, the division of labor, the rules, the artifacts and tools, and the community. The activity system is characterized by constant interaction and change, with tensions and mediations (called contradictions) within and between system elements, that can generate change and innovation, often responding to external influences.

11. Further information can be found on the project site www.edite.eu.

# REFERENCES

Arnove, Robert F. and Carlos A. Torres. 1999. *Comparative Education. The Dialectic of the Global and the Local.* New York: Rowman & Littlefield.

Biesta, Gert. 2012. "The future of teacher education: evidence, competence or wisdom?" *Research on Steiner Education*, 3: 8–21.

Bonal, Xavier and Xavier Rambla. 2003. "Captured by the Totally Pedagogised Society: teachers and teaching in the knowledge economy." *Globalisation, Societies and Education*, 1 (2): 169–84.

Bronfenbrenner, Urie. 1979. *The Ecology of Human Development. Experiments by Nature and Design*. Cambridge, MA: Harvard University Press.

Caena, Francesca. 2014a. "Comparative Glocal Perspectives on European Teacher Education." *European Journal of Teacher Education* 37 (1): 106–22.

Caena, Francesca. 2014b. "Teacher Competence Frameworks in Europe: from Policy-as-Discourse to Policy-as-Practice." *European Journal of Education*. DOI: 10.1111/ejed.12088.

Caena, Francesca and Ugo Margiotta. 2010. "European Teacher Education: a Fractal Perspective Tackling Complexity." *European Educational Research Journal*, 9 (3): 317–31.

Charmaz, Kathy. 2006. *Constructing grounded theory. A practical guide through qualitative analysis*. Thousand Oaks, CA: Sage.

Cochran-Smith, Marilyn. 2006. *Policy, Practice, and Politics in Teacher Education*. Thousand Oaks, CA: Corwin Press.

Cochran-Smith, Marilyn and Kim Fries. 2005. "Researching teacher education in changing times: politics and paradigms." In *Studying teacher education*, edited by Marilyn Cochran-Smith and Ken Zeichner, pp. 69–110. Mahwah, NJ: Lawrence Erlbaum.

Commission of the European Communities. 2007. *Communication from the Commission to the Council and the European Parliament. Improving the Quality of Teacher Education*. Brussels, 3.8.2007. http://europa.eu/legislation_summaries/education_training_youth/lifelong_learning/c11101_en.htm.

Conle, Carola, Hsin-Fen Changa, Chao Jia, and Michelle Boone. 2006. "Interpretation, Teaching and Rationality." *European Journal of Teacher Education*, 29 (1): 99–123.

Council of Europe Committee of Ministers of Foreign Affairs. 2008. *White Paper of Intercultural Dialogue: Living together as equals in Dignity*. Strasbourg: Council of Europe. http://www.coe.int/t/dg4/intercultural/source/white%20paper_final_revised_en.pdf.

Council of the European Union. 2009. *Council Conclusions on a Strategic Framework for European Cooperation in Education and Training*. 2941th Education, Youth and Culture Council Meeting, Brussels, 12 May 2009. http://www.consilium.europa.eu/uedocs/cms_data/docs/pressdata/en/educ/107622.pdf.

Crossley, Michael and Keith Watson. 2003. *Comparative and International Research in Education. Globalisation, Context and Difference*. London: Routledge Falmer.

Cummings, William K. 2003. *The Institutions of Education. A Comparative Study of Educational Development in the Six Core Nations*. Providence, MA: Symposium Books.

Darling-Hammond, Linda. 2006. "Constructing 21st-century teacher education." *Journal of Teacher Education*, 57: 1–15.

Darling-Hammond, Linda and John Bransford (Eds.). 2005. *Preparing teachers for a changing world. Report of the Committee on Teacher Education of the National Academy of Education*. San Francisco: Jossey-Bass.

Edwards, Richard and Robin Usher. 2008. *Globalisation and Pedagogy: Space, Place and Identity*. 2nd Edition. London/New York: Routledge.

Engeström, Yrjö. 1999. "Activity theory and individual and social transformation." In *Perspectives on activity theory*, edited by Yrjö Engeström, Reijo Miettinen, Raija-Leena Punamäki, pp. 19–38. Cambridge: Cambridge University Press.

European Commission. 2012a. *Rethinking Education: investing in skills for better socio-economic outcomes*, COM(2012) 669/3. http://eur-lex.europa.eu/legal-content/EN/TXT/?qid=1389778594543&uri=CELEX:52012DC0669.

European Commission. 2012b. *Supporting the Teaching Professions for Better Learning Outcomes*. Strasbourg, 20.11.2012, SWD (2012) 374 final. http://eur-lex.europa.eu/LexUriServ/LexUriServ.do?uri=SWD:2012:0374:FIN:EN:PDF.

European Commission. 2013. *Supporting Teacher Competence Development for Better Learning Outcomes*. Brussels: EC. http://ec.europa.eu/education/policy/school/doc/teachercomp_en.pdf.

European Commission DG Education and Culture. 2005. *Common European Principles for Teacher Competences and Qualifications*. Brussels. http://www.atee1.org/uploads/EUpolicies/common_eur_principles_en.pdf.

Eurydice. 2006. *Quality Assurance in Teacher Education in Europe*. Brussels: EACEA.

Eurydice. 2013. *Key Data on Teachers and School Leaders in Europe*. Luxembourg: Publications Office of the European Union.

Giddens, Anthony. 1999. *Runaway World: How Globalization is Reshaping Our Lives*. London: Profile.

Glaser, Barney G. and Anselm L. Strauss. 1967. *The discovery of Grounded Theory: strategies for qualitative research*. Chicago: Aldine Transaction Books.

González, Julia and Robert Wagenaar (Eds.) 2005. *Tuning Educational Structures in Europe II. Universities' contribution to the Bologna Process*. University of Deusto & University of Groningen.

Green, Andy. 2002. "The many faces of lifelong learning: recent education policy trends in Europe." *Journal of Education Policy*, 17: 611–26.

Hagger, Hazel and Donald McIntyre. 2006. *Learning Teaching from Teachers. Realizing the Potential of School-based Teacher Education*. Maidenhead: Open University Press.

Hudson, Brian. 2007. "Comparing Different Traditions of Teaching and Learning: what can we learn about teaching and learning?" *European Educational Research Journal*, 6 (2): 135–46.

Kelly, Michael and Michael Grenfell. 2004. *European Profile for Language Teacher Education. A Frame of Reference*. University of Southampton, UK.

Korthagen, Fred, John Loughran, and Tom Russell. 2006. "Developing fundamental principles for teacher education programs and practices." *Teaching and Teacher Education*, 22 (8): 1020–41.

Paquay, Léopold and Marie-Cécile Wagner. 2001. "Compétences professionnelles privilégiées dans les stages et en vidéo-formation." In *Former des Enseignants Professionnels. Quelles Stratégies?Quelles Compétences?* Edited by Léopold Paquay, Marguerite Altet, Éveline Charlier, and Philippe Perrenoud, pp. 153–79. Bruxelles: De Boeck.

Schwille, John and Martial Dembélé. 2007. *Global perspectives on teacher learning: improving policy and practice*. Paris: UNESCO.

Shulman, Lee S. 1986. "Those who understand: knowledge growth in teaching." *Educational Researcher*, 15 (2): 4–14.

Shulman, Lee S. 1987. "Knowledge and Teaching: foundations of the new reform." *Harvard Educational Review*, 57 (1): 1–22.

Snoek, Marco and Irene Žogla. 2009. "Teacher Education in Europe: Main Characteristics and Developments." In *Becoming a Teacher Educator. Theory and Practice for Teacher Educators,* edited by Anja Swennen and Marcel van der Klink, pp. 11–27. The Netherlands: Springer.

Star, Leigh S. and James R. Griesemer. 1989. "Institutional Ecology, 'Translations' and Boundary Objects: Amateurs and Professionals in Berkeley's Museum of Vertebrate Zoology, 1907–1939." *Social Studies of Science*, 19: 387–420.

Tatto, Maria Teresa. 2006. "Education Reform and the global regulation of teachers' education, development and work: A cross-cultural analysis." *International Journal of Educational Research*, 45: 231–241.

Tatto, Maria Teresa. 2007. *Reforming Teaching Globally*. Didcot: Symposium Books.

Wenger, E. 1998. *Communities of practice: learning, meaning and identity*. Cambridge: Cambridge University Press.

Williamson McDiarmid, G. and Mary Clevenger-Bright. 2008. "Rethinking Teacher Capacity." In *Handbook of Research on Teacher Education. Enduring questions in changing contexts*, edited by Marilyn Cochran-Smith, Susan Feiman-Nemser, and Donald McIntyre, pp. 134–156. New York/Abingdon: Routledge/Taylor & Francis.

*Chapter Eleven*

# Teaching *International Struggles for Critical Democratic Education*

## Wangari P. Gichiru and Matthew Knoester

### INTRODUCTION

*International Struggles for Critical Democratic Education* is incredibly timely and significant. Its thoughtful and engaging chapters vividly depict "on the ground" struggles for democratic education across very diverse contexts. While chapters illuminate how the web of neoliberalism cuts into communities that are distant and different from each other, chapters also show the potency of democratic visions for challenging neoliberalism.

—Christine Sleeter, California State University-Monterey Bay (emerita)

A growing literature in teacher education focuses on issues of globalization and globally—competent teaching (Brooks & Normore 2010; Collinson et al. 2009; Knoester 2012a, 2013; Robertson 1995; Zhao 2010). These authors explore how the concept of glocalization—a meaningful integration of local and global dynamics—can be used by educators to enhance their pedagogy and practice to best reach and teach the full diversity of their students for life opportunities increasingly influenced by global forces. Nevertheless, there remains a critical need for additional research and understanding on using international and comparative education studies to inform local educational practices in teacher education.

The quotation at the beginning of this chapter refers to a book that the authors of this chapter helped to write and edit, titled *International Struggles for Critical Democratic Education* (Knoester 2012a). In this chapter, we describe why and how this book has been instrumental as a primary textbook for two university teacher education courses we taught in different educational contexts, both focusing on teaching the "glocal" in teacher education. This will be followed by a detailed description of the purposes and processes of these courses, evaluating their successes and limitations, and arguing for why teaching international and comparative education is important for preservice or in-service teachers.

*International Struggles for Critical Democratic Education* is a collection of research-based stories and arguments focusing on educators in six different countries committed to educating in ways that interrupt the reproduction of inequalities from one generation to the next. All of the authors in the book see themselves as part of the Freirian tradition of education for critical consciousness, or teaching for understanding and for the purpose of interrupting social forces of inequality in various settings. The educators profiled in this book are attempting to do this work, but it is a struggle, and not all are completely successful. Nevertheless, these stories, detailing the struggle—as opposed to the more common narrative of outstanding educational success—demonstrate that the powerful forces of globalization include social inequalities based upon race, gender, class, nationality, and religion, and they are not easily interrupted.

In the first chapter, for example, author Assaf Meshulam describes a bilingual, binational, multicultural school educating both Jewish and Arab students in Israel. Drawing on interviews and observations at the school, along with his personal experience in similar situations, he provides a critical analysis of the many difficulties involved with providing equitable education to both Jewish and Arab students in Israel, even after the school had been created and managed to survive, despite great odds, for more than twenty years.

In another chapter, written by Min Yu, she describes the problem—almost never discussed outside of China—of the enormous migrant population within China and the lack of educational rights and opportunities for children of migrant workers. Having taught in a migrant school herself, and drawing on observations and document analyses, Yu is able to capture and describe the challenges of being an urban migrant without legal status—a situation that tens of millions of people are currently experiencing in China—and the difficulty of providing adequate educational resources for these children.

A third chapter, written by Mi Ok Kang, describes educational struggles within a country that has been widely recognized for chart-topping educational performances on international tests, such as PISA and TIMSS. South Korean children do well on these tests, but as Kang, a former teacher in South Korea, describes in this chapter, the pressure of the high-stakes tests in Korea often has the effect of creating misery among children, including a high suicide rate among youth. Kang describes the organized resistance to high-stakes tests among educators, parents, and children in Korea. (See appendix A for the complete table of contents of the book.)

The eight authors of the chapters that make up the edited volume are former schoolteachers who were fortunate to attend graduate school in education together at the University of Wisconsin-Madison between about 2004 and 2011 and were working on educational research focusing on our "home countries," and often situated within the schools where we once taught. The idea for this book came from our realization that although we were focusing on different educational contexts around the world, we noticed many shared commitments to liberatory and justice-oriented pedagogy and educational work, and often opposed to the same or similar global forces of neoliberalism, racism, or gender discrimination. The chapters complement each other in interesting and unexpected ways; and many of the book's readers responded positively, including the committee that awarded the Critics' Choice Book Award from the American Educational Studies Association, as well as the Jackie Kirk Book Award committee of the Comparative and International Education Society, which named the book a finalist for its award.

The current chapter is written by two contributors to the above-mentioned volume, both of who completed PhDs in curriculum and instruction and are now teaching undergraduate preservice teachers, as well as graduate in-service teachers, in two universities in the United States. We independently decided to use the edited volume within our classes focusing on comparative and international education. There are, of course, many ways to go about teaching international and comparative education. For example, one approach might be to compare the educational systems of just two countries in depth. Another might be to focus on what appears to be the "top performing" nations worldwide, according to international tests. By choosing this book as the primary textbook for these two classes, we chose to focus on a myriad of sociopolitical complexities involved with educating children in these six countries and in their situated contexts. Some chapters focus on countries that are honored for their high achievement on indicators such as international tests, while other countries under focus here are not. This approach prevents simple comparisons but requires careful thought about the specific social contexts of teaching and learning.

One of the main purposes of the edited volume was to avoid reductionism or overgeneralizations. This approach can often lead to stereotyping and overly simplistic understandings. Instead, the chapters in this book are grounded in intensive research, drawing on empirical qualitative methods and theoretical frameworks that help to explain complex phenomena related to educational and social processes and written by natives of the country under focus. The book does not look only to OECD or wealthy countries as the source of knowledge about education. Several chapters of the book look to the "global south" for enlightening struggles for more critical democratic—inclusive and responsive—education for effective democratic citizenship.

In this chapter we further reflect on and discuss how we have used this volume similarly and differently in our classes. In the tradition of practitioner inquiry (Cochran-Smith & Lytle 1992, 2009), we describe the purposes of our courses here, the goals and understandings that are the focus of our teaching, the various approaches to teaching that we have taken, and how we assess our students' learning and development over time. We believe this chapter can be useful to other teacher educators who hope to teach their education students to think "outside the box" in terms of looking for solutions to current problems in teaching and education, and to learn from a broader spectrum of contexts and practitioners who share similar educational goals. It is also possible to sometimes understand our current context only by looking (perhaps more "dispassionately" and with an outsider's view) at the challenges faced by people living in other countries. Both of the authors of this chapter have personal experiences with this way of knowing, which are worth sharing briefly here.

The first author of this chapter (Gichiru) was born and raised just outside of Nairobi, Kenya. She immigrated to the United States after she had already acquired a teaching license and was a successful teacher for five years in Kenya. When she immigrated to the United States in 2002, she noticed many things about the country that also helped her to better understand her experiences in Kenya. Upon first arriving she was shocked at the plentiful food and drink that seemed to be taken for granted in the United States, at the cold weather that people endured in Wisconsin, and the long distances between major cities. However, she also noticed the segregation of race and class in the United States, and wide disparity between the richest and poorest, but this also helped her to better understand her own country. Kenya was not a utopian mix of races and classes; divisions and disparities existed, even as the narrative of a unified and perfectly harmonious country continued.

The second author (Knoester) was born in the United States, to a father who immigrated from the Netherlands as a child and to a mother who was born in the United States but whose father was also a Dutch immigrant. When Knoester lived for a summer in the Netherlands as a teenager he noticed many aspects of life that were both similar to and different from his upbringing in western Michigan. He noticed for the first time that "what it means to be Dutch" did not have to be conservative Christianity, as he had assumed and understood in Grand Rapids for example. He found a social liberalism in Amsterdam that allowed him to rethink his own "roots." Similarly, he had the opportunity to study for a semester in Guatemala and Colombia while in college. There, his professors pointed out various sectors of the economy, inequalities, and ideologies that could be seen and understood in another country, and "mapped" onto the various places where he had lived in the United States but were somehow previously invisible—like water to fish. Spending time learning in and about different countries and contexts often provides the opportunity to better understand one's own context in the world.

Although both of the examples described above focus on the authors of this chapter traveling across the world, the important insights gained from a better understanding of disparate cultural contexts do not have to include traveling. Learning about various cultural contexts can also take place within one's own country, but a concerted effort must take place to look outside of one's own assumptions and viewpoints. Viewing cultural environments outside of one's own, whether via traveling or using multimedia-based studies and discussion, can allow rigorous new thinking about one's own cultural context. This chapter focuses on university teacher education courses that attempted to carry out this work.

## INTERNATIONALIZING THE TEACHER EDUCATION PROGRAM

The central purposes of the courses under focus here were to communicate or to remind preservice or in-service teachers that what they see in front of them is not inevitable—that there are many models available of thoughtful educational struggles and practice; it is sometimes necessary to "think outside the box" to problem-solve in terms of looking outside our current contexts for solutions. Further, they were to encourage students to think critically and divergently by providing them with comparative research, multimedia material, speakers, topical papers, and other publications relating to international and comparative education. This was done so as to sensitize and create a general awareness of different social issues around the world in which schools became the social sites to contest these struggles. In addition, we wanted to encourage students to better understand and address global issues in a local context because, as teachers, they will be confronted with the ever-changing population dynamics in their classrooms (e.g., the case of refugees and immigrants), and other forms of cultural and experiential diversity found in schools. Lastly, we wanted to let students start conceptualizing themselves as global citizens who have the power to act on global social issues, perhaps interrupting forms of social inequality, albeit from a local context, by asking what lessons can be learned from these global issues that can be applied to local schooling contexts. The chapters of *International Struggles for Critical Democratic Education* richly illustrate how educators carry out this work. They have served as an excellent jumping-off point for further inquiry and discussion in these courses.

## SETTINGS AND PARTICIPANTS

Gichiru teaches at Central Connecticut State University, a regional comprehensive public university in New Britain. The school has an enrollment of approximately 11,000 students with 9,000 in the undergraduate level and 2,000 in the graduate level. Two percent of the total headcount of students are international.

Gichiru's international education course is a graduate course taught every fall semester. Gichiru has taught this course twice, in the fall of 2012 and 2013. Both were small classes with an enrollment of five students in 2012 and eight students in 2013. All students were female. The classes met every Tuesday evening from 4:30 p.m. to 7:10 p.m. All students in both sections were Caucasian except two: one was Chinese and the other was African American. All students had different educational careers or were planning to enter the teaching profession. One was a lawyer looking to found a new school, another worked for the state's bilingual program, another was a school principal, and the rest were all classroom teachers at various grade levels.

Knoester teaches at the University of Evansville, a private regional university with an enrollment of approximately 2,500 students, approximately 9 percent of whom are international, located in a midsize city in southern Indiana. Knoester has taught two versions of his international and comparative course, one for noneducation majors and another for education majors. This chapter focuses on the course for education majors. Six students were enrolled in the course, and they took the course as an elective; it was not required for their teaching major or for licensure to teach. Five of the students were female and one male. All students were white and originally from midsize or small cities or towns in the Midwestern part of the United States. While education students are at the university they have practical and student teaching experiences in schools that qualify for significant Title I federal funding, a proxy measure for low income. The students are often confronted with students with many cultural differences and assumptions as compared with where they are from. These experiences are often the base of knowledge from which many connections are made with the course material in the comparative and international education class discussions.

Methods of instruction that were used in classes taught by both Gichiru and Knoester included discussions, films, readings from *International Struggles for Critical Democratic Education* as well as from other selected readings, the United Nations website, student presentations, guest speakers, and a final written assignment. Knoester's course also included a ten-day travel-abroad component to England. Five of the six students in the class signed up and paid the fee to participate in the study-abroad experience to the University of Evansville's British campus, Harlaxton College. The British component of the course included visits to two primary schools, two secondary schools, and two universities, tours of historic sites and cities, tours of two museums in London, attendance at a musical in London, and discussions with British educators and historians. In the following section, the first and second authors will each reflect on their own classroom experiences.

The course syllabus of Gichiru's class included this list of goals for her students: By the end of this course, students will be able to: 1) identify and discuss the nature and major objectives of international and comparative education as a field of study in general terms; 2) demonstrate understanding of the complex nexus of ideology, political economy, and formal and informal educational institutions in different societies; 3) articulate the role and importance of ethics (and especially professional ethics) in different educational traditions; 4) explain the overall structure and objectives of public schooling in the United States; and 5) articulate the role of cultural, linguistic, and ethnic diversity in the educational process of various societies.

Overarching questions for Knoester's course, included in his syllabus, were: How are education systems and views of teaching similar or different around the world? What are the best ways to evaluate the quality of teaching and schools? What are the benefits and drawbacks of international tests like PISA and TIMSS? How do inequalities based on class, income, race, gender, nationality, and ability affect educational outcomes? How have basic assumptions about education changed over time in various countries?

## TEACHING PRACTICES IN TWO
## INTERNATIONAL TEACHER EDUCATION COURSES

### The Case of Gichiru

For her course(s), Gichiru created an audiovisual aspect for most readings, such as providing or showing a film demonstrating a similar issue in a different context to accompany a particular chapter. Gichiru generally assigned one chapter from *International Struggles for Critical Democratic Education* for each week of classes. For some chapters, Gichiru supplemented the readings with a guest speaker for one of the readings. She also organized two formal debates. She also regularly facilitated roundtable discussions. Gichiru required students to be responsible for part of the class facilitation starting from the fourth week. She spent the first three weeks helping students understand how to facilitate discussion by modeling facilitation skills and informing students that each one of them would take a turn in facilitating part of the class at least twice during the semester.

On the first day of each of these classes (fall 2012 and fall 2013), Gichiru asked the students to think, reflect, and write down on a piece of paper, a) one reason why they chose to take this class and b) what they hoped to learn from the course by the end of the semester. She then asked them to share their responses with the rest of the class. For the first question, in both sections of this course, some replied that they wanted to learn what education was like in other countries. One wanted to learn about different "forms of education." A few others replied that they needed three credits before their master's thesis projects, or that the class looked interesting from the course catalog. For the second question, most students wanted to know what education was like in other countries, and a few of them named specific world regions, mostly because of family ancestry reasons, that they wanted to learn about. What was interesting is that none of the students wrote that they saw themselves, or their native country, the United States, as part of the global narrative. Rather, they seemed to see themselves as a "we" versus "them out there" and "how can we help them to make their education better?"

In selecting this book to read, as well as the film and speakers for this class, Gichiru made certain that not only different regions of the world were represented, but that there was a combination of social issues to consider, like displacement, religious issues, poverty, contested areas, gender issues, and other aspects that affect the education of children. In addition, Gichiru made sure to include discussions about different kinds of education, including formal and nonformal, religious education, indigenous education, and mainstream education, all of which were represented in the various course activities and discussions. Because the chosen text did not adequately address various important types of education, such as indigenous education, Gichiru added relevant readings and films concerning these topics. This means she selected readings and films based on the region, the type of education, and the social issue in question. As such, she did not cover all readings in the class text so that she could make room for the additional selected readings. For example, when examining the topic "Educational quality/inequality: Looking at education through the eyes of the dispossessed," Gichiru assigned the book chapters by Min Yu and Gichiru on the "struggle and the social influence of migrant children schools in contemporary China" and "challenges and prospects of providing critical educational opportunities for Somali refugees in the United States," respectively. Two films also accompanied these readings, namely, *Making the Grade: Beijing Migrant Schools* (BON 2011) and *God Grew Tired of Us* (Quinn 2006), respectively. Similarly, when examining the topic on "gender and education in developing nations," the chapter reading by Gupta on "gendering Muslim girls into religious and cultural values" was accompanied by the film *Educating Lucia*, which focused on the plight of girls in three regions of Africa (Richards & Metcalf 2000).

At the beginning of each class, Gichiru led a discussion about the assigned film and either showed the movie's trailer or short snippets of the film. Gichiru then asked students questions such as: What was the most striking thing that you noticed in the reading and film? What similarities and differences do you notice about the reading and the film? For the most part, as the course progressed, students were increasingly able to deconstruct complexities surrounding the various kinds of educational struggles and the tenacity that these children and their teachers put forth just to receive a basic education. One student commented after watching a film about Chinese migrant schools: "These children are working harder than anything I have ever witnessed . . . even despite social and political quagmire they face."

To situate the book in context, Gichiru first introduced the students to the Millennium Development Goals, which are eight international development goals developed by the United Nations in order to provide students with a global viewpoint with which to place different topics in relation to wider goals concerning those issues in the world. All students said that they had never heard about the Millennium Development Goals. As one student remarked, "I did not realize that there was actually a blueprint that almost every nation in the world followed in an effort to make things better for everyone." During many of the class discussions, Gichiru asked the question, "What kinds of effort or plans of action are required, if any, to accelerate the commitment to some of the Millennium Development Goals targets?" This question generated responses that progressed from outright frustration from the enormity of the struggle of education worldwide, despite it being a basic human right, to the increased desire to start where they were and take positive action.

Gichiru encouraged students to think widely in terms of their term papers, which were to be eight to ten pages in length, so that they could choose educational issues which held their interest and cut across national boundaries (i.e., international in character). Even though she encouraged them to explore educational issues in at least two countries, this was not a requirement. She emphasized that whatever issue was chosen, it should not merely be reported in descriptive fashion. She encouraged them to critically analyze the issue or topic from a combination of historical, contemporary, social, cultural, political, and/or economic perspectives.

An analysis of the papers that were written by students revealed that they addressed a wide range of topics. For example, one student wrote a paper on overcoming inequality through educational reform for the Ainu people in Japan. One student completed a comparative study of elementary education in India and the United States and asked what lessons the United States could learn from India's elementary education, and another wrote on lessons that teachers could learn from African refugees' motivation to learn in the United States. Another asked what lessons the United States could borrow from the education system of Finland.

Gichiru also asked students to write their papers in successive stages, so that the entire process could be less overwhelming and allow for greater support from the instructor. Gichiru listed the stages as such in her syllabus: a) identify an educational topic in international context; b) conduct a thorough literature search via computer databases, library research, and World Wide Web; c) create a working bibliography, citing the works you found from your literature search that you are likely to use for your paper; d) obtain actual articles, book chapters, and other materials to read; e) share your research themes and some preliminary findings via an informal class; f) presentation; g) write your final comparative education paper organized via these themes; and h) present your final comparative education paper via a formal class presentation.

Even though writing the paper assignment in this way was laborious for the instructor because of the many successive stages involved, it was also advantageous because the students were able to expand on their knowledge of writing as the class progressed. In the end, each student was able to produce a great paper that fulfilled the objectives of the course. As one student commented in the final evaluation, "the final paper was given and presented to students appropriately and gradually. Step by step, the teacher led the students toward our goals."

## The Case of Knoester

Knoester's class used many of the same approaches to teaching as did that of Gichiru, including films and guest speakers to accompany the readings. However, it must be noted that the course led by Knoester was a bit more informal than that of Gichiru. This was likely due to the course being an elective and a required part of attending the ten-day travel component to England. Several students also took the course for just one credit, rather than the usual three credits. For this reason, the course was not as heavy in research and writing as those of Gichiru.

Nevertheless, the course involved intensive analysis of educational challenges and approaches in each of the countries named above, with a few additional countries. The part of the course taking place at the University of Evansville began with the reading of several newspaper articles regarding U.S. education in comparison to other countries. All of the articles made reference to either PISA or TIMSS scores. Knoester then gave students a copy of the most recent rankings of countries on these international tests. He then asked students: "If you were going to write a headline about the PISA scores, what would it be?" One student replied: "America is average." This response echoed what several of the newspaper articles wrote.

Knoester then read aloud from Diane Ravitch's recent book, *Reign of Error* (2013), in which she argues that the international tests are taken far too seriously and generally misread. For example, if poverty were controlled for in the rankings, the United States would rank much higher. If other inequalities were accounted for, the rankings would be much different. Further, there are outstanding schools and miserable schools found in many countries, and the tests may be misleading. In short, Knoester and his students problematized the rankings. This was how the course began (after basic introductions), and this process continued throughout the rest of the semester.

The first chapter Knoester's class read from *International Struggles for Critical Democratic Education* was that of Min Yu, titled "History, Struggle, and the Social Influence of Migrant Children Schools in Contemporary China." As mentioned above, this chapter focused on the children of migrant workers in China and the precarious situation of schools built for these children. What is essential to this story is the understanding that families living in the major cities of China must hold what are called urban *hukou*, or official status within the urban area. Only children from these families are entitled to the official school system in the major urban areas. So when Shanghai is listed at the top of the international rankings it is important to consider what this means. Several questions arise. First, why is a city listed on this comparison of countries? Second, does this city represent every child in Shanghai, or are only the children of urban *hukou* included?

In Knoester's class, several short videos were shown from YouTube, some showing migrant workers' schools and others the "official" schools in large cities. The disparities are stark. Knoester asked the following question of his students: "What do you notice about the film about China, and Min Yu's chapter in the book?" Student responses included: "Some of China's cities do well on the PISA and TIMSS, but they are very selective about who gets tested." Another student stated: "There is a lot of struggle to provide education for everyone."

This description of Knoester's class reading and watching short films about education in China was a familiar routine in the course. During most weeks, a chapter of the textbook was assigned to read before class and a short film was shown to provoke comparisons and deeper discussion. Students were asked to analyze both the chapter and the film in juxtaposition. Each of the chapters in the book pointed to various complexities within the countries under focus that demanded greater attention, rather than simply stating, "That country has a great (or bad) education system." Social inequalities within each country were always raised, and the struggles that particular educators or schools waged to create a more equitable or powerful educational opportunity were presented.

One example from the United States (from chapter 5 of the book) focused on the struggle of one particular school, the Mission Hill School in Boston to educate a racially and culturally diverse student body within a deeply segregated city. The second author of this chapter, Matthew Knoester, wrote the chapter. As a former teacher in the school, and someone who conducted an in-depth qualitative study of the school, Knoester (2012b) was able to describe fifteen specific approaches used by the school to build trust and foster an integrated, welcoming, and democratic school setting. Examples of those approaches included placing issues of race and diversity at the center of the curriculum at various points; conducting whole-school forums for discussing difficult issues around race and class; celebrating families of all colors, shapes, sizes, and traditions through the curriculum and the various forms of messaging used in the school; and hosting regular "family nights" that focused on student work but included food, music, and other ways of educating and celebrating diversity. A professional filmmaking crew spent many hours in the school during the 2011–2012 school year and created a film series titled *A Year at Mission Hill* (Valens & Valens 2013). Knoester's class at the University of Evansville watched several of these short films together, which raised many questions for students as to how to create a trusting and integrated multicultural school environment when these types of schools are increasingly rare in Boston and in the United States.

The last several weeks of Knoester's course were spent preparing for the ten-day travel experience in England. The British campus of the University of Evansville, Harlaxton College, is a large country manor in the Lincolnshire region of England, about an hour north of London by train. The manor was built by a wealthy industrialist named Gregory Gregory over the course of several years and completed in 1845. The University of Evansville began using the manor for educational purposes in 1971 (it was owned by a member of the university's Board of Trustees) and it was given to the university outright in 1986. Harlaxton College follows the semester calendar of the university based in Indiana, allowing U.S.-based students to spend a semester studying at Harlaxton. During the summer months, shorter courses are held based on availability of rooms and often designed by individual professors or school groups. Knoester has led three ten-day courses based at Harlaxton, each with an educational focus.

Knoester wanted his students to understand before traveling to England a basic outline of British education and some of the challenges facing British educators, especially the difference in educational resources and expectations of students from different socioeconomic classes. Although one chapter of *International Struggles for Critical Democratic Education* refers to British education—specifically comparing higher education in Britain to that of the United States in terms of cost and regulation—Knoester wanted to focus much more on primary and secondary education in Britain. To do so, students read additional chapters from John Oakland's book *British Civilization: An Introduction* (2011), as well as chapters from Charlie Caroll's *On the Edge: One Teacher, a Camper Van, Britain's Toughest Schools* (2010). In both of these readings students were able to begin to understand the basic types of schools in Britain, how children matriculate, and some of the various inequities found in schools, generally related to social class. Students also watched several films in the class, including part of the first episode of PBS's *Downton Abbey* (Neame et al. 2011) which depicts the class structure within a large country manor in the early twentieth century, similar to Harlaxton Manor. Students also watched the first three episodes of *The Up Series* (Apted 1986) a documentary series that depicts British youth from various class backgrounds reflecting on their educational and social lives at the ages of seven, fourteen, and twenty-one. Knoester wanted students to understand some of the different life trajectories of youth in Britain before traveling there.

Upon arriving in Britain, the students lived in the manor and could clearly see the class differences in the house between where the servants lived and where the "master" and his family lived in Harlaxton Manor when it was first built. Further, two contrasting schools at the primary, secondary, and university level were chosen for visits, which allowed students to begin to see how children with different family resources are treated.

For the second-to-last class period, Knoester asked a colleague who was born and raised in Trinidad to guest lecture for the class. This colleague was able to describe how Trinidadian education, based on the British system, was similar in many respects to that of the British system today. He described the schools that he attended and also was able to reflect on the differences between British education and education in a British colony. He described the strong racial segregation he knew in Trinidad, and the fact that the white managers lived "up on the hill" of his town, while those who were darker-skinned, like him, lived "at the bottom" and were generally unable to move into management positions, often even in spite of high performance in schools. This perspective allowed us to see that even as class is the most prominent form of inequality found in England, that England's influence has reached far outside of its country's borders and has created racial divisions, in addition to class divisions, in colonies such as Trinidad. This is another reason why it is important to not only look to wealthy countries for answers to our educational problems, but to look elsewhere as well, where racial and cultural inequalities might be viewed differently.

## COURSE EVALUATIONS AND ANALYSIS

In both courses, the instructors found that through these activities, there was evidence of rich learning, discussion, thinking, and challenging of basic assumptions students might have had about students and teachers in other countries.

## The Case of Gichiru

Overall, in Gichiru's courses, the students clearly appreciated the videos that accompanied the readings. Students insisted that every topic was eye opening. As mentioned before, none of the students had heard of the UN's Millennium Development Goals before this class, let alone how to use them as a yardstick when discussing various issues in different contexts. On many occasions, the class was in a somber mood after the continual realization of the struggles that many people have to go through in search of an education around the world. The students also marveled as to just how complex the political and social issues were as they played out in different educational contexts around the world. All students appeared to be refreshed and very motivated by the different ways Gichiru presented material to them. They seemed to realize that after being teachers for several years (two of them had a teaching experience of over fifteen years), they had neglected to take advantage of instructional resources such as those presented in this course that could enhance the quality and relevance of their students' educational experiences through raising their students' critical awareness of their world conditions (Freire 1974). As one student who was a fifth grade teacher said toward the end of the semester, "I will teach my students about these issues and as a class, we will figure out strategies on how we can contribute to this struggle."

As they continued to gain confidence, some of the students clearly loved the opportunities to challenge opinions and viewpoints of authors, and of each other. One student was especially strong in her critique of the Millennium Development Goals as a yardstick to measure all nations' progress. "Given the unique complexity of each nation's educational struggle, these goals are difficult for me to interpret," she said. Students also appreciated the numerous opportunities to improve on their work in progress as they continued to gain more insight through class discussions.

In the beginning, many of Gichiru's students seemed to be oblivious to "the way that local and global forces interact to shape the context of the lives of those responsible for delivering quality instruction for student learning and the school and communities in which they lead" (Brooks & Normore 2010, p. 55). In the end, Gichiru witnessed real transformation in their thinking. The students slowly grasped the effects of "power, influence, and authority in the allocation of scarce and valued resources at various levels of the education sectors" (Brooks & Normore 2010, p. 56). As already mentioned, this resulted in many of the students starting to seek ideas of how they can act as empowered participants in their schools to influence international decisions from a local level. Gichiru marveled when students started thinking of these ideas in terms of "communicating clearly what the issues are." They started seeing how they themselves were indirectly embroiled in these struggles through the various immigrants and refugees that they taught in their own classrooms. They talked of how they can "take action" where they were in their own classrooms so that they can make a positive global impact. This is synonymous with what Freire (1974), in his work *Pedagogy of the Oppressed*, referred to as "*problem-posing education.*" One student went out of her way to write an e-mail to Gichiru that included this statement: "I can't be the same person I was after your course last semester in comparative and international education. I think I told you I don't know what I am going to do with that knowledge but I am forever changed by it." This former graduate student is now hoping to join Gichiru for a study-abroad trip that Gichiru will be leading to Tanzania in 2015.

In the student evaluations of Gichiru's course, the students were clearly happy to understand a new perspective of the world and education outside the United States. Many students stated that class discussions were stimulating, eye opening, and enjoyable. Finally, several students wrote that the amount of work was appropriate for a graduate course, and the various steps of preparing the paper were appreciated. As one student stated, "the final paper was given and presented to students appropriately and gradually. Step by step the teacher led the students toward our goals."

Students whose areas of interest were not well represented wanted more of those areas in the future. How to present a balance so that all areas of interest are better represented remains an issue for this class.

One student offered the following response in reaction to the guest speaker in Gichiru's class: "It was neat to engage in a discussion with someone who taught there [at the school under focus for the reading] when he spoke to us via Skype. He was able to clarify every question we had about the school," an acknowledgment that it often helps to speak with people personally to better understand and to probe the issues under focus.

One final note on Gichiru's class: As suggested above, even though Gichiru did not have a study-abroad component in her two classes, students over the two semesters suggested that an "excursion to bring some of these topics to life would be a great idea." This prompted the instructor to submit a study-abroad proposal to various countries in West and East Africa. The first trip will commence in the summer of 2015 to Arusha, Tanzania.

## The Case of Knoester

Similarly, Knoester witnessed students thinking critically about important issues and making connections that were likely only possible with an international and comparative perspective. Students in Knoester's class unanimously gave the course the top grade in their student evaluations (5/5), and Knoester was impressed by the level of oral discourse and writing that was produced by students, even as many took the course for just one credit.

Upon returning from England, students in Knoester's class wrote what he calls a "pedagogical paper," which means a paper with reflections on what the students learned throughout the course. The students were asked to include as many of the readings, films, and experiences as possible in their responses. Here are a few responses written by students:

One student wrote, "Studying abroad opened my eyes and heart to new ideas. I was excited to learn more history through our visits to London, Cambridge, churches, and schools. There is richness in having such deep roots. I am excited this year to put into action the ideas I observed and to share my new knowledge with my colleagues and students!"

Another student wrote, "As I began reading about the British education system, I found that the titles given to schools was different compared to those used in the United States. I gained better insight from educators we encountered on our school visits or from guest speakers visiting Harlaxton. As shared at the London Nautical School, there are public schools: the elite and expensive schools such as Eton, St. Paul's, and Bedford; private schools: independent schools free to operate outside of government regulation; and state schools that are funded by taxes and must follow the national curriculum."

It is possible to see in these responses that these students were able to see and to connect their readings and experiences to form new understandings of the world around them. They were also able to see U.S. roots and history in their visits to schools and historical sites in Britain. It is helpful to see these aspects as they continue their teaching careers and realize that nothing that exists came from nowhere; and there are reasons, sometimes wise and sometimes faulty, for carrying out educational processes the way that they are.

Another student reflected on the multiple layers of inequalities that exist in countries around the world, a frequent topic of discussion in the course, and wrote the following in her final paper:

> The biggest thing I've taken away from this semester is that education alone is not a fix for society. . . . The United States needs to learn from countries like South Korea and Finland to equalize educational opportunities. Unfortunately, even fixing the education system will not change inequality within the entire society . . . relying on education as the solution to poverty places the responsibility for destroying the socioeconomic hierarchy on the people at the bottom of it.

This statement demonstrates that this student made important connections that are generally found outside of mainstream discourse about education. Educators and others are often led to believe that education can fix all of society's ills, but closer examination reveals that schools are a part and a reflection of the larger society. Educators should not be blamed for the poverty and inequalities that schools did not create but must nevertheless work to interrupt these forces as a new generation comes of age.

## IMPLICATIONS

The implications for this work are potentially enormous for the students involved. As stated above, we hope that students who matriculate through these courses are able to "think outside the box" and realize that what they see in their local schools is not inevitable. We hope that they can see the connections among countries in terms of historical colonization, in terms of the global economy, and in terms of shared cultural knowledge and finding solutions to common problems. Our education students are or will be teaching students who are themselves diverse in many respects, in fact, it is not a stretch to assume that many of these students will be immigrants from another country. We believe it is a teacher's responsibility to understand as much about his or her students as possible, in terms of their experiences in the world, their cultural understandings and assumptions, their languages and ways of being, and so much else.

Finally, we hope our students are better able to view themselves as global citizens, as people who are intricately connected to people around the world and able to see common aspirations for our shared humanity and for one another. By learning about people in various contexts—and with an anti-reductionist and anti-inequality lens—it is possible to deepen our shared commitments to equality and to education for connected and responsive citizenship.

## CONCLUSION

In conclusion, it is a powerful and important act to challenge preservice and in-service teachers to compare their current educational and cultural understandings with the way education is conducted and understood in various countries and contexts around the world. This chapter has described how two U.S.-based teacher educators have "internationalized" their teacher education programs and have brought "glocal" teaching opportunities and viewpoints to U.S. education students. Both drawing from the book *International Struggles for Critical Democratic Education*, among other resources, the courses described in this chapter demonstrate that it is possible to provide comparative and international educational exposure and challenging course material to undergraduate and graduate students in a way that does not simplify or provide stereotypical depictions of various countries and their educational systems. Rather, what these courses have done is demonstrate that there are always more questions to ask, stories to tell, and complexities to explore when comparing different educational systems or approaches. This book and these courses focus on hearing the educators from various parts of the world tell their own stories, and to focus critically on their situations, continually asking, how can committed educators provide effective educational opportunities for all children?

## APPENDIX A

**Table of Contents for *International Struggles for Critical Democratic Education***

Chapter 9: Global Capitalism, Neoliberalism, and "Reactionary Postmodernity": Responses from the MST's Teacher Education Program in Brazil
*Júlio Emílio Diniz-Pereira*

## REFERENCES

Apted, M., Almond, P. (Directors). (1986). *Seven up!/Seven plus seven/21 up/28 up/35 up/42 up.* [Motion Picture Series]. London: First Run Features.

BON (Producer). (2011). *Making the grade: Beijing migrant schools* [Motion Picture]. Retrieved from http://www.youtube.com/watch?v=5gf3JjOnlAQ.

Brooks, J. S. & Normore, A. H. (2010). Educational leadership and globalization: Literacy for a global perspective. *Educational Policy, 25* (1), 52–82.

Caroll, C. (2010). *On the edge: One teacher, a camper van, Britain's toughest schools.* London: Monday Books.

Cochran-Smith, M. & Lytle, S. (1992). *Inside/outside: Teacher research and knowledge.* New York: Teachers College Press.

Cochran-Smith, M. & Lytle, S. (2009). *Inquiry as stance: Practitioner research in the next generation.* New York: Teachers College Press.

Collinson, V., Kozina, E., Lin, Y. H., Ling, L., Matheson, I., Newcombe, L., & Zogla, I. (2009). Professional development for teachers: A world of change. *European Journal of Teacher Education, 32* (1), 3–19.

Freire, P. (1974). *Pedagogy of the Oppressed.* New York: Seabury.

Knoester, M. (Ed.) (2012a). *International struggles for critical democratic education.* New York: Peter Lang.

Knoester, M. (2012b). *Democratic education in practice: Inside the Mission Hill School.* New York: Teachers College Press.

Knoester, M. (2013). The flat world and books about education reform. *American Journal of Education, 119* (4), 633–639.

Neame, G., Eaton, R., Fellowes, J., Trubridge, L., Pearce, A., Goddard, A., Kelly, B., et al. (2011). *Downton Abby: Season One.* London: Carnival Film and Television Limited.

Oakland, J. (2011). *British civilization: An introduction.* London: Routledge.

Quinn, C. D. (Writer). (2006). *God grew tired of us* [Motion Picture]. In M. B. Pace, C. D. Quinn, and T. Walker (Producer). Sudan.

Ravitch, D. (2013). *Reign of error: The hoax of the privatization movement, and the danger to America's public schools.* New York: Knopf.

Richards, J. (Executive Producer), and Metcalf, C. (Director). (2000). *Educating Lucia* [Motion Picture]. United States: Bullfrog Films.

Robertson, R. (1995). Glocalization: Time-space and homogeneity. In M. Featherstone, S. Lash, and R. Robertson (Eds.), *Global modernity* (pp. 25–44). London: Sage.

Valens, A. & Valens, T. (Producers and Directors), Chaltain, S. (Producer). (2013). *A year at Mission Hill* [Motion Picture]. United States: Tom and Amy Valens.

Zhao, Y. (2010). Preparing globally competent teachers: A new imperative for teacher education. *Journal of Teacher Education, 6* (5), 422–431.

*Chapter Twelve*

# Exploring the "Glocal" in Urban Teacher Education

*A Journey in Unpacking One Teacher Education Course*

Alison Price-Rom

## INTRODUCTION

In many introductory preservice teacher education courses and teacher education programs, the context of study is the state system of education first and foremost, with some attention to education policy on the national level. However, preservice teacher education programs rarely emphasize teacher education or education systems in societies outside the United States, or the impact that an increasingly globalized world is likely to have on future teachers and their students. Global perspectives of significance to teacher education include such topics and themes as foreign language skills and cross-cultural sensitivity, understanding the impact of large-scale, multinational assessments such as the PISA exam or TIMSS on education policy in the United States, the emergence of new and powerful economies in China and India, and an explosion of information technology that is profoundly reshaping the working world. Today's teachers should be equipped with a new set of knowledge, skills, and attitudes that would enable them to prepare their students for this increasingly competitive and interconnected global community. At institutions of higher education in the United States there is a growing campus internationalization movement that has largely bypassed teacher education programs. Global and international themes have long been a part of teacher education programs but have often been confined to social studies education. However, in recent years leading scholars in the field of teacher

education have noted this deficit and have begun to support internationalizing teacher education programs.

## PURPOSE OF THE CHAPTER

The purpose of this chapter is to examine the literature on the internationalization of teacher education and to use that literature review as a framework
for analyzing my own reflections on an introductory teacher education course
that is regularly taught at a university in the greater New York City area. This
analysis of my own reflections on an introductory teacher education course
will determine students' attitudes toward integrating global and international
elements into a particular preservice teacher education course. The analysis
will help determine how I might go about creating a global or international
component for this specific course and the extent to which these changes
might be applied to teacher education courses at other institutions. Given the
logistical challenges of providing all students with study-abroad experiences,
this chapter will instead discuss the global potential of local or "glocal"
resources for globalization—resources that teacher educators can find on any
university or college campus as well as in the surrounding community. The
more long-range objective of the study is to offer suggestions to teacher
educators in general for ways in which to incorporate global elements into
their introductory courses in such areas as historical foundations, philosophy
and sociology of education as well as teaching methods across the content
areas.

## SETTING AND PARTICIPANTS

In order to maintain the confidentiality of participants in this study, this
article will refer to the university in question as Normal University and will
identify the course being discussed as Teach 101. Every semester the preservice teacher education program at Normal University offers several sections
of Teach 101, each of which is partnered with a school located in a nearby
urban school district. Students in Teach 101 are asked to complete thirty
required hours of observation at the partnering school and district, which
includes a half-day orientation, shadowing a teacher, completing community
service, and attending administrative meetings such as advisory board or
departmental meetings. Different instructors devise their own approach to
teaching this course, but in general all assign the students group and individual projects designed to help them reflect on their field experience, and
ultimately on their choice of teaching as a profession. For example, one
faculty member regularly asks students to collect their partnering school's
demographic data while others ask students to reflect back on their own high

school experience; some instructors expect students to keep a journal or take extensive field notes during their teacher observations, or write a weekly blog about specific topics relevant to urban education. Students read articles and books focused on school as a social institution, democracy in schooling, urban education, diversity, politics and education policy while tracking current events related to education, such as the debate over Common Core Curriculum Standards, efforts to promote charter schools, and debates about universal pre-kindergarten.

Readings for Teach 101 vary depending on who is teaching. Instructors assign a wide range of materials designed to engage students in thinking about the role and purpose of education, primarily within the context of U.S. schools. Thus students read the works of Nell Noddings, bell hooks, James Banks, John Dewey, Lisa Delpit, Gloria Ladson-Billing, Gregory Michie, Diane Ravitch, Walter Parker, and Pedro Noguera, to name a few. In addition, students review laws and policies ranging from "No Child Left Behind" to the New Jersey Education Law Center's website on the Abbot Schools legislation to the current Common Core Curriculum Standards. Each instructor has a slightly different approach, but all succeed in thoroughly immersing students in the concept of school as a social institution with emphasis on social justice and urban education in the United States.

Normal University's teacher education program asks that all of its students become familiar with a set of standards encompassing what the faculty consider ideal attributes of a teacher in a democratic society. In this study we will refer to these as *Standards of Excellence*. These standards are designed and regularly monitored by a center at the university's College of Education, and include such attributes as having thorough disciplinary knowledge, knowledge and understanding of how adolescents learn and develop, understanding the practice of culturally responsive teaching, critical thinking and problem solving skills, the ability to be reflective practitioners, and promotion of social justice. Students enrolled in all sections of Teach 101 are expected to familiarize themselves with all of the *Standards of Excellence*, which are discussed at length in class.

In Teach 101, as in many teacher education courses at U.S. universities, aspiring teachers learn about education at the state and national level, preparing them to teach within the local, state-level context. The course also provides students with insight into national-level debates in education policy and some discussion of the purpose of education within the context of U.S. society. In addition, students learn to be aware of the racial and ethnic diversity of their local schools, and of the importance of culturally responsive teaching. Because culturally responsive teaching is key to a course that introduces students to urban schools, this theme is emphasized throughout class discussions and readings. According to Geneva Gay, culturally responsive teaching gives guidance to educators who are trying to improve the academic achievement of students from diverse racial, ethnic, cultural, linguistic, and social class groups (Gay 2000). Thus in Teach 101 a great deal of attention is given to this topic by requiring students to think about and discuss the diversity of the K–12 schools they themselves attended as well as the diversity of their Teach 101 partnering school. A number of readings for the course model best practices in culturally responsive teaching, such as Gregory Michie's *Holler if You Hear Me* (2009), the author's memoir of his experience teaching in Chicago's inner-city schools.

What the course does not do as extensively, however, is provide students with a wider, more global perspective on the purpose of education in the global and international context, with its variations from one society to another. Some instructors require students to read the research of multicultural and social studies education scholars such as James Banks and Walter Parker, with emphasis on global education as it relates to civics and citizenship education and social justice. A number of scholars and researchers in the field of teacher education also have a long history of researching teaching as it relates to global and international education and/or cross-cultural awareness. An examination of recent literature on internationalization of teacher education will reveal the many reasons why it is imperative that teacher educators at all levels and in all content areas be more cognizant of global and international elements and incorporate them throughout their teacher education courses.

## LITERATURE REVIEW

According to the Longview Foundation's report *Teacher Preparation for the Global Age* (Longview Foundation 2008), most teachers begin their careers with little knowledge of the world in an age when one in five jobs are linked to international trade. While U.S. teacher preparation courses have not typically emphasized global and international approaches to education, conversely, much of the research in the field of comparative and international education has emphasized macro-level comparative analyses of systems of education around the world, or has examined the impact of international development projects and policies but has not emphasized teaching and teacher education. Only in recent years has research in the comparative education field begun to examine micro-level classroom interactions in comparative contexts. In the field of teacher education, conversely, research on teaching has traditionally avoided international and global contexts. This approach began to change in recent years, starting with social studies education in the 1990s, and has more recently expanded to encompass teacher education in general terms. An indicator of the convergence of these two fields took place in 2012, when two veteran researchers of teacher education in the United States edited the November edition of *Comparative*

*Education Review*, the flagship journal for research in comparative and international education in the United States.

In their introductory article for the November 2012 edition of *Comparative Education Review*, editors Lynn Paine and Kenneth Zeichner contended that teaching is not immune from global forces, and that as educators we rarely think about public schooling as being affected by global trends, noting that globalization has altered the skills that are imperative for the next generation of teachers and learners. They point out that policies and practices internationally do not support a claim that there is in all places a single vision of a "good teacher" or what it means to support the development of such teachers (Paine & Zeichner 2012). In other words, there is no international standard of what it means to be a good teacher along the lines of the *Standards of Excellence* Normal University sets for its own teacher education students.

Paine and Zeichner further argue that teaching is a "situated practice"; and even though teaching is "situated within a global context of shared discourses," teaching is also shaped by its more local (national and subnational) contexts. The authors argue that both national and local, historical and cultural practices, traditions, and institutions require globally informed policies and reforms. In short, they contend that it is time to examine the impact of globalization on the teaching profession and define new standards to produce globally competent teachers who can in turn prepare their students to be teachers who act as citizens, not just of the United States but also of the world.

In an earlier address to the National Association of Foreign Student Advisors (NAFSA) Colloquium on the Internationalization of Teacher Education, Zeichner asked what globally competent teachers should be able to do. He asserted that there should be more discussion of the rationale behind including global perspectives in teacher education as well as what such global perspectives should be like. He noted that U.S. institutions of higher education are well on their way to internationalization across the curriculum, yet with a few exceptions, such efforts have largely bypassed teacher education programs (Zeichner 2010).

James Banks argued in favor of globalization of teacher education within the framework of citizenship education with a specific focus on social justice. In his article "Diversity, Group Identity and Citizenship Education in a Global Age" Banks asserted that citizenship education should help students to develop an identity and attachment to the global community and a human connection around the world. He viewed this process as becoming "cosmopolitan." He maintained that students have become globally competent only when they view social justice and equality on a global level. It is this process that Banks referred to as "Transformative Citizenship Education."

Walter Parker offered another perspective in his article "Internationalization: What's in a Name." Parker discussed trends in internationalization of teacher education and argued that in recent years international education discourse has been dominated by national security concerns focused on building up both economic security and defense. Thus U.S. students' limited knowledge of the world has implications for U.S. economic competition in a global economy, while a lack of knowledge of languages has implications for defense and has led to measures such as the 2006 National Security Language initiative to support the learning of strategic languages such as Arabic, Korean, and Farsi. Parker argued that internationalization of education is necessary for students to develop "perspective consciousness," or "awareness on the part of the individual that he or she has a view of the world that is not universally shared" (Parker 2008, p. 199). Like Banks and Zeichner, he thought that educators should help students become citizens of the world first. In order to accomplish this, Parker proposed building international education on the demographics of the student body in U.S. schools in order to help both students and teachers be more aware of the diversity within their midst and be able to extend a more localized multicultural awareness and cross-cultural understanding to the global context. International education should "liberate multiculturalism from its national container," and begin at the local level by taking advantage of a vibrant immigrant population (Parker 2008, p. 199).

In her studies of preservice social studies and global education teachers, Merry Merryfield similarly argued in favor of an approach to global education that places students at the center of instruction by helping teachers make instructional decisions based on students' background and interests. She argued for beginning with students' own cultures before other cultures and for connecting local and global injustices and inequities across time and space. Merryfield advocated the use of cross-cultural experiential learning based on local global cultures, asserting: "The process of making connections between global and local creates constant comparisons and an appreciation of the complexities of cultural borrowing and change" (Merryfield 1998, p. 365). Merryfield called the development of global awareness and cross-cultural sensitivity "worldmindedness." According to Merryfield, we know we are "worldminded" when we form the habit of thinking about the effects of our decisions on people across the planet, when we care about how others view our nation, and when we use "us" to refer to people from many places, not simply our own nation (Merryfield 2008).

Scholars like Zeichner and Paine, Parker, Banks, and Merryfield would agree that the key to linking teacher education with globalization or to the internationalization of teacher education is to tap into the potential of students as global citizens and promote education for social justice on a local as well as global scale. Parker, Zeichner, and Merryfield in particular contended that preservice teacher education programs should help teacher education candidates develop what has been called perspective or sociocultural consciousness where students learn that their way of thinking, behaving, and being is influenced by their social and cultural location—race, ethnicity, gender, social class, language, nationality. Future teachers need to develop humility about their own point of view and understand that what they believe as U.S. citizens is not necessarily shared by others throughout the world.

Villegas and Lucas (2002) have similarly found that teachers cannot connect with students across social and cultural perspectives without sociocultural consciousness that their world view is influenced by location in relation to markers such as gender, social class, ethnicity, race, and religion. In a more recent study, Biraimah and Jotia (2013) pointed out that effective teacher preparation for a global age should include such competencies as inclusive pedagogical practices, cultural and contextual knowledge, instruction that meets the needs and challenges of a culturally and linguistically diverse student community, approaches to address stereotypes and prejudices as well as conceptualizations to address global interconnectedness and cultural sensitively. In short, globalization of teacher education is needed to bridge the consciousness of cultural awareness and help teacher education students understand that American views are not shared by others around the world.

Many of the competencies researched and discussed by the scholars in this literature review have similarity to the attributes found in Normal University's *Standards of Excellence*, and specifically those that relate to culturally responsive teaching, sensitivity to cultural and linguistic diversity, and approaches to address stereotypes. Teach 101 is meant to convey the basic principles and standards outlined in the *Standards of Excellence* and is in that sense well on its way to addressing the development of sociocultural consciousness among preservice teacher education students. However, the standards stop short of providing preservice teachers with a standard for global competence.

It is common for teacher education programs to focus on development of a sociocultural consciousness as part of preparing students to become teachers in their state-level school system as well as at the national level. However, as previously mentioned, few preservice programs seek to extend this cultural awareness beyond the borders of the United States, nor do they actively seek to make students aware that such competencies are needed in a rapidly globalized world.

What can we do to better prepare our future teachers for global competency? Overseas travel on the part of preservice social studies or language teachers can motivate teachers to improve instructional practice in teaching about the world, while teachers with cross-cultural backgrounds have a greater awareness of the importance of promoting cross-cultural understanding in the classroom (Merryfield 1998). Given the costs and time commitments involved in overseas travel, it makes the most sense to focus efforts on promoting local, cross-cultural understanding in preservice teacher education programs, and thereby develop global awareness and perspective consciousness through local or "glocal" approaches to teacher education.

The course Teach 101 might therefore benefit from the addition or expansion of culturally responsive pedagogical theory and practice for all preservice teachers that would include strategies for building instruction on students' own cultures and for connecting the local community with global cultures through cross-cultural experiential learning. How can future iterations of Teach 101 take cross-cultural and multicultural education out of its "national container" by helping teacher education students make these local-global connections? The following analysis will attempt to answer this question by exploring the "glocal" potential of Teach 101 as a model for internationalization of general and introductory teacher education courses.

The following analysis is in response to two research questions:

1. What are students' attitudes toward incorporating "glocal" elements into Teach 101?
2. How may students' attitudes help to create a "glocal" component for the class?

## DATA COLLECTION AND ANALYSIS

Data collection for this chapter involved a triangulation of data sources. Some of the most creative research uses models eclectically; combining aspects of various data sources' results in a more valid research design (Le-Compte & Preissle 1993). Although this is a case study of a single course, data sources extend outside the course to include the wider departmental, school, and university community, as well as affiliated partnering school districts. I used anecdotal records taken after classroom conversations and discussions; biweekly journal entries where I reflected on all aspects of the class (students' assignments, presentations, practicum experiences, and their understanding of the assigned readings); and all personal written correspondence regarding this project (e-mail, faculty meetings, and other meetings regarding the class).

Data analysis used an emergent theme analysis approach: I read and re-read all the written materials I gathered during the semester looking for emergent themes and potential coding categories, made notes in the margins of my reflective notes and materials looking for overarching themes as they emerged as part of the reflective process (Lincoln & Guba 1985). During my reflections, I began to notice that preservice teachers in the course developed a great interest in cultural sensitivity and culturally responsive teaching that they observed in their reading, assignments, and classroom observations. My thoughts stem from course syllabi and materials, and my notes on my evaluations of student work and field-based activities during a semester of Teach 101. I view this study as a pilot: these reflections will form the basis of a more extensive and deliberative study of multiple sections of this course, and emergent themes will form the basis of more formal coding categories. This study will prepare the groundwork for the larger study by means of a preliminary literature review and reflective analysis of course activities.

## FINDINGS

The following section includes the research questions followed by their findings.

### Research Question 1

1. What are students' attitudes toward incorporating "glocal" elements into Teach 101? My reflective analysis of the data determined that (a) students equate global and international with occasional culture fairs, exposure to diversity, and study-abroad experiences; (b) students felt they had sufficient exposure to a local "melting pot" of international cultures and did not need global elements in their teacher education course; and (c) the majority of students demonstrated a deep understanding of the importance of culturally responsive teaching and did not see the need to add global elements to their preservice courses.

a. Students equate global and international with occasional culture fairs, exposure to the diversity, and study-abroad experiences:

A closer look at my reflections on student comments throughout the semester indicated that some preservice teacher education students' conceptions of global or international education were limited to cultural fairs, parades, or social studies classes. For example, a common theme that emerged was that schools students attended while growing up adequately addressed global education through their annual international culture days and parades. I recall some students commenting that it is not necessary to study foreign languages since everyone in the world studies English, while other comments were made indicating that state and local communities were already sufficiently diverse to provide students with a global perspective, implying that there was really no need to add such a component to teacher education courses.

My reflections on preservice teacher education students' attitudes about "glocalizing" Teach 101 further indicated that in regard to university-level education, the existing culture clubs and activities on the Normal University campus were good and sufficient sources of campus internationalization, as was the presence on campus of a multinational teaching staff. The consensus was that the state is already a "melting pot," and its schools already have enough cultural diversity to provide students with global competency without necessarily making such themes a requirement of teacher education courses or programs.

In spite of the consensus discussed above, there were some student comments that showed awareness of and interest in internationalization of teacher education. In my reflections on a classroom activity in which students were asked what global or international experiences they would add to their studies at Normal University, I recall some students suggested that teacher education programs should require more classes in cross-cultural awareness or multicultural education to help future teachers develop global perspectives. Some student comments suggested that teacher education students be asked to do a presentation on their own cultural heritage as a way of developing cultural awareness as a potential "glocal" element. Nearly all of the students' comments indicated that they thought study abroad or some form of overseas experience was an important means of developing global awareness, demonstrating a tendency to equate global and international with travel.

b. Students felt they had sufficient exposure to a local "melting pot" of international cultures and did not need global elements in their teacher education course, and related experiences.

In my own reflections on the in-class exercise described above, I noted that five students thought teaching about education in other countries would be helpful in developing global awareness, while six students thought it would be useful to have the university's visiting scholars and other individuals with overseas teaching experience come to class to discuss education in their country of origin. Although they did not explicitly label it as such, these students showed "awareness of comparative and international education through expressing interest in studying transnational comparisons of education systems throughout the world" (A. Price-Rom, personal communication, April 25, 2014). In general, those students whose comments supported globalization demonstrated that they understood global education was not the purview of social studies alone. For example, music education students' reflections demonstrated their awareness that music instruction should not be overly focused on Western European traditions, and that children should be exposed to a variety of conceptions of music in other cultures. Physical education was thought to be without cultural boundaries, and the Olympic Games and World Cup in particular were viewed as ways to "unify diverse cultures with activities that were of value to all" (A. Price-Rom, personal communication, April 25, 2014). In the reflections of mathematics teachers it was noted that math, like physical education, is a universal topic that can be compared across cultures.

Finally, a few students observed that the presence of two other students in the course who had recently emigrated to the United States provided Teach 101 students with a different perspective and actually helped eliminate assumptions about education in the United States. For example, it was helpful for students to hear about the numerous local languages spoken in the country of origin of a student of West African origin: "The student noted that French and English were both official languages of instruction in her country of origin, and that in addition there were in 24 major African language groups" (A. Price-Rom, personal communication, May 6, 2014).

    c. The majority of students demonstrated a deep understanding of the importance of culturally responsive teaching at the local level.

After reviewing anecdotal records taken from evaluations of student presentations, it was evident that a significant number of students in Teach 101 demonstrated understanding of culturally responsive teaching. During the first few weeks of Teach 101, students were asked to analyze the individual statements from Normal University's *Standards of Excellence*. Groups of two to three students were assigned to each of the statements and asked to write a brief analysis. At the end of the semester students reviewed their statements a second time and wrote a few lines about how the teachers they observed at the partnering school exemplified each of the *Standards of Excellence*. In their reflections about which statements were important to them as teachers, a majority of the students mentioned the standard for culturally responsive teaching.

In my notes on final project reports, I found that students demonstrated the ability to identify culturally responsive teaching in the classrooms they observed. Half of the students enrolled in the course chose to write about the *Standard of Excellence* for culturally responsive teaching in their final report, which stipulates that the ideal teacher should understand the practice of culturally responsive teaching, have skills for learning about the diverse students they teach, and use knowledge of students and their lives to design and carry out instruction that builds on students' individual and cultural strengths. Student thoughts about culturally responsive teaching clearly demonstrated their belief that "good teachers need to create learning environments in which students feel safe enough to contribute to class discussions without being denied an equal learning opportunity due to race, culture, diversity or socio-economic status" (A. Price-Rom, personal communication, April 25, 2014).

In reviewing my notes on students' final project presentations, I found that nearly every Teach 101 student had commented on the ability of the teachers they observed at the partnering school to empathize with their students by using culturally relevant assignments, such as one art teacher's creation of a mural reflecting the local community, and the use of culturally relevant posters and motivational quotes that were hung on the classroom walls. A few students "noted a music teacher's choice of culturally relevant music, willingness to adapt instruction as well as dedication to helping economically disadvantaged students have access to musical instruments" (A. Price-Rom, personal communication, May 12, 2014).

Course readings related to cultural awareness also made an impression on students in Teach 101, who in their reflections frequently referred to Gregory Michie's 2009 memoir *Holler if You Hear Me*, and specifically to episodes where Michie tapped into his students' cultural backgrounds to engage them in learning, or considered his students' circumstances when they were having difficulty in school. Finally, Teach 101 students were also cognizant of the political situation in their partnering school's district and made note of the high school students' involvement in social justice movements at the school, such as a student walkout protesting district policies.

## Research Question 2

2. How may students' attitudes help to create a "glocal" component for the class? My reflective analysis of the data determined that the development of a glocal consciousness to promote social justice is a crucial task for the class. This consciousness would build upon students' understanding of culturally responsive teaching at the local level and extend it to the global level to foster what Merryfield calls "world-mindedness."

Clearly the students in Teach 101 were in the process of developing sociocultural consciousness, affirming views toward diversity and an understanding of culturally responsive teaching, and it is this element in the course that may open the door to helping beginning teachers become more culturally competent on a global as well as local scale. Students demonstrated their potential to take culturally responsive teaching a step further to develop what James Banks called an "identity and attachment to the global community and a human connection around the world" (Banks 2008). As Banks argued, students become globally competent only when they view social justice and equality on a global level. The students in Teach 101 did not consistently equate diversity and culturally responsive teaching with global education, perhaps because the course was very much focused on the U.S. education context. Therefore, the task of future sections of this course is to help students extend their local understanding of social justice and cultural competence to the global level.

Future iterations of Teach 101 and similar introductory preservice courses may build upon the concepts of transformative citizenship and socio-cultural competence and develop what Villegas and Lucas call "socio-cultural consciousness of the global self" (Villegas & Lucas 2002) by including some of the students' own recommendations for incorporating global elements into teacher education courses, as well as recommendations from scholars of citizenship education and multicultural education. We have noted that study abroad is not always affordable or feasible for college students; however there are local "glocal" alternatives that might re-create the experience of living and/or student teaching in another cultural context.

Merryfield's study of social studies teachers' decision-making processes noted that not only teachers but also students themselves play a significant role in shaping their teachers' instructional decision making; and she found that teachers made decisions based on particular characteristics of students— race, ethnicity, religion, class, experiences, interests, or behavior and noted that effective teachers make curriculum relevant to students' lives. She suggested that teacher educators must deal with the realities and contextual factors that have shaped their own perspectives and those of the teachers with whom they work. This means that systematic reflection may be an important first step in helping teacher education students develop sociocultural consciousness and ultimately global competence. Merryfield asks her own teacher education students to identify and reflect upon the values, beliefs, and experiences that have shaped their own multicultural and global perspectives through a "Tree of Life" exercise in which they trace their cultural connections and heritage (Merryfield 1994).

In her 1998 study Merryfield noted the contradiction between what students learned about global education on campus in contrast to their field experiences. In this study of three groups of global studies teachers the guiding theory shared by all teachers was that students need knowledge and appreciation of multiple perspectives, multiple realities, and conflicting viewpoints on issues, events, and people under study. This then enables them to develop a perspective consciousness and move away from parochialism. She pointed out that for teachers in homogeneous settings, school experience in a heterogeneous school setting is critical in helping students overcome parochialism. A number of the students in Teach 101 were from homogenous suburban school districts with little diversity. Thus the required practicum in an urban district was instrumental in connecting these students with heterogeneous classrooms and with practicing teachers who modeled culturally responsive teaching in those contexts.

Merryfield's ideas for global education teachers apply to teachers in all content areas and to students in introductory preservice courses like Teach 101. In Teach 101, students and their backgrounds, interests, and experiences should be at the center of instruction wherever possible, and instructors should be prepared to build upon those experiences. Using an exercise similarly to Merryfield's "Tree of Life" at the beginning of the course would help identify students' interests and experiences early on. The presence of students educated in different countries who regularly contributed their perspectives to the class might also contribute to class meetings in more formal ways by being given the opportunity to give a lesson or lead a discussion on the differences between schools in the United States and schools in their country of origin. An examination of common education-related issues in other parts of the world would provide students with a more global perspective and enable them to connect issues and topics related to U.S. schooling with those in the global community. Thus access and equity to education in the United States could be discussed in relation to those issues in West Africa or South America, while the civil rights movement and education in the United States could be compared with education and the end of apartheid in South Africa.

There are numerous other ways to design cross-cultural learning that brings teacher education students together with teachers and students from other cultures both on and off campus. University campus offices that support international students and visiting scholars can be a wealth of resources and information about overseas partnering schools and universities as well as visiting scholars and students from around the world. Introductory teacher education courses can easily build in a guest lecture or discussion with international visitors to learn about schooling in global contexts and potentially develop long-term partnerships that could result in both real and virtual classroom experiences, observations, discussions, joint research projects focused on action research, team teaching, or lesson planning in a given content area and working on a social justice project with a group of teacher education students in another part of the world.

Instructors for Teach 101 might easily tap into resources in the local community, such as a variety of practicum experiences at schools where instruction is in languages other than English, tutoring opportunities in refugee education programs such as the International Rescue Committee or the Jewish Federation, and involvement with the education-related activities of the local World Affairs Council, Peace Corps offices, and various international exchange organizations. Assignments to visit local communities where students can experience another culture would also be helpful for students from suburban districts. Spending time in predominantly Spanish- or Arabic-speaking schools and their surrounding communities would give students a different cultural perspective and could be one of several cross-cultural requirements for the course.

## CONCLUSION

This reflection serves as a preliminary exploration of the potential to infuse one teacher education course with local/global elements, but due to time constraints does not pretend to be a comprehensive study. It is intended to prepare groundwork for a more elaborate study of Teach 101 and a variety of introductory, preservice teacher education courses. The latter will involve a more thorough review of several sections of Teach 101 in addition to similar courses taught at representative teacher education programs in other parts of the country, including interviews, focus groups, and a small survey questionnaire in order to determine whether the recommendations of this chapter are applicable in other contexts.

Internationalization of teacher education programs is essential in helping future teachers cross the "us/them boundary" and in understanding that American perspectives are not always shared by others around the world. Global competence among teacher education students means understanding that diversity and culture both at home and abroad mean more than an annual culture fair or occasional culture course and should be integrated across and throughout the teacher education curriculum. Although some students in the Teach 101 course expressed an interest in study-abroad opportunities, and those are important, more localized opportunities for global interaction provide all students with access to international perspectives regardless of their ability to pay or find time to travel. Whatever the "glocal" teacher education experience is, it must be one that enables students to develop awareness that a person's view of the world is influenced by location in relation to gender, social class, ethnicity, race, and religion. This may mean requiring students to participate in a project that promotes social justice in another part of the world, it may mean connecting students with visiting international scholars and students at Normal University to make them aware of differing cultural perspectives, or discovering what their own region has to offer by way of cross-cultural experiences.

## REFERENCES

Adamson, B. (2012). International and comparative studies in teaching and teacher education. *Teaching and Teacher Education 28*: 641–648.

Banks, J. A. (2008). Diversity, group identity and citizenship education in a global age. *Educational Researcher 37*(3): 129–139.

Biraimah, K. and Jotia, L. (2013). Longitudinal effects of study abroad programs. *Journal of Studies in International Education 17*: 433–454.

Gay, G. (2000). *Culturally responsive teaching: Theory, research and practice.* New York: Teachers College Press.

Koziol, S., Greenberg, J., Williams, L., Niehaus, E., & Jacobson, C. (2011). *Internationalizing teacher education: A systematic initiative.* Paper presented at the International Conference on Education for Teaching. Glasgow, Scotland.

LeCompte, M. & Preissle, J. (1993). *Ethnography and qualitative design in educational research.* New York: Academic Press.

Lincoln, Y. & Guba, E. (1985). *Naturalistic Inquiry.* Beverly Hills, CA: Sage Publications.

Longview Foundation. (2008). Teacher preparation for the global age: The imperative for change. Silver Spring, MD: Author.

Merryfield, M. (1994). Shaping the curriculum in global education: The influence of student characteristics on teacher decision making. *Journal of Curriculum and Supervision 9*(3): 233–249.

Merryfield, M. (1998). Pedagogy for global perspectives in education: Studies of teachers' thinking and practice. *Theory and Research in Social Education 26*(3): 342–379.

Merryfield, M., Lo, J., Po, S., & Kasai, M. (2008). Worldmindedness: Taking off the blinders. *Journal of Curriculum and Instruction 2*(1): 6–16.

Michie, G. (2009). *Holler if you hear me: The education of a teacher and his students*. New York: Teachers College Press.

Paine, L. & Zeichner, K. (2012).The local and the global in reforming teaching and teacher education. *Comparative Education Review 56*(4): 569–583.

Parker, W. (2008). International education: What's in a name? *Phi Delta Kappan*, 90, 196–202.

Parker, W. & Camicia, S. (2009). Cognitive praxis in today's "international education" movement: A case study of intents and affinities. *Theory and Research in Social Education 27*(1): 42–74.

Villegas, A. M. & Lucas, T. (2002). Preparing culturally responsive teachers: Rethinking the curriculum. *Journal of Teacher Education 53*(1): 20–32.

Villegas, A. M. & Lucas, T. (2007). The culturally responsive teacher. *Educational Leadership 64*(6), 28–33.

Zeichner, K. (2010). Preparing globally competent teachers: A U.S. perspective. Colloquium on the internationalization of teacher education. NAFSA: Association of International Education.

*Chapter Thirteen*

# Positionality and Glocal Encounters in Social Studies Teacher Education

## Steven Camicia and Marialuisa Di Stefano

I would like U.S. students to be aware of the "not-so-good" relationship between the Filipinos and the Americans before as the latter were once one of
our colonizers. Later on however, when the Japanese invaded our country and
brought terror, the Americans were in our side against the mighty forces of
Japan. Until present, these two countries remain in good terms. (Filipina student, discussion board post)

One of the central components of social justice is the recognition of people
and their perspectives when considering histories and policies that impact
their lives. This is especially true for people who have been or are currently
marginalized through histories and policies. Inequitable power relations
based upon actual or perceived identities such as race, ethnicity, gender,
language, sexual orientation, ability, and geopolitical belonging are reflected
in histories and policies. The recognition of these inequitable relations and
the perspectives connected with them is a critical attribute of democratic
communities that are committed to social justice. Camicia (2012, 2014) describes this as an *ethic of recognition*. The discussion of public issues with an
ethic of recognition can be an important part of teacher education in general
and internationalizing social studies teacher education in particular. Preservice teachers in social studies methods courses learn how to prepare their
future students to participate in democratic, multicultural, and global communities.

In this chapter, we illustrate the ethic of recognition in two ways. First,
our illustration is grounded in our positionalities as social studies teacher
educators and authors in accordance with duoethnography methodology,
which highlights the positionalities of the authors as a form of rigor in data

analysis (Camicia & Zhu, 2012; Lund & Nabavi, 2008; Norris, 2008; Sawyer & Liggett, 2012). Rather than detached participants and observers, our positionalities are central within the network of power relations surrounding curriculum design and implementation. Second, we illustrate recognition through our description, analysis, and interpretation of a project where preservice teachers in social studies methods courses in the Philippines and the United States discussed issues through an online discussion board. Our purpose in presenting these two facets of recognition is to show how students, teachers, curriculum developers, and researchers can be recognized in the process of curriculum design and implementation.

The unique history between the Philippines as a colonized country and the United States as a colonizing country provided the context for creating glocal spaces within teacher education programs in both countries. Preservice teachers communicated through an online discussion board about issues such as colonization, language, politics, and gender. Social justice was a main component of this project as students discussed inequalities related to their different global positionalities. The discussion opened a third space where global and local combined, and as a result, privileged and marginalized people and perspectives had the opportunity to communicate.

Although the project was brief due to technological limitations, we discuss implications for interactions between glocalization, technology, teacher education, social studies education, and social justice. We, the authors, a male born in the United States and a female born in Italy, discuss our differing interpretations of the project and the topics discussed as a way to place and recognize our positionalities. We conclude from the project that glocal teacher education can increase student understanding of global issues and the power inequities inherent in such issues. Teacher educators and curriculum designers of international experiences can use this issue-based model of recognition to promote global citizenship and understanding oriented toward social justice.

## THEORETICAL PERSPECTIVE

### The Range of Multicultural and Global Perspectives in Curriculum

An awareness and recognition of multiple perspectives is increasingly valued in state standards as is reflected in the Common Core State Standards Initiative and C3 Framework for Social Studies State Standards. This recognition is also an important aspect of authentic and equitable dialogue in democratic communities. An issues-based curriculum encourages students to deliberate as members of a democratic community (Camicia, 2009; Gutmann, 1987; Hess, 2008; Parker, 2006). Discussion of public issues provides students opportunities to view public issues from multiple perspectives. Since the recognition of people, identities, and their perspectives is vital to the legitimacy of a democratic community, curriculum aimed at such inclusion is central to social studies education and education for democracy.

Unfortunately, schools are often places where dominant cultural groups and identities exclude the perspectives of nondominant groups and identities (Apple, 2000; Banks, 2002). Although curriculum can appear democratic to dominant groups, a closer look often reveals an underlying restriction of the range of perspectives found in the curriculum. For example, Camicia (2007, 2009) found that social studies instructional materials teaching students about immigration policy, deliberation, and citizenship lacked a recognition of multicultural and global perspectives. Although the instructional materials that he examined claimed to provide multiple perspectives on immigration policy for students to use in classroom deliberation, the materials did not recognize nondominant identities and perspectives.

From a global perspective, this lack of recognition took the form of a nationalistic perspective. All the choices of immigration policies were aimed at enriching the United States. The range of global perspectives could have been increased by including a broader understanding of the causes of human migration related to inequitable power relations. For example, students could have recognized perspectives on human migration related to globalization and inequitable trade policies (Bigelow, 2006; Bigelow & Peterson, 2002). From a multicultural perspective, the restriction in the social studies instructional materials took the form of monoculturalism. Although one of the sets of instructional materials discussed how racism has shaped U.S. immigration policy, this perspective was not recognized explicitly in the policies and perspectives offered for student discussion. The perspectives of marginalized people related to identities such as gender, sexual orientation, language, ability, and geopolitical belonging were also absent from the instructional materials. Although the materials claimed to foster democratic deliberation through choice of policies, students were primarily given very few choices when recognizing the possible range of multicultural and global perspectives.

Alfredo Bayon, a social studies education professor at Southern Leyte State University in the Philippines, and Steven Camicia, a social studies education professor at Utah State University in the United States, started a collaboration that was intended to increase the range of multicultural and global perspectives in teacher education curriculum. They wrote an account that focused upon the process of their collaboration (Camicia & Bayon, 2012). We, the authors of the current chapter, extend Steven and Alfredo's project by focusing upon implications for internationalizing social studies teacher education.

## Positionalities and Teacher Education

Our project is composed of the positionalities of students, teachers, and curriculum developers in the discussion of social issues. Our understanding of positionality is guided by feminist epistemologists (Code, 1991; Collins, 2000; Harding, 1993; Hekman, 1997; Lather, 1992) and postcolonial theorists (Bhabha, 2003; Mohanty, 1984; Spivak, 1996) who understand knowledge as situated within a specific context. In every classroom, each student and teacher has a unique positionality. The question becomes whether all these positionalities are recognized in classroom conversation or only dominant positionalities are recognized. For example, are the perspectives of white students recognized more than students of color? Are the perspectives of male students recognized more than the perspectives of female students? Are the perspectives of students who speak English as their first language recognized more than the perspectives of students who are learning English as an additional language? Social justice in classrooms relies upon recognition of these various positionalities during discussion of public issues. Maher and Tetreault (1993) describe positionality this way:

> Gender, race, class, and other aspects of our identities are markers of relational *positions* rather than essential qualities. Knowledge is valid when it includes an acknowledgement of the knower's specific position in any context, because changing contextual and relational factors are crucial for defining identities and our knowledge in any given situation. (p. 118)

We created an issue-centered teacher education experience that placed our positionalities as curriculum designers and the positionalities of students as a central strand that would support the opening of a third space (Bhabha, 2003). Our methodology of duoethnography, which we discuss in more detail later, is our attempt as teacher educators to place our positionalities within this third space as we ask our students to do. Soja (2009) writes that third spaces resist definition but can be thought of as "an invitation to enter a space of extraordinary openness, a place of critical exchange where geographical imagination can be expanded to encompass a multiplicity of perspectives that have heretofore been considered by the epistemological referees to be incompatible, uncombinable" (p. 51). We recognize glocal spaces as third spaces with possibilities for internationalizing social studies teacher education. Rather than discussing issues that were primarily national in scope, we opened glocal spaces where students discussed issues related to colonization, language, and gender on an online discussion board. We begin our discussion of the project by reflecting upon our positionalities as teacher educators, as well as developers of curriculum in the areas of multicultural, global, civic, and language education.

The following questions guide our chapter:

1. How can our sharing/discussing of positionalities (as teacher educators and students) lend authenticity to the discussion of glocal issues and increase social justice?
2. How do these discussions increase the range of multicultural and global perspectives in social studies teacher education courses?

## DUOETHNOGRAPHY METHODOLOGY

Duoethnography is a way for researchers to use their unique positionalities to improve the rigor of research. Under many traditional research methodologies, researchers view rigor through a lens of triangulation. According to this view, validity is increased when data sources are consistent in their perspective of an experience or phenomenon. When multiple researchers describe, analyze, and interpret data separately and arrive at the same findings, validity is also increased. This is where duoethnography contrasts itself with many traditional viewpoints. Sawyer and Liggett (2012) write:

> [Duoethnography's] method is framed by a poststructuralist approach to research. Such an approach rejects the notion of a single, fixed, and absolute reality existing independently of human consciousness and imagination. Instead, meanings are constructed in the process of interpretation. Drawing from this philosophy, duoethnographers engage in multiple interpretations as they use self as a site of analysis of socio-cultural meanings and influences. (p. 629)

When researchers/authors enter the research process with an eye toward converging multiple voices into a single disembodied voice, as is traditional in the process and reporting, some voices, identities, positionalities, and interpretations are lost. Those that are marginalized are lost first. This is a central concern in any research process and to a greater extent in research surrounding issues of social justice. In the following sections, we present our positionalities as authors and teacher educators in order to foreshadow each of our analyses and interpretations in the findings section. Along this journey, we hope to increase an ethic of recognition in our understanding of the dialogue project and construct a glocal space within this chapter where we, preservice teachers, and readers can dynamically insert their unique positionalities.

### Marialuisa's Positionality

I am a female doctoral student, Sicilian in ethnicity, Italian in citizenship, and a permanent U.S. resident. I am multilingual and moved to the United States originally for professional development in journalism and mass media communication. My first academic experience in the United States was as an exchange student and Rotary International Ambassadorial scholar at the University of Idaho. I was selected to promote international understanding and friendly relationships among people of different geographical areas. As a result of my cultural interactions with Latin American students and professors on campus, I quickly became proficient in Spanish and I found a great passion for their cultures. I quit my job as Web writer and reporter in Italy and I started teaching Spanish and Italian languages and cultures at Washington State University. As part of my MA program in foreign languages and cultures, I especially focused on Caribbean studies and migration. I approached my journey as student and teacher in the United States comforted that my positionality would put me in a favored position. I was wrong. While I was taking up the defense of all races and ethnicities of immigrants, refugees, and minorities, I was unconsciously and proudly carrying my white privilege. I had in my travel kit my European business-class immigrant privileges and those charms or myths that linger around my Italian heritage. This caused a lack of recognition.

My thinking and my way of knowing have been informed by the Eurocentric, patriarchal, heterosexual doctrine in which I have been trained for the first twenty-seven years of my life until I moved to the United States. I was raised in a middle-class society that officially recognizes equal self-determination rights for women, as long as we learn to self-censor when we are stepping into male roles or pretending to obtain social status and job positions without the right connections. Looking back at my original positionality, I can see that I failed to deconstruct my Western standpoint, which led to a lack of recognition of other standpoints. But the Western position was the only perspective that I could use at that time to recognize a radically open perspective.

While arguing about the importance of creating intercultural spaces, I was only encouraging my Sicilian community to share privileged spaces with marginalized people for their occasional cultural celebrations. In a certain way, we were proud of allowing Sri Lankans, who are the most numerous migrants in my hometown, to celebrate their heritage day once a year in a public fair. Likewise, we were happy to accept Catholic Filipinos and connect with them by sharing Sicilian patron saints days. In other words, it was pretending that they were recognized and could all "pass" for locals. From this perspective, our Sicilian community could build an inclusive society by simply recognizing our similarities while ignoring our differences. In the same vein, this perspective advocated for the creation of an artificial identity that we conferred on others to make them more suitable to our sociocultural expectations. This "openness" built upon a lack of recognition masked an attempt to impose the perspectives of a dominant culture upon a marginalized culture.

During the last four years, I gradually engaged in a critical and postcolonial journey that unveiled a completely different perspective on recognition. I started becoming and recognizing my hybrid cultural identity, produced by the integration of Sicilian-Italian, Latin American, and U.S. cultures, languages, and values. My dual immersion in U.S. and Latin American languages and cultures in a small liberal college town in the Northwest hybridized my identity even further. I felt relieved of this spiritual culpability of not being able to choose what was naturally good for me and that had always coincided with what my heritage culture wanted for me: being a strong and intelligent, but not too ambitious, docile spouse and mother.

In the global setting, I recognize myself as part of Western academia, writing in English about the rest of the world. In the local context, my multiculturalism and exotic background are perceived as good skills to engage in bilingual and diversity discussions in my teacher education courses. Trading my position as European Union citizen with a position in the privileged minorities in the United States entailed a multicultural perspective.

However, my foreign accent and my not-white-enough status do not facilitate my attempt to unlock and recognize the concept of whiteness and white privilege for white preservice teachers. They usually master the concept of whiteness better when it is taught by teachers who are recognized as more white. In order to negotiate meanings with students and other scholars every day, I have to recognize and elaborate a glocal dimension of myself that acknowledges my international experience in a predominantly white U.S. setting.

To interpret our project with preservice teachers in the Philippines and the United States, I started reflecting on the cultural boundaries and hybrid identities that are built in liminal spaces. These hybrid identities belong to specific populations but involve different cultures. In addition to my reconsideration and recognition of identities, my positionality led me to unlearn the notion of the nation-state and space. In this project, I listened to the insights of students and colleagues in our teacher education program. I became committed to continuous reflection that values social justice and cross-cultural understanding. I valued the conversations generated by class discussions even when they challenged me as a student and as a teacher. As a researcher, my journey will lead me to consider how I can contribute to dialogue between cultures, and what languages I can use in order to deconstruct dichotomies and prejudicial thought.

## Steven's Positionality

My awareness of my identities has been limited by the ways that they mirror the dominant culture in the United States during my lifetime. As a white, English-speaking, middle-class, cis male, U.S. citizen, my positionality has been privileged in local and global communities. As a result of this unearned privilege, I have limited understanding of what it is to be marginalized as a result of racism, classism, sexism, ableism, cisgenderism, nationalism, or language. The school curriculum mirrored most of my identities through a historical metanarrative of European, American, and male exceptionalism. This metanarrative was maintained through many aspects of my education ranging from who was recognized in instructional materials to who was recognized in classroom discussions.

While these identities were privileged in the curriculum, my identity as a queer male was never recognized in the curriculum or classroom discussion. Heteronormativity in society yielded my identity as a queer male as unrecognizable. This lack of recognition was policed by a violent code of masculinity and patriarchy that saw any differences in sexuality as threats to society. This was also codified by most of the religions that I knew of growing up. In this case, misrecognition of my queerness was a bad thing because it marked me as ill or evil. The combinations of these cultural forces that denied my recognition through threat of physical and mental abuse lead me to live most of my life under a blanket of depression. My positionality as having mostly privileged identities and one marginalized identity increased my interest in the role of positionality and recognition within educational settings.

I first started recognizing my unearned privileges during a viewing of the *Color of Fear* in one of my first teacher education courses (Lee, 1994). This film and other experiences at the University of Nevada, Reno, increased my awareness of my privilege as a white male and the resulting ignorance of oppression that was attached to these identities. During my time as a sixth-grade teacher, I looked for ways to include multiple perspectives and identities in my curriculum. This involved an increased interest in multicultural and social studies education. I decided to enroll in a PhD program at the University of Washington in Seattle in order to study with my mentor, Walter Parker, and James Banks. My doctoral studies increased my commitment to democratic, multicultural, and international education.

My interest in the dialogue project between preservice teachers in the Philippines and the United States was in creating a dialogue where global issues could be discussed. I wanted this discussion to increase the range of perspectives in teacher education courses. My positionality as a white male from the United States was problematic. During the colonization of the Philippines, the United States used language and education as tools of colonization. English is still an official language in the Philippines, and the scope and sequence of the education system still mirrors the U.S. system. I wondered if this project was another form of colonization by a white male from the United States. I believed that attention to issues of social injustice and a transparency of identity and positionality was a way to proceed. I wasn't interested in teacher educators or preservice teachers discussing global issues in a disembodied debate. In order for authentic dialogue to occur, there needed to be transparency related to historical and contemporary relations of domination and marginalization.

To some, this consideration can be seen as too theoretical, but this is often the viewpoint of someone from a dominant group or positionality. As a queer male, I don't see LGBT issues in classrooms as theoretical. It is only such to people who have the privilege to deny recognition of such perspectives. In this way, an awareness of the ways that curriculum excludes cultural or global perspectives is the first step in social studies teacher education toward consciously including those perspectives.

## SETTINGS AND PARTICIPANTS

The participants for our project included preservice teachers in the Philippines and the United States and us, as teacher educators and authors. Preservice teachers in our social studies education courses participated in an asynchronous online discussion board. Although student dialogue was limited due to logistical and technological limitations, the participation of preservice teachers illustrates the potential for technology to internationalize teacher education toward an orientation of global social justice. Sixteen preservice teachers in the Philippines and sixteen preservice teachers in the United States took part in our project, but the number of students who actually discussed issues was much lower. The project only lasted for three weeks due to different semester schedules, student teaching, and technical issues. We discuss the technical issues in more detail later. Participation in the project was also not graded, something that we would consider changing in future iterations due to a low participation rate. From the beginning of the project, we were aware from discussions that the Filipino preservice teachers knew much more about the United States than the preservice teachers in the United States knew about the Philippines.

When introduced to another country's culture, preservice teachers in our program in the United States often make comments such as: information about other countries is not taught in public schools unless they are directly related to the United States; or I have never had the opportunity to learn anything about it because I have never really had any reason to know the geography or the history of that specific country. This illustrates the privilege that the United States carries internationally. This privilege was also apparent in the use of English as the language of the discussion board. Because language expresses cultural interpretations of the world, the use of English forced a particular architecture of discussion. It is within these contexts, settings, and our positionalities that we next discuss the findings that emerged from our interpretation of the discussion board.

# FINDINGS

In the following sections we first present the themes that emerged related to positionality, glocal understanding, and multiple perspectives on social issues. The themes of dialogue, American exceptionalism, and gender inequalities form a focal point for an increased recognition of identity, positionality, and power asymmetries in a glocal space of asynchronous discussion. We present illustrative quotes of each theme and follow the quote with each of our interpretations. In the process, our purpose is to show ways that our unique positionalities as social studies teacher educators can increase perspectives and reflection more than traditional reporting where, although different, our narratives are collapsed into a single narrative. An ethic of recognition asks us as social studies teacher educators to recognize our positionalities in glocal spaces as we ask the same of our students.

## Dialogue

> Such dialogue between these two institutions helps promote a congenial atmosphere among them. Such atmosphere promotes greater chances to communicate, which will eventually allow the exchange of ideas between them with respect to their historical backgrounds and of their curriculum. (Filipino student, discussion board post)

> I think that it will open doors to different viewpoints about the world. Too often a person's views are trapped by what is around them and they do not bother to look outside of themselves to find a different answer, even if it isn't one that they want. By participating in this dialogue I hope to get out of my Utah mindset and become a more worldly and effective person. (American student, discussion board post)

*Marialuisa*

These posts reveal the different global and local dimensions with which students in the Philippines and in the United States connect. The dialogue between students of different countries is perceived as a great opportunity from both sides. However, the Filipino students connected it to a community level, as a chance for institutions to get in contact, share information, and build relationships. In this sense, students are vehicles that promote cooperation first between higher education institutions, and consequently between countries. In contrast, U.S. students first perceived their individual dimension; they wish to expand their personal mind-set and become more "worldly." This extra step is possible only if students "bother to look outside themselves," as the American student commented. Acknowledging that each of us has a specific viewpoint is the first step to open the horizon to multicultural perspectives. Nevertheless, it has to be connected to the local and the global dimension in order to engage in a real cross-cultural dialogue.

Both students recognize the relevance and the influences of sociocultural background in the development of personal standpoints and identities. The Filipino student mentioned taking into consideration the "historical background" of other students, while the American student refers to "what is around" people. The Filipino student's articulated definition reveals a structural understanding of the notion of sociocultural background, something that is taught in the formal and informal curriculum. In contrast, the American student's comment reveals a general perception of this cultural background with which they might not have engaged in depth. Nevertheless, in both cases it is evident that students' standpoints cannot be considered outside their specific contexts.

This last consideration is important at multiple levels. The Filipino and the American students will have to consider their specific backgrounds when engaging in communication with each other and with their respective future students. At the same time, I, as teacher educator and student, have to consider my peculiar positionality while considering students' developing positionalities as they emerge in their comments.

*Steven*

The Filipino student first communicates the primacy of a "congenial" relationship. This is an indication that he understands dialogue to be built upon authentic communication within the context of openness and hope. His focus on the conditions for cross-cultural dialogue represents an awareness of historical and contemporary communication between the Philippines and the United States. In my collaborations with colleagues in the Philippines, it was important in the process that I recognized in our conversations the inequitable power relations between the two countries. These were ongoing and important components that fostered authentic dialogues about colonization and curriculum. The Filipino student quoted above who references history and curriculum emphasized this, and in his statement he views history and curriculum as connected. The quote from a Filipina student at the opening of this chapter illustrates a similar understanding of colonization and the complex nature of historical and contemporary relations between colonized and colonizing people and nations. From a very young age, students in the Philippines are aware that the curriculum and English as a language of instruction have been used as tools of colonization by the United States. However, this specific recognition is lacking with the American student who sees a need to recognize different perspectives as a way to become "a more worldly and effective person" but lacks the historical understanding to connect colonization and curriculum. Her emphasis upon individual improvement and contemporary rather than historical perspectives communicates a lack of recognition of the inequitable power relations between Filipinos and Americans. However, in the quotes in the next section, American students see this lack of understanding and recognition.

## American Exceptionalism

> When history is presented in a cut and paste fashion where only one side is shown, the U.S. is in the right 98% of the time. At least that is how it is in the United States. I'm sure in most countries it is the same with the people in charge being able to do no wrong and the "bad" guy is always on the opposing force. The children always get to hear of the atrocities caused by the other side but hardly ever hear of the bad choices that the U.S. has made in conjunction with those "bad people." With a more rounded version of events everyone can get a much more accurate view of the world and the past as a whole, not just the sunny, we are awesome version that likes to be told. (American student, discussion board post)

> I'm really interested in hearing about American history from your point of view. I know that in my schools, when I learned about the different wars and the terrorist attacks, America was always the good guy. Like the article [(Kumashiro, 2004)] said, we always learned that the United States saved the world. I want to know how other countries see the US history. (American student, discussion board post)

### *Marialuisa*

As an Italian, I have seen that numerous European countries consider the United States to be one of the most contradictory and certainly the most powerful countries. The United States is portrayed as a place in which people can achieve anything they want if they work hard, but at the same time they can easily go bankrupt because of traps such as credit cards, mortgages, and the health care system. Occasionally, the United States is seen as the country that can save the world from oppressors, some of whom they have historically supported and armed. To the purpose of this project, it was very beneficial for the students to challenge the perception of their home country and engage with different points of view. They looked at the different stories that contribute to building what is recognized as the "official" history of the United States.

### *Steven*

In our social studies methods courses we examine how historical narratives vary depending upon a person, group, or nation's positionality. The American students quoted above communicate an understanding of the ways that history has portrayed the United States as a force for good while uncritical of social inequalities perpetuated by, for example, inequitable environmental policies. This metanarrative of exceptionalism also focuses upon leaders as the agents of change while downplaying the roles of social movements and marginalized identities as agents of change. In addition, the leaders and agents of change are mostly portrayed as male and disproportionately portrayed as white. When the United States is examined as a colonizer, it is often portrayed as a liberator with social justice as an intent and not national enrichment. In the case of the Philippines, the United States is often portrayed as instituting public education during colonization. However, public education had an effect of devaluing the languages and cultures of the Philippines. The American students in the quotes above illustrate the beginning of authentic communication and recognition locally and globally. This understanding of history as a matter of positionality and perspective opens the possibility of a third space of the glocal where a hybridity of local and global identities can be recognized in teacher education courses.

## Gender Inequalities

> Women in the Philippines, before, were just shadows of men. Parents tended not to send their daughters to school because they would just end up being housewives. They thought "what's the use of the diploma you earned when you are just going to end up as a housewife?" Things have change now. Women are taught that we are equal to men. We can be bosses too not just being bossed around. Do you think United States will have a woman president? Just a thought. . . . (Filipina student, discussion board post)

> I really think that in current social studies curriculum, women are being empowered. Girls are being taught that they can do anything a man can do, that we all have the same rights. (American student, discussion board post)

### *Marialuisa*

Social studies curriculum may teach that women and men have the same rights and deserve equal opportunities. However, real choices for women are still very limited; women are not making it to the top of their professions in many countries in the world (Sandberg, 2010). Women have to face harder decisions, especially when they have to choose between their career and their family. As I stated in my positionality section, women tend to self-censor in order to assume the predetermined partnership and motherhood roles that society makes incompatible with a fully developed professional life. Sandberg encouraged women to sit at the table with men, and negotiate their duties and rights, and to make their partners real partners to share family responsibilities. Finally, she suggested that women not disregard professional development opportunities in advance, thinking they would not be able to accomplish them in the future because they would be too busy with their spouse and mother roles.

With regard to politics, women are often associated with the role of mediator. The necessity of mediation and negotiation in politics almost permit or justify the presence of women, who otherwise would not fit in because of their pseudo-innate emotional instability. In the same vein, the expression of emotions in politics and their interpretation in mass media are very much related to gender perception. For example, a male senator who cries in public is sensitive while a female senator would be judged as unstable. A male senator talking too loudly is considered a good fighter for people's rights while a female senator in the same situation is simply a hysterical woman. Women cannot be just intelligent. In order to succeed, especially in politics, they have to be judged beautiful and intelligent, and they have to constrain expressions of masculinity so as not to be judged as perverse.

*Steven*

The Filipina student's question above about a female president of the United States illustrates some of the complexity that we hope to extend to future projects. While the discourse of colonization often misrecognizes colonized people as not progressive or advanced, the Filipina student offers a chance to recognize the Philippines as progressive on gender inequalities. The fact that the Philippines has had two female presidents and the United States has had none indicates an inequality and disrupts simple dichotomies of progressiveness assigned to colonizing and colonized nations. The American student quoted above illustrates that there have been increased efforts to recognize females in history and other social studies curriculum. The quote also illustrates a connection between empowerment and recognition. The curriculum can be a form of empowerment when an ethics of recognition guides the perspectives and identities that are represented. In future iterations of our project, we will include demographic and other information about global gender inequities that will serve as discussion points for students. While the above student comments communicate an awareness of gender inequities, more information could deepen discussions surrounding sexism and topics such as education, economics, media, and politics.

## CHALLENGES AND OPPORTUNITIES

The asynchronous discussion board provided a platform with challenges and opportunities. We initially created a discussion board that had multiple capabilities for discussion and graphics that is common among social media sites. However, after our first iteration of the project, we discovered that the bandwidth of the Southern Leyte State University (SLSU) campus was not large enough to accommodate the discussion board that we planned because the graphic information took too long to download. This cut the amount of time that students were able to participate in the project because we had to find a discussion board that required little bandwidth and was mostly text based. Because the school year in the Philippines ends during mid-spring, most of the responses needed to be posted by the student teachers while in their field placements. Many of the schools that the Filipino students were assigned did not have computers, and some had limited times for access to electricity even if student teachers had access to a computer.

These challenges in implementing the program were connected to an opportunity for increased understanding of global inequalities with Utah preservice teachers. The inequalities related to resources were a powerful illustration of how privilege is related to ignorance. Our assumptions as curriculum developers and teacher educators concerning the resources in the Philippines were wrong. The preservice teachers in Utah initially had trouble understanding why there was such a time delay between posts. This led to an increased understanding of the digital divide and global inequalities.

Finally, the discussion board took on a new meaning by opening a third space of glocality that synthesized local and global recognition related to privilege and marginalization. The combination of historical, contemporary, and resource inequalities with positionality provided new ways for preservice teachers and us, as social studies teacher educators, to increase the number of cultural and global perspectives in the curriculum. Recognition of identity and positionality provides a glocal space of departure and return as educators and students understand public issues with an eye toward power and social inequalities.

This understanding of glocality is supported by an ethics of recognition. Through our methodology of duoethnography, we found opportunities to reflect on our understanding of glocal curriculum. We hope our journey shows ways that teacher educators involve themselves and their positionalities as central components of a curriculum planned, implemented, and reflected upon in a glocal space aimed at improved understanding and social justice.

## CONCLUSIONS

In our brief encounter with the discussion board project, we see possibilities for using technology and discussion as tools for social justice. We have argued for transparency in the discussion of social issues through an ethics of recognition that seeks to create a third space of glocality. It is a space where students and teachers, as Soja (2009) writes, are provided "a place of critical exchange where geographical imagination can be expanded to encompass a multiplicity of perspectives" (p. 51). It is a space where glocalization, technology, and social studies teacher education interact to increase recognition and social justice.

In our introduction to this chapter, we presented two research questions that guided our reflections on our project. Our first question concerned the ways our sharing/discussing of positionalities (as teacher educators and students) lends authenticity to the discussion of global issues and increases social justice. Acknowledging our positionality unveiled our strength and vulnerability as teachers. We encourage teacher educators and preservice teachers to acknowledge their positionalities and help their students develop, understand, and learn about their own positionalities. The journey we embraced is a continuous reconsideration of our ethnic, social, and professional identities. The education process is part of this identity development that we share with our students and we co-construct with them. By revealing the source of stereotypes and social injustice, we hope to promote a more just learning environment that combines and increases local and global understandings to form third spaces of glocality.

In our second question, we asked how a discussion between students from different countries might increase the range of multicultural and global perspectives in social studies teacher education courses. Curricula that claim to provide multicultural and global perspectives often restrict the range of possibilities to simplistic descriptions and cultural stereotypes. The different positionalities of the students in different countries in our project provided an opportunity for discussion of issues from multiple perspectives.

Engaging in authentic dialogue with students from different areas of our globe gave preservice teachers an opportunity to understand and engage with multiple perspectives through dialogue. This hands-on activity was an opportunity for both groups to experience a glocal dimension of social studies education through engaging with themes such as gender inequalities. The glocal space that opened through an ethic of recognition was a hybrid place where marginalized and privileged students could dialogue about local and global issues. The disruption of colonizing discourses such as the discourse of progress can be achieved through this recognition of multiple perspectives and the deconstruction of hegemonic discourses. Although the discussion was brief due to the challenges we discussed in the previous section, the study has implications for future projects where positionality serves as a focal point to increase the number of perspectives in social studies teacher education curriculum.

We also found that technology helps or hinders communication between students at different universities. Technology contributed to the development of a glocal space of multicultural and global dimensions. This glocal space resisted a rigid definition that would confine its natural flexibility, but it was a hybrid space composed of the local and global dimensions that can be manifest in online environments. Glocality in this case was a borderland where public issues formed the focal point for engagement with different positionalities and their multiple perspectives. Although students were engaging with their computers locally, the online discussion board opened a space where multiple glocal perspectives were opened through engaging with issues from multiple global and cultural perspectives. Technology helped to visualize a virtual place for glocal communication between preservice social studies teachers at different universities.

Preservice teachers could not have shared their perspectives without technology, but we found that different semester schedules and the digital divide between the United States and the Philippines technology infrastructures caused some delays in the project. This last point illustrated how technology, instead of being an equalizing instrument, revealed once more the differences between privileged and marginalized people. These discrepancies, however, shouldn't lead us to abandon online discussion board projects between preservice teachers different countries. On the contrary, we should encourage more student discussion in glocal spaces as tools to promote social justice and cross-cultural communication. An examination of the inequalities related to technology and resources provided a platform for this glocal space.

In conclusion, our project helped us consider the implications that our study has for our future projects that help teachers incorporate social justice, international/global education, citizenship education, and multicultural education in their social studies classrooms. As a result of our, the authors', recognition of our positionalities and the recognition of various perspectives in the project, we hope to include the following as guides for future iterations of similar projects and classroom practices:

1. An issue-centered curriculum provides the structure to increase student understanding of glocality composed of different cultural and global perspectives.
2. An examination of privilege, marginalization, and positionality should play a central role in internationalizing social studies teacher education.
3. Based upon this examination, social studies teacher educators and curriculum developers should purposefully include unrecognized cultural and global perspectives in order to create glocal spaces of social justice.
4. Technology can provide a vehicle for dialogue and a glocal third space, but privileged partners in such collaboration must examine assumptions about resources and capacity.

We plan to develop our teacher education program to include more global partners in these types of conversations. In addition to other global partners, we see much room for curriculum development surrounding, but not limited to, global issues such as education, migration, culture, economics, energy, health, development, human rights, trade, the environment, and globalization. This issue-based curriculum will be based upon an ethics of recognition surrounding the social inequalities that are inherent in these issues.

# REFERENCES

Apple, M. W. (2000). *Official knowledge: Democratic education in a conservative age* (2nd ed.). New York: Routledge.

Banks, J. A. (2002). Race, knowledge construction, and education in the USA: Lessons from history. *Race, Ethnicity, and Education, 5*(1), 7–27.

Bhabha, H. K. (2003). On writing rights. *Globalizing rights: The Oxford Amnesty lectures 1999* (pp. 162–183). Oxford University Press, USA.

Bigelow, B. (Ed.). (2006). *The line between us: Teaching about the border and Mexican immigration*. Milwaukee, WI: Rethinking Schools Ltd.

Bigelow, B., & Peterson, B. (Eds.). (2002). *Rethinking globalization: Teaching for justice in an unjust world*. Milwaukee, WI: Rethinking Schools Press.

Camicia, S. P. (2007). Deliberating immigration policy: Locating instructional materials within global and multicultural perspectives. *Theory and Research in Social Education, 35*(1), 96–111.

Camicia, S. P. (2009). Identifying soft democratic education: Uncovering the range of civic and cultural choices in instructional materials. *The Social Studies, 100*(3), 136–142.

Camicia, S. P. (2012). An ethics of recognition in global and teacher education: Looking through queer and postcolonial lenses. *International Journal of Development Education and Global Learning, 4*(1), 25–35.

Camicia, S. P. (2014). My pedagogical creed: Positionality, recognition, and dialogue in democratic education. In S. Totten (Ed.), *The importance of teaching social issues: Our pedagogical creeds* (pp. 166–175). New York: Routledge.

Camicia, S. P., & Bayon, A. (2012). Curriculum development collaboration between colonizer and colonized: Contradictions and possibilities for democratic education. In T. C. Mason & R. J. Helfenbein (Eds.), *Ethics and international curriculum work: The challenges of culture and context* (pp. 73–92). Charlotte, NC: Information Age.

Camicia, S. P., & Zhu, J. (2012). Synthesizing multicultural, global, and civic perspectives in the elementary school curriculum and educational research. *The Qualitative Report, 17*, 1–19.

Code, L. (1991). *What can she know? Feminist theory and the construction of knowledge*. Ithaca, NY: Cornell University Press.

Collins, P. H. (2000). *Black feminist thought: Knowledge, consciousness, and the politics of empowerment*. New York: Routledge.

Gutmann, A. (1987). *Democratic education*. Princeton, NJ: Princeton University Press.

Harding, S. (1993). Eurocentric scientific illiteracy: A challenge for the world community. In S. Harding (Ed.), *The "racial" economy of science: Toward a democratic future* (pp. 1–22). Bloomington, IN: Indiana University Press.

Hekman, S. (1997). Truth and method: Feminist standpoint theory revisited. *Signs, 22*(2), 341–365.

Hess, D. E. (2008). Controversial issues and democratic discourse. In L. S. Levstik & C. A. Tyson (Eds.), *Handbook of research in social studies education* (pp. 124–136). New York: Routledge.

Kumashiro, K. K. (2004). *Against common sense: Teaching and learning toward social justice*. New York: RoutledgeFalmer.

Lather, P. A. (1992). Critical frames in educational research: Feminist and post-structural perspectives. *Theory into Practice, 31*(2), 87–99.

Lee, M. W. (Writer). (1994). *The Color of Fear.* In StirFry Seminars and Consulting (Producer). United States.

Lund, D. E., & Nabavi, M. (2008). Duo-ethnographic conversation on social justice activism: Exploring issues of identity, racism, and activism with young people. *Multicultural Education* (Summer), 27–32.

Maher, F. A., & Tetreault, M. K. (1993). Frames of positionality: Constructing meaningful dialogues about gender and race. *Anthropological Quarterly, 66*(3), 118–126.

Mohanty, C. T. (1984). Under Western eyes: Feminist scholarship and colonial discourses. *Boundary, 12/13*(3/1), 333–358.

Norris, J. (2008). Duoethnography. In L. M. Given (Ed.), *The Sage encyclopedia of qualitative research methods* (pp. 233–236). Thousand Oaks: SAGE Publications, Inc.

Parker, W. C. (2006). Talk isn't cheap: Practicing deliberation in school. *Social Studies and the Young Learner, 19*(1), 12–15.

Sandberg, S. (2010). Why we have too few women leaders. Retrieved April 25, 2014, from TED http://www.ted.com/talks/sheryl_sandberg_why_we_have_too_few_women_leaders.

Sawyer, R. D., & Liggett, T. (2012). Shifting positionalities: A critical discussion of a duoethnographic inquiry of a personal curriculum of post/colonialism. *International Journal of Qualitative Methods, 11*(5), 628–651.

Soja, E. W. (2009). Toward a new consciousness of space and spatiality. In K. Ikas & G. Wagner (Eds.), *Communicating in the third space* (pp. 49–61). New York: Routledge.

Spivak, G. C. (1996). Subaltern studies: Deconstructing historiography. In D. Landry & G. MacLean (Eds.), *The Spivak reader* (pp. 203–235). New York: Routledge.

# Recommendations, Policy, and Practice Supplication

## David Schwarzer and Beatrice L. Bridglall

This volume summarizes powerful experiences that committed teacher educators in different contexts have implemented in order to internationalize their teacher education programs with a social justice framework. Some of the projects were collaborative projects and some were individual ones. Some were very successful and some were not as much. In this final conclusion chapter, the editors of the book would like to talk about some lessons learned from the different projects as well as to discuss some future steps to internationalize our profession.

### LESSONS LEARNED

This section will summarize some of the major findings across all the research projects in this book. Several lessons about internationalizing teacher education programs that were learned from the different accounts are:

1. Logistics, planning, and flexibility are crucial
2. Expect challenges
3. Misconceptions should be made explicit
4. Pedagogy and curriculum are key
5. Internationalization is a worthwhile and transformative experience

### Logistics, Planning, and Flexibility Are Crucial

Careful and thorough planning of the international experiences in this book is a clear first lesson. Authors seem to agree that certain aspects of the planning are crucial for its successful implementation. We could not find a particular order in which these elements should be followed. However, the following checklist with questions may be useful for teacher educators interested in fostering such collaborations.

1. What are the main experiences that this international collaboration will entail? What are the stages for the implementation of the international experience?

    Be concise and clear. Assign times and responsibilities so each one of the members is clear about his own responsibilities. Take into consideration ample time to talk about every possible aspect of the experience *before* you get started.

2. What are the anticipated goals for the program? Are the goals the same for both "sides" of the collaboration, or are they different?

    Be explicit about goals that might be shared between both sides; some may serve one side and not the other. More importantly, reciprocity is key. Try to find how each aspect of the experience can be a win-win situation for all sides involved.

3. What are the expected outcomes for the program? Do we have a model that can explain this collaboration?

    Again, the outcome may be similar or different for different participants. Try to use a model that already exists, or create your own model to frame the international experience. Make these goals/model explicit to all the participants since it is central to the long-term success and implementation of the insights gained during this experience into teachers' future classrooms.

4. How are these outcomes going to be assessed or evaluated? What is the research plan?

    Plan a pilot study research plan that allows you both accountability and a certain flexibility based on unexpected challenges that many of the chapters report as commonplace.

5. What are other researchers recommending for similar experiences? Is there a gap in the literature that this experience is trying to fill?

    Make deep theoretical connections to research studies and other literature that has dealt with the same challenges and opportunities you are facing. See if your experience is similar or different than others already described in the literature review. Since internationalizing efforts for teacher education programs is a fairly new research area, do not be surprised if your project is filling a gap in the literature.

6. What sustainable structures are you creating for this project to be repeated again? What type of institutional support do you need?

Even at the beginning stages and pilot planning of your international experience, start thinking about the next experience. Invite key administrators and colleagues to participate as much as possible in the experience. Disseminate your results as well as pictures, artifacts, and other documents as much as possible. Most importantly, students who participated in the experience are the best ambassadors within your institution.

## Expect Challenges

All the projects documented in this book mentioned some challenges they encountered and how the authors overcame them. As stated throughout the chapters, challenges will come in a variety of forms. Flexibility is important—plan for it!

The following list demonstrates challenges and some of the ways that the authors of the book were able to account for them.

1. Cultural challenges: Some of the challenges are cultural in nature. Making decisions about time and length of a session, deciding deadlines and leading roles, making descriptions of the task and the rubrics used for its evaluation months in advance are all viewed differently in different educational contexts and countries. One funny and yet valuable recommendation we heard from a very seasoned international expert was that when deciding on an international partner for a project, you should be mindful of the cultural characteristics of the context where we reside. If the collaboration is between a U.S. team (in which planning in advance and having detailed conversations about outcomes is the usual way to conduct business) and, let's say, an Argentinean team (in which planning is not always done in advance and the details sometimes develop as the project is conducted)—choosing a more "flexible" U.S. partner and a more "rigid" Argentinean one might be a possible solution to alleviate this possible cultural challenge in the way the project is conducted.
2. Technological challenges: Using technology as a way to foster a world-minded teacher candidate's understanding of teaching and learning is a plausible tool. Several chapters experience some challenges while exploring this kind of experience. Sometimes the technology froze, sometime the students were not able to properly connect

during the class times, and so forth. A way to alleviate this challenge is to experiment and try the technologies before they are used in the project. Make friends and allies with the technology groups at your institution. Plan for several different options so at least one of them will work during the actual experience. If nothing else works, you can always resort to simple technologies to promote the experience (using e-mail, posting projects on a Web-based platform, etc.). Remember that the overarching goal of these experiences is to create a space within your class where you and your students transcend the classroom walls—that can be achieved with very simple technologies or with complex and sophisticated ones.

3. Idiosyncratic challenges: While all the plans always have some expected challenges, some are completely random. As stated in the chapters, some of the challenges were weather-related issues (typhoon, unexpected snowstorms, or Hurricane Sandy), time zone differences, and personal preferences in terms of language. To alleviate these kinds of challenges, plan with plenty of time and options so if a hurricane hits or a snowstorm prevents your class from using the Internet, some other options are available.

Other idiosyncratic challenges might be a change in the housing options (last minute), the classroom or school visit that does not happen because the teacher is sick are some of the challenges study-abroad teachers may need to address. Be ready for alternative plans for these kinds of challenges. Create a schedule of activities with options in mind to address the above-mentioned challenges.

Some of these challenges are simple to bridge. For example, a very seasoned international expert in the United States clearly preferred Latin American countries for technology-enhanced collaborations since the time zone differences with the United States are minimal.

Overall, although there were many challenges while crafting a world-minded teacher education program, some of the chapters also discuss the transformative power of the experience.

## Misconceptions Should Be Made Explicit

Some teacher educators and administrators interested in developing and sustaining international experiences for student teachers may hold some misconceptions that may need to be revisited and made clear.

1. Placements should be limited to English-speaking countries *only*.

   Some administrators believe that student teaching placements and international experiences should be limited to English-speaking countries. However, that is not required. Student teachers could be placed in international schools in a variety of countries. Moreover, they can have international student teacher experiences in the English as a foreign language classes in a variety of school systems regardless of the language of the country. All of these experiences have the potential to transform students' perceptions of social justice and their understanding of teaching and learning in both a local and global perspective.

2. Internationalization is more than culturally responsive teaching.

Another misconception is that some teacher educators and student teachers equate global and international experiences with culturally responsive teaching. Some teacher educators believe that understanding teaching and learning as a global phenomenon with a local "taste" is not needed for student teachers in the United States. Moreover, the occasional exposure to diversity, cultural fairs, and some community-based experiences is equated to creating a world-minded educator. Expanding the definition of culturally responsive teaching in general and adding a "glocal" sociocultural consciousness to promote social justice is important while discussing international perspectives with teacher educators and student teachers.

3. Internationalization efforts are very costly.

Although many teacher education programs are interested in internationalization efforts, many of them see study abroad or exchange programs as the preferred way. These types of programs cost quite a lot of money both for the students and the institution. However, as demonstrated in two sections in this book, technologically-enhanced globalization efforts as well as glocal efforts are virtually free options to internationalize teacher education programs. They are costly in terms of the commitment of time and effort from the participants, but not in terms of monetary resources.

By engaging in meaningful and clear conversations with administrators and peers to address some of the misconceptions listed here, more internationalization experiences will be available for teacher candidates in a variety of teacher education programs in the United States and in the world.

## Pedagogy and Curriculum Are Key

Many of the experiences explored in this book report on cutting-edge peda-gogical experiences and curriculum development to enhance the academic experiences of teacher candidates. Following is a list of some of the salient pedagogical and curriculum experiences that should be taken into considera-tion while planning an international experience.

1. Experiential learning

   Many of the book chapters use some kind of experience that be-came very influential in the way students understand teaching and learning in a globalized world. As part of the experiential learning it is important to mention the power of place. Visiting the house of Anne Frank or a concentration camp is a transfor-mative experience for all teacher candidates, but surely for so-cial studies teacher candidates in particular. In the same vein, visiting a Costa Rican school, teaching in an American school in Africa are powerful experiences. However, finding a "third space" using technology might be an important option to con-sider. For example, conversing and collaborating on a project over the Internet with a student in Israel or Spain are some experiences that have the potential to expand teacher candi-dates' understanding of teaching and learning for social justice in a globalized world.

2. Project-Based Learning (PBL)

   One of the pedagogies used by many authors in this book is pro-ject-based learning. Many of the chapters centered on a project (a presentation, a poster, or some other project agreed by the collaborators) to create a shared task to promote the comparison and contrast between the educational systems in the collabora-tion. PBL has the potential to create a space for small groups of students to interact in meaningful ways during the class and even after its completion. Reflecting on the PBL experiences in the book, they seem to be the most meaningful and useful tool to promote world-minded educators.

3. Common education experience across contexts

   Many of the collaborations across contexts developed a shared educational experience for students in both countries. The expe-riences ranged from reading the same book, to watching an online education documentary, or researching some pedagogi-cal practices. These common experiences were used as a catalyst to help students compare and contrast the ways in which different educational systems deal with similar issues. For examples, conversations about the widespread use of drugs in the United States for students with disabilities were very different than the reality students encountered in the Spanish education system.

4. Varied types of forums for collaborations

It was astonishing to see the variety and diversity of forums, formats, and types of collaborations to internationalize the curriculum of teacher education programs. Some of the projects portrayed in this volume used only asynchronous forums for collaborations (e-mail, websites, and blogs), some used only synchronous forums (Skype and Vimeo scheduled meetings), and some used both synchronous and asynchronous ones. Moreover, some of the discussions were whole-group discussions, some were small-group discussions, and some were pair discussions. Finally, some of the forums were public (Facebook) and some were password protected and more private (Ning). Like regular teaching, the variety of forums, formats, and types of collaboration has the potential of enhancing the overall achievement of the internationalization efforts.

## Internationalization Is a Worthwhile and Transformative Experience

Internationalizing the curriculum of teacher education programs is not a simple task. As stated before, it requires monetary and personal investments from the faculty and the institution. However, it is clear from all the chapters presented in this volume that it has the potential to be a transformative experience. Following is a list of insights that students can gain from the efforts described before:

1. Comparative understandings of teaching and learning

Many of the experiences described in this volume suggest that teacher candidates developed both general and content-specific understandings of teaching and learning. Teacher candidates were faced with alternative ways to approach the same challenge across the world. For example, student teachers needed to deeply consider issues of history and how it is represented and commemorated across cultures. Moreover, these efforts and experiences may seriously affect their ability to effectively help their school students in becoming productive members of a global society.

2. Comparative understanding of social justice and schooling

> Teaching underrepresented communities, immigrant populations, marginalized and minoritized groups are global concerns. For example, by engaging student teachers with immigrant populations and the intersection of Latino culture and the social atmosphere of Costa Rican schools, students developed a commitment to social justice as a worldwide concept. Moreover, it might promote an international understanding of social class and poverty as a globalized challenge that is being addressed in different ways by the different educational systems.

3. Personal and professional intercultural understanding

> One of the most robust findings is the long-term, enduring, and transformative cultural awareness that the international experiences offered teacher candidates. For example, student teachers reported that the international experiences influenced them through: (a) professional relations and collaboration; (b) enthusiasm for teaching; (c) exposure to multiple nationalities and unique perspectives; (d) second language speakers and differentiated instruction; and (e) increased self-awareness. Overall, the process of internationalization has the potential to open student teachers' eyes to global issues in education. Moreover, when the teacher candidates involved were part of a minority group in the United States, student candidates made connections between their own cultural backgrounds and the ways in which they saw this represented in the international context. This led them to think deeply about how to create a classroom environment in which both social and academic objectives would be addressed.

4. Personal and professional cross-linguistic language proficiency

> Students engaged in a personal and professional experience with a peer who speaks English as a second language was a powerful experience for the U.S.-based students in all the projects described here. This experience suggests that U.S. student teachers were compelled to better understand issues related to second language learning such as adapting their language to the second language learners. Student teachers became more aware of their language choices, jargon, and assumptions while collaborating with an international peer. From the international peer experience, having an authentic international experience increased the international counterparts' motivation to use English as a

foreign language. For example, some findings suggest that motivation and learning are closely linked to cooperation between international participants.

5. Comparative understandings of critical issues in education

Through this international and comparative experience between settings, student teachers were able to reflect and show indications of growth in their understanding of critical issues in education. For example, conversations about gender inequality across the contexts were highlighted. Similarly, many participants in technology-enhanced collaborations were able to demonstrate that they recognized the concepts and issues involved in the use of technology at local and global levels and the importance of helping their students understand digital citizenship. A very important topic that was present in most chapters in the book was the positionality and American exceptionalism that many times engulfed the global conversations. However, many of the projects showcased in this book also illustrate some of the ways to recognize and embrace multiple and divergent perspectives that play a central role in promoting social justice and the internationalization of teacher education.

6. The development of an emergent understanding of global-local connections

Some of the chapters in the book are great examples of the importance of helping student teachers to see the *glocal* tensions (between *global* influences on teacher education and *local* cultures) reflected in teacher education curriculum makeup, delivery, and, above all, outcomes. The profile of a world-minded teacher in the twenty-first century requires a different set of knowledge, skills, and values to meet the new global challenges (inclusion, diversity, multilingualism, and intercultural issues in the classroom) to guarantee social justice and education for all.

In conclusion, promoting international perspectives in teacher education is a long overdue task. As noted before, there are many challenges for this implementation, but the rewards are immense. We are hoping that more and more teacher educators begin to explore these transformative experiences in their own programs throughout the United States and the world.

# Index

# About the Contributors

**Perien Joniell Boer** is lecturer in educational technology, University of Namibia, Faculty of Education. Dr. Boer holds a doctorate in education with specialization in instructional technology and media from Teachers College, Columbia University, in New York City. She is currently teaching the master's of education program in educational technology at the University of Namibia. Her interests in educational technology focus around school change, policy implementation, and understanding by teachers. She contributes to the national education technology sector in various capacities at the Ministry of Education and Industry.

**Alexandra Leman Brown** is adjunct professor of education, Department of Secondary and Special Education, and adjunct professor, Spanish Department, Montclair State University. Alexandra Brown has been a member of ASCD and a member of FLENJ and ACTFL, Sigma Delta Pi Spanish Honor Society and Kappa Delta Pi International Education Society. During the academic year 2013–2014, she has taught two undergraduate courses to students in their field work and student teaching semesters titled, Teaching for Learning One and Two. She has taught a graduate-level course for the M.A.T. program and has been teaching Spanish for the Spanish Department at MSU. She organized a "Symposium on the Teenage Brain" in 2011 in which the science editor of the *New York Times* came to speak about emerging research on the adolescent brain. She has been with the university for five years and prior to this, was a high school Spanish teacher for eleven years. She received a master's degree in curriculum and teaching from Montclair State University in 2006 and graduated at the top of her class from Vanderbilt University.

**Marya Burke**, Montclair State University, is independent consultant for PRISM (Professional Resources in Science and Mathematics). Burke is an experienced researcher, evaluator, and editor specializing in educational programming. She received her doctorate from the University of Illinois at Urbana-Champaign in education policy studies. Her primary interests include equity studies, teacher education, parental involvement, and approaches to assessment. Some programs she has worked with include: the Rainforest Connection, PRISM; Cognition Works, Inc.; the Orpheum Children's Science Museum; GearUp of Newport News, Virginia; the Division of Disability Resources and Educational Services, WaterCAMPWS, and the Nano-CEMMS center, all at the University of Illinois.

**Francesca Caena**, University Ca' Foscari, Venice, is contract lecturer and teacher educator (University of Venice) and in-service teacher trainer (Ministry of Education/LEA). Caena has extensive experience as a teacher educator (ITE and CPD) and an EFL teacher (primary and secondary schooling). She has had relevant opportunities to study and participate in the development, implementation, and analysis of European education policy as a consultant for the European Commission as well as a European project manager. She was awarded a PhD education degree (Padua University) in 2010, defending a thesis on European teacher education. Her interests focus on European education policies, comparative studies, teacher education, and foreign language teaching/learning.

**Steven Camicia** is associate professor, School of Teacher Education and Leadership at Emma Eccles Jones College of Education and Human Services, Utah State University. Camicia earned his PhD in curriculum and instruction from the University of Washington where he was mentored by Walter Parker and James Banks. He is currently associate professor of social studies education at Utah State University. Camicia's research focuses on curriculum and instruction in the areas of perspective consciousness, postcolonial theory, queer theory, global education, and social justice as they relate to democratic education. He is currently using these lenses to examine LGBTQ-inclusive curriculum and instruction in different political contexts. In 2012, he secured funding from the Bureau of Educational and Cultural Affairs, State Department Teaching Excellence and Achievement Program, to bring twenty-two teachers from nineteen countries to Utah State University. During their two-month stay, the international teachers co-taught in Utah schools where they formed lasting collaborations with Utah educators. Camicia taught sixth grade in Reno, Nevada.

**Marialuisa Di Stefano** is a doctoral student and research assistant at Emma Eccles Jones College of Education and Human Services, School of Teacher

Education and Leadership, Utah State University. She is currently working on integrating perspective between global education and dual language immersion programs using postcolonial theory framework. She earned her master of art in foreign language and cultures from Washington State University, where she was mentored by Ana María Rodriguez-Vivaldi. She has been teaching Italian and Spanish languages and cultures, English as a second or other language, and foundation of education for elementary preservice teachers. She is also a co-facilitator of preservice teachers' seminars about diversity inclusion, issues of poverty, ethnicity, religion, and gender in education, along with learning differences, including those related to the historic marginalization of underrepresented groups in our society.

**Wangari P. Gichiru** is associate professor at Central Connecticut State University. She is a former high school teacher in Kenya. She received a master's degree in special education from the University of Wisconsin Eau Claire, and a master's degree in international public policy and a PhD in curriculum and instruction from the University of Wisconsin-Madison. Her research focuses on understanding the perspectives of key stakeholders regarding the education of African immigrant students, examining key stakeholders' perspectives on the meaning of democracy and its application to classroom practice, particularly its implications for equity and access for at-risk African immigrant students.

**Efrat Harel** is lecturer in the EAP Department at Kibbutzim College, Israel. Dr. Harel is a researcher in the domain of language acquisition among bilingual children, compared to monolingual peers. Her PhD dissertation focused on the linguistic profile of typically developing bilingual children in preschool years. In addition, Efrat takes part in an international project whose aim is to create a diagnostic tool designed for the bilingual population. Efrat trains student teachers in Kibbutzim College to deal with issues of multilingualism and multiculturalism at preschools and schools in Israel. In her recent course, Efrat instructed a project which involved collaboration between Israeli and American students of education, from Israel and New Jersey, initiated by Dr. Tina Waldman (Israel) and Dr. David Schwarzer (United States). This collaboration enabled a meaningful cultural exchange for students.

**Matthew Knoester** is assistant professor of education at the University of Evansville. He is a National Board Certified Teacher in the United States and former teacher in the Boston Public Schools. He is author of the book *Democratic Education in Practice: Inside the Mission Hill School* and editor of *International Struggles for Critical Democratic Education*. His research focuses on issues of inequality and access in literacy and citizenship education.

**Katrina Macht**, is a sixth-grade science and English teacher in the Bridge-water-Raritan School District and consultant to PRISM (Professional Resources in Science and Mathematics) at Montclair State University. She is a curriculum specialist who is recognized throughout the United States for her expertise in environmental education. For the past several years she has worked with PRISM to link scientists in the field to classrooms throughout the United States by way of interactive video broadcasts. Katrina is currently a doctoral candidate in the EdD in pedagogy program at Montclair State University.

**Alan S. Marcus** is associate professor of history education at the Neag School of Education, University of Connecticut, where he runs the social studies/history education program. He is a University of Connecticut Teaching Fellow and a former high school social studies teacher. Alan earned his doctorate at Stanford University. His scholarship focuses on museum education and teaching with film. Alan collaborates with museum educators across the United States and internationally. He also partners with the history education program at the University of Nottingham in England and runs a study-abroad field experience for his preservice teachers to WWII historic sites and museums in Europe. He recently coauthored *Teaching History with Museums* (2012) and *Teaching History with Film* (2010).

**Leigh Martin** is assistant professor in the Department of Teaching, international student teaching coordinator, coordinator of MAE for International Educators, and professional development consultant at Korea International School, University of Northern Iowa. Martin currently lives in Seoul, South Korea, where she coordinates the International Student Teaching Center for the University of Northern Iowa (UNI). She oversees partnerships and student teaching placements in various international schools throughout the world such as India, Tanzania, Brazil, Singapore, and South Korea. She also co-coordinates the UNI master's degree program for teacher leaders in American international schools. Leigh completed her student teaching in Cairo, Egypt, and taught in international schools in Egypt and Brazil for eight years. She holds a bachelor's degree in elementary and early childhood education and a master's in international education. She completed her PhD in education leadership from Iowa State University. Her dissertation focuses on the intercultural development of educators who completed their student teaching in non-Western cultures and the impact of those overseas experiences on their classrooms during their first year of teaching.

**David M. Moss**, PhD, is associate professor on the faculty of the Neag School of Education at the University of Connecticut. Specializing in curriculum studies, his research interests are in the areas of culturally responsive teaching, global education, and environmental literacy. His books include *Preparing Classroom Teachers to Succeed with Second Language Learners* (in press); *Reforming Legal Education: Law Schools at the Crossroads* (2012); *Critical Essays on Resistance in Education* (2010); *Interdisciplinary Education in an Age of Assessment* (2008); *Portrait of a Profession: Teachers and Teaching in the 21st Century* (2005, 2008); and *Beyond the Boundaries: A Transdisciplinary Approach to Learning and Teaching* (2003). Dr. Moss has served as a keynote speaker at scholarly societies and national conferences. He has extensive K–16 curriculum development and assessment experience, and has directed a teacher education internship-based study-abroad program in London, England, for over a dozen years. Dr. Moss was named a teaching fellow at the University of Connecticut, the highest honor awarded for instructional excellence and leadership.

**Alison Price-Rom** is adjunct faculty, Departments of Secondary and Special Education and Modern Languages and Literature, Montclair State University. Price-Rom received her EdD in international education and development from Teachers College, Columbia University, and has both an MA in international studies and a K–12 teaching certificate from the University of Washington. Since completion of her EdD in 1999, Dr. Price-Rom has managed several international teacher education projects, including a U.S. State Department citizenship education exchange for Eurasian teachers and a USAID education project in Central Asia. Her college-level teaching background includes lectureships in the International Education Program at the University of Maryland and Montclair State University's Departments of Educational Foundations and Secondary and Special Education. She has traveled widely and lived and worked in Russia and Belarus.

**Mary Petrón** is associate professor of Bilingual/ESL education in the Department of Language, Literacy & Special Populations at Sam Houston State University in Huntsville, Texas. Her research interests include transnational populations, biliteracy development, and bilingual/ESL teacher education.

**Sarah Thomas** is assistant professor in the Secondary Education and Professional Programs at Bridgewater State University. Prior to accepting the position at BSU, Sarah spent six years living and working in Brussels, Belgium. While in Brussels, Sarah was an English teacher at the International School of Brussels, and it was here that her interest in overseas teaching and its influence on teaching decisions was developed. In addition to teaching, Sarah serves on the board of greenlight for girls, an international NGO dedicated to inspire girls to pursue STEM subjects. When not teaching or pursuing her research, Sarah enjoys spending time with her husband and two children. Sarah can be contacted at sarah.thomas@bridgew.edu.

**Tina Waldman** is head of English for Academic Purposes Unit, Kibbutzim College of Education, Technology and the Arts. Dr. Waldman's research interests include applied corpus linguistics, vocabulary learning in an additional language, and the dynamics of foreign language writing. She heads the English for Academic Purposes Unit at Kibbutzim College of Education, Technology and the Arts in Tel Aviv, Israel, where she also lectures in vocabulary acquisition and writing pedagogy to preservice English teachers. Her publications include a chapter on the status of vocabulary acquisition research in a foreign language in *Issues in Language Teaching in Israel* (2014); collocation use in writing among Israeli learners in *Humanizing Language Teaching Magazine* (2013); and verb-noun collocations in second language writing in *Language Learning* (2011).

**Hilary Anne Wilder** is professor in the Department of Educational Leadership and Professional Studies in the College of Education at William Paterson University of New Jersey in the United States. She teaches undergraduate and graduate courses in educational technology and also directs an MEd and graduate certificate program in learning technologies. Since 2001, she has worked on a number of curriculum development projects with the Ministry of Education in Namibia and the University of Namibia. Her research includes the use of Information and Communication Technologies (ICTs) in teacher education programs in developing nations as well as looking at ways of using ICTs to facilitate international collaborations in education and provide global perspectives and authentic cross-cultural experiences for K–12 students and preservice and in-service teachers.

**Eleanor Vernon Wilson** is associate professor of curriculum, instruction, and special education at the Curry School of Education in the University of Virginia where she teaches in the elementary teacher education program, focusing on curriculum and instruction. She has led an international student teaching placement in Cambridge, England, since 2009 for a group of six to eight elementary preservice students from the Curry School of Education. Her interest in designing experiences for students to earn credit for full-time student teaching placements internationally has led to a focus on creating ways in which preservice students reflect, interpret, and apply pedagogical knowledge in domestic and international settings.

**Jacalyn Giacalone Willis** is director of PRISM (Professional Resources in Science and Mathematics), Montclair State University. Willis is a biologist with forty years experience in tropical forests, and twenty years as a professional developer in K–12 science education. Dr. Willis founded PRISM, a professional development center for STEM education, with a staff of scientists, mathematicians, former K–12 teachers, and administrative personnel. PRISM and earlier programs designed by Dr. Willis have served over 5,000 teachers and more than 60,000 students since 1994. She is an early innovator in the use of Internet STEM education programming, especially videoconference technology to connect K–12 classrooms globally with researchers at the Smithsonian Tropical Research Institute in Panama and students in Belize, Australia, Madagascar, and Thailand.

# About the Editors

**Dr. David Schwarzer** was born in Buenos Aires, Argentina. He began his academic career in Tel Aviv, Israel. He worked in several different positions in schools: as a school counselor, a reading coach, a lecturer at Levinsky College and Beit Berl, and as the principal of Bialik Elementary School (featured in the award-winning Oscar documentary movie *Strangers No More*).

David Schwarzer received his PhD from the University of Arizona in the area of language reading and culture. He is currently working at Montclair State University where he was the chairperson of the Department of Secondary and Special Education in the College of Education and Human Services for four years. He is now associate professor in the same department.

His research interest focuses on the role of the monolingual teacher in multilingual and transnational learning communities. More recently, he is interested in redefining the boundaries between literacy, biliteracy, and multiliteracy. He is exploring the idea of "translingual" and "transliteracy" education as a possible solution.

Dr. Schwarzer is the author of four books: *Noa's Ark: One Child's Journey into Multiliteracy* (2001) is a case study about his daughter's literacy development in English, Spanish, and Hebrew in a bilingual first-grade classroom; *Research as a Tool for Empowerment: Theory Informing Practice* (2005) is an edited volume that includes an array of research-based chapters in the area of innovative and cutting-edge foreign and second language education; *Research informing practice—Practice informing research: Innovative teaching methodologies for world language teachers* (2011) is an edited volume in which teacher research accounts of innovative classroom practices in second and foreign language education are presented; he is currently editing a book called *Promoting Global Competence and Social Justice in*

*Teacher Education: Successes and Challenges within Local and International Contexts* (in press).

He has also published and presented multiple articles in Hebrew, Spanish, and English in local, national, and international journals and conferences.

David is married to Taly and is most proud of his three multilingual children: Noa, Ariel, and Tamar.

**Dr. Beatrice L. Bridglall** is chair of the Student Success Initiative in Higher Education in New Jersey, which is sponsored by the Office of the New Jersey Secretary of Higher Education. She is also faculty affiliate at New York University—East China Normal University, Institute for Social Development at NYU Shanghai. Her most recent book, *Teaching and Learning in Higher Education: Studies of Three Student Development Programs* (2013), explores the teaching and learning processes that enable high academic achievement in the Meyerhoff Scholars Program at the University of Maryland, Baltimore County; the premedical program at Xavier University in New Orleans; and the Opportunity Programs at Skidmore College in New York. Prior books include: *Supplementary Education: The Hidden Curriculum of High Academic Achievement* (2005), which makes the conceptual argument that high academic achievement is closely associated with exposure to family and community-based activities and learning experiences that occur outside of school in support of academic learning; and *Affirmative Development: Cultivating Academic Ability* (2008), which argues that academic abilities are not simply inherited aptitudes but rather can be developed through pedagogical and social interventions.

A Fulbright specialist in higher education, Dr. Bridglall's research draws on multiple disciplines (including educational, social, and developmental psychology; neuroscience; anthropology; and sociology) to understand the phenomenon of student academic development/socialization, curriculum, assessment and instruction, educational/organizational systems and conditions that impact successful learning (including parental involvement), learning and cognition, faculty expertise, and student motivation and cognition.

Dr. Bridglall obtained her doctorate in education and health psychology from Teachers College, Columbia University, in 2004; and in 2014, a master's in fine arts from Fairleigh Dickinson University.